AF400817

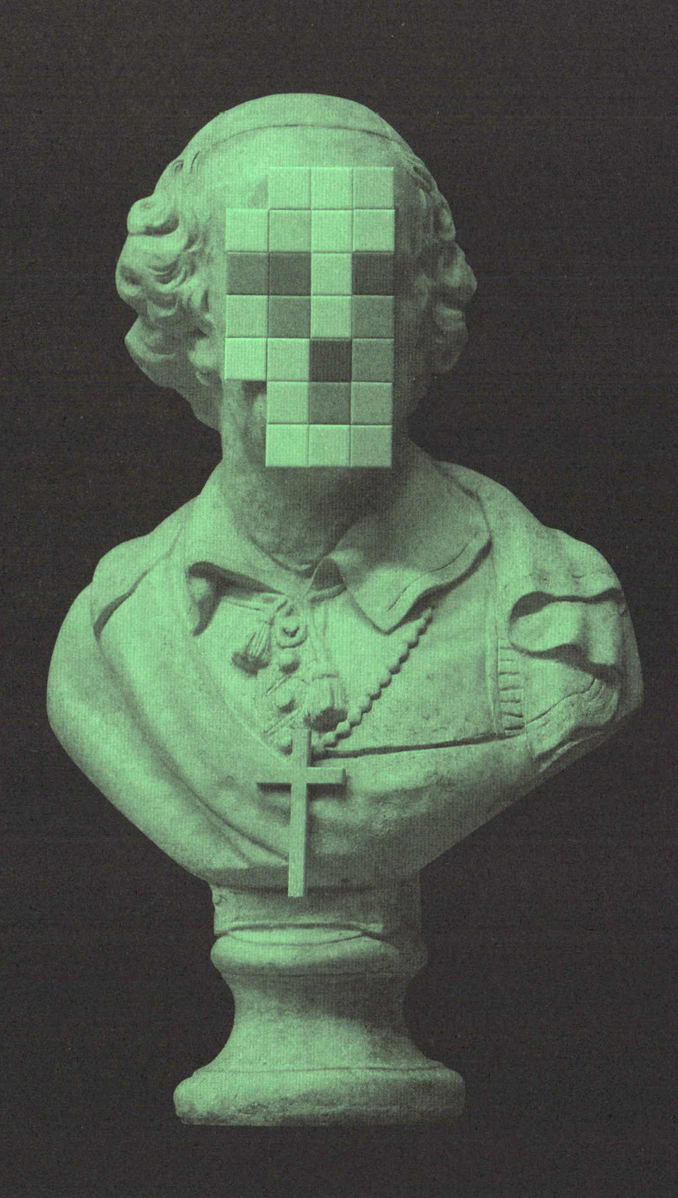

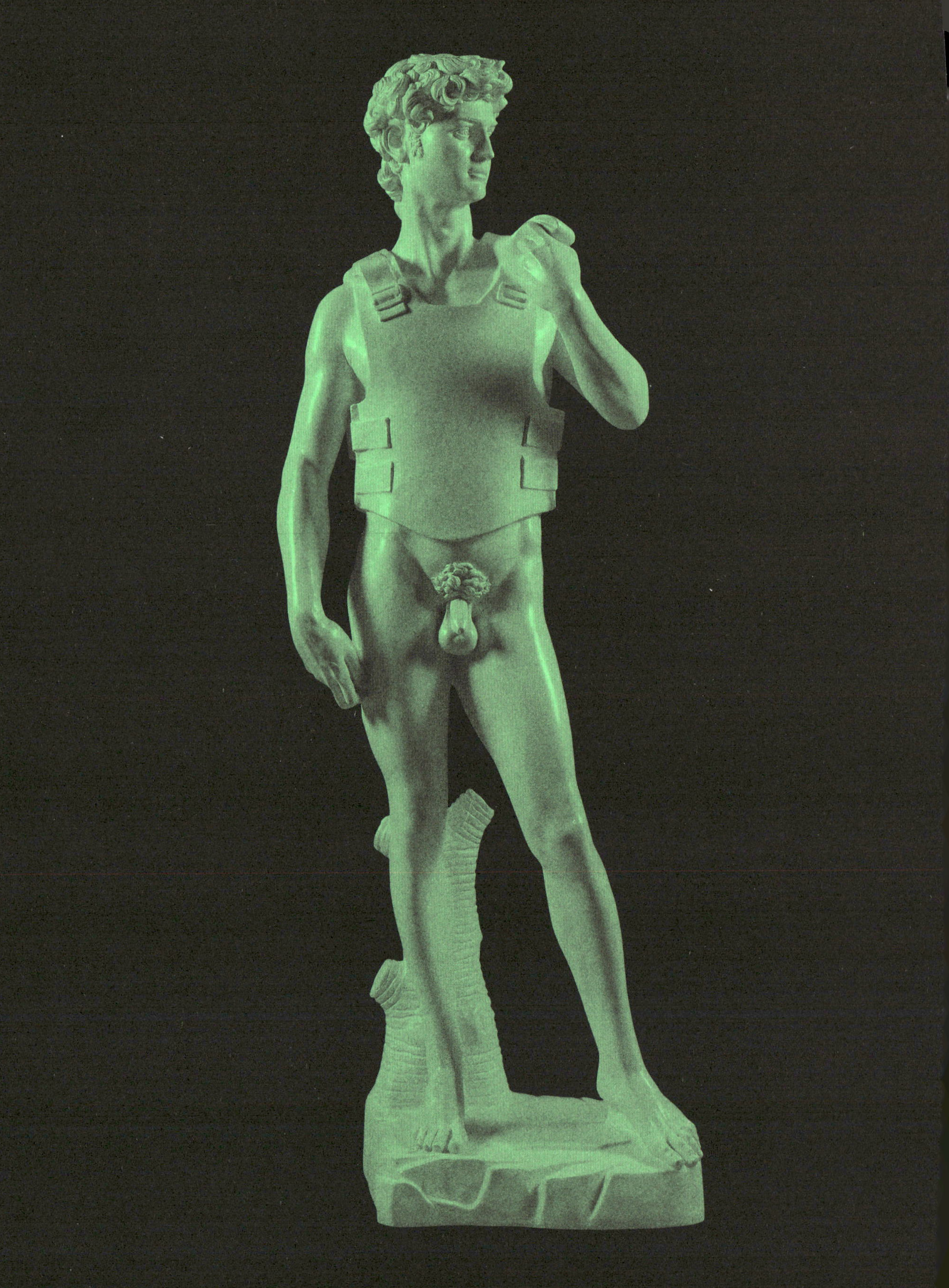

HOW BANKSY SAVED ART HISTORY

KELLY GROVIER

WITH 139 ILLUSTRATIONS

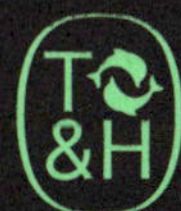

CONTENTS

IS GRAFFITI ART
OR VANDALISM?
THAT WORD
HAS A LOT
OF NEGATIVE
CONNOTATIONS
AND IT ALIENATES
PEOPLE...

…SO NO, I DON'T
LIKE TO USE THE
WORD 'ART'
AT ALL'

BANKSY

INTRODUCTION

Banksy doesn't borrow from art history. He shoves it up against a wall and mugs it. For decades, Banksy has lured one unsuspecting masterpiece after another down dark alleyways to strip them of the smug and superficial gloss that has, over time, tarnished their tired surfaces. Paintings and sculptures that we have long taken for granted, from Michelangelo's *David* to Claude Monet's *Water Lilies*, are not politely appropriated by Banksy, merely alluded to or echoed in his irreverent murals, canvases, sculptures, drawings and prints. They are abducted, radicalized and turned against us.

Banksy's spray-can has become a kind of enslaving syringe with which he injects himself into milestones of cultural history, from the Great Sphinx of Giza to Mary Cassatt's *Children Playing on the Beach*, from Johannes Vermeer's *Girl with a Pearl Earring* to Jean-Michel Basquiat's *Boy and Dog in a Johnnypump*. What Banksy leaves behind is something duffed-up and dangerous, cast in a new and dingy light: darkly witty mirrors of society's selfishness and hypocrisy. Far from damaging or debasing the works into which he intrudes, however, Banksy rescues these weary icons from an accelerating irrelevance. He infuses them with the raw energy and edgy urgency that, for many, they ceased to have long ago. He saves them.

When Banksy emerged from the underground street-art scene in Bristol, England, in the early 1990s, art history was struggling, strung out, and left by many for dead. Recent high-profile controversies in America over public funding of critically acclaimed artists, such as Andres Serrano, who infamously dunked a crucifix in a beaker of urine, and Robert Mapplethorpe, who photographed himself in the guise of the devil with a bullwhip jammed up his bottom, stoked wider cynicism about whether art had any future at all. In 1991, the German psychologist and theorist Rudolf Arnheim published a collection of essays whose very title is indicative of a state of crisis: *To the Rescue of Art*. Arnheim, who confessed to being aghast at the 'nihilistic attitude prevailing' in the arts,[2] wasn't the first intellectual to sound the alarm. Less than a decade earlier, the prominent American philosopher and art historian Arthur Danto had pronounced that humankind had in fact reached 'The End of Art'[3] — a provocative sentiment that had begun to sink into the minds and muscles of artists and scholars, critics, and casual admirers alike.

What exactly did Danto mean by his now famous phrase? For centuries, every generation had succeeded in advancing the story of art by reacting (or overreacting) to the art that had come before it. There was a logic and order to art's evolution, however shocking or unexpected the emergence of each art movement may have seemed at the time. Post-Impressionism gave birth to Cubism, Cubism to Surrealism, Surrealism to Conceptualism, and so forth, as the art of the past always remained a vital energy and inspiration in the art of the present. But Danto sensed that something had changed in the mid-1960s. It was then that in a New York gallery he stumbled across Andy Warhol's perfect replicas of the commercial packaging of Brillo-brand steel scouring pads, a controversial work that appeared to collapse the distance between a thing represented and the thing itself. In Danto's mind, Warhol's work marked a *see* change, as it were, in the way we perceive the making and meaning of images. New art was no longer a conversation with works that came before. The past was cut off umbilically from the future. Old masters and old masterpieces that once were fundamental to the unfolding of art ceased to be essential to understanding its significance. Art history had reached an end.

Danto was not the first to detect that something had shifted. In 1952, the Italian Futurist artist Bruno Munari came close to reaching the same conclusions when he reflected on a modern world in which everyone is accustomed to seeing images not in museums or galleries, but 'in the cinema, in illuminated advertising, in the great three-dimensional publicity signs of the international fairs'. 'So is art dead', Munari asked, 'or has it just altered aspect without many people noticing? What would Leonardo be doing today?' 'Art is not dead', Munari ultimately decided, 'it has merely altered course and this is where we must look for it. It no longer responds to the old.'[4] But for Danto, art's response 'to the old' is, in fact, its defining feature. Art is, at its heart, a discourse, a give-and-take, between the present and the past. Remove the old and the conversation ceases. You reach 'The End of Art'. The implications of Danto's startling thesis began to spread. By 1992, the American political scientist Francis Fukuyama took things a step further by elevating the phrase 'the end of history',[5] which had been knocking around in cultural discourse since the 19th century, to the bold title of his blockbuster book *The End of History and the Last Man*.

Enter Banksy. In Banksy's work, the famous icons of the past are neither exhausted nor inert. They hold limitless potential. But the dialogue Banksy strikes up with the past is not quite like anything that ever came before. It is as if he salvaged the history of art from a fusty catacomb where its half-remembered milestones have been festering for centuries, waiting to be rediscovered – coarser than we recalled, a little dirtier, and more real. Everything from Leonardo da Vinci's *Mona Lisa* to Damien Hirst's spot paintings is reprogrammed and redeployed in an elastic, illicit language, one that recalibrates what we thought we knew about them. Taken together, the myriad memorable images that Banksy has created over the course of the past thirty years – from his poetic portrait of a little girl reaching hopelessly for a heart-shaped balloon as it floats away to the paradox of a masked protester aggressively hurling a bouquet of

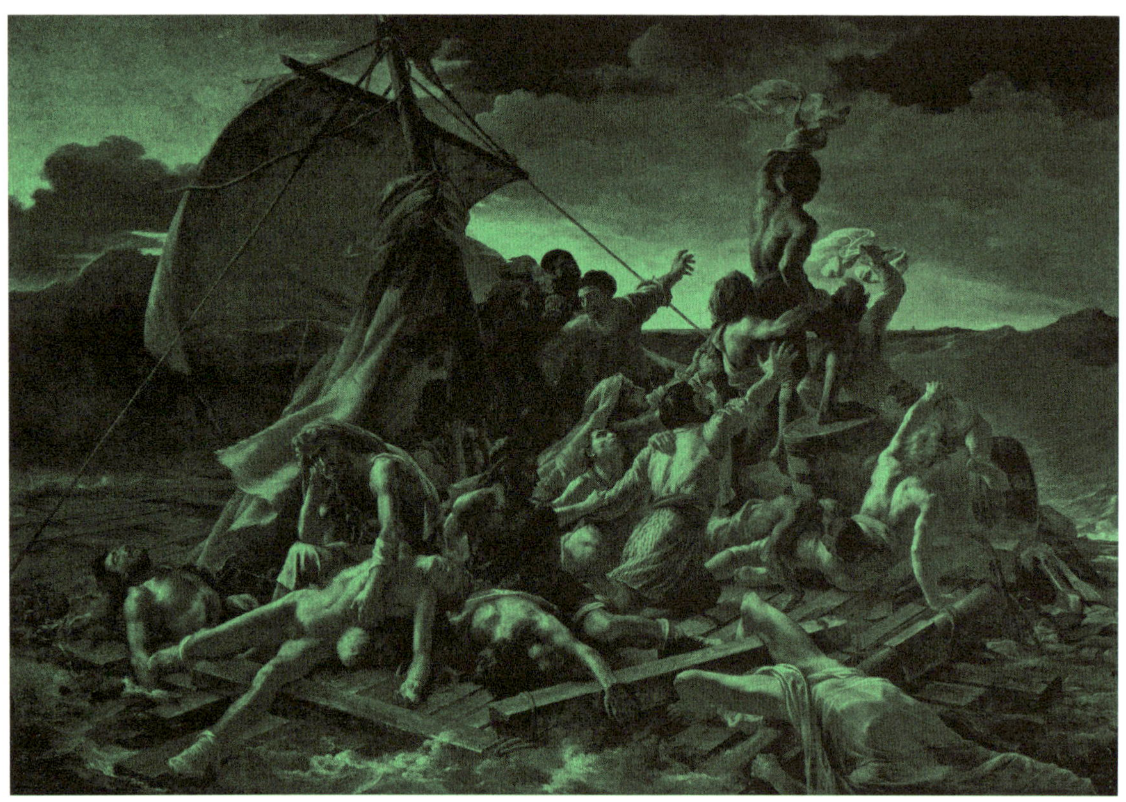

Théodore Géricault, *The Raft of the Medusa*, 1818–19

flowers as if it were a Molotov cocktail – comprise a shrewd and highly original commentary on the history of image-making, from prehistory to the present.

Armed with little more than a clutch of rumpled stencils, rucksacks of nerve, and an anonymizing cloak of after-hours darkness, Banksy succeeded in forging an unrivalled identity for himself as an incorrigible prankster who doesn't embrace tradition, but shreds it. Think of Banksy and you think of scruffy city walls far removed from the pristine white cubes of elite galleries and the vaulted spaces of privileged museums where great art is conventionally found and often left to languish. Through the dark, satirical lens of Banksy's imagination, the history of art can be glimpsed afresh and brought into unexpected focus. From his elaborate replication of Palaeolithic cave paintings (which he envisions being erased by a street cleaner with a pressure hose) to his reinvention of French Impressionist Claude Monet's enchanting Japanese footbridge over a water-lily pond out of which steel skeletons of stolen shopping trolleys and discarded traffic cones jut, Banksy's iconoclastic works force us to reassess our affection for, and appreciation of, the great works of art that define cultural history. While his urban murals and dripping canvases may often appear rough, rushed and reckless, they are in fact deftly conceived –

hardwired with incisive insight into the genius of the works they appear, at first glance, to be flippantly debasing.

No master is spared Banksy's simultaneously eviscerating and invigorating gaze. From Da Vinci to Degas, everyone is grist for his unmerciful mill. Rather than being diminished in their significance, however, the iconic works that Banksy parodies are ironically refurbished by his insolent interventions. Renowned paintings, sculptures and photographs that have become fatigued from being looked at too much and too often are suddenly made pertinent again when displaced by Banksy. Take, for example, a work that Banksy unveiled in Calais, France, in 2015 – a mural based on Théodore Géricault's tragic seascape *The Raft of the Medusa* (1818–19), which depicts the aftermath of a French shipwreck, whose raft-clinging survivors were decimated by starvation before being rescued at sea. Invoked by Banksy in the context of the struggles facing migrants stranded in overcrowded camps in Calais, many of whom risked perilous Channel crossings, Géricault's original canvas is imbued with a new urgency – one that rescues it from the ever-rising waters of over-familiarity and cultural indifference.

By manipulating small details in Géricault's tragic tableaux, Banksy not only constructs a devastating statement on contemporary callousness, but also leaves an indelible mark on the underlying work, one that our mind's eye cannot unsee. The excitement of such frictions – of the present shaping the past – is what motivates *How Banksy Saved Art History*. Traditionally (before, that is, art was deemed to have reached its end), a key benchmark of an artist's impact was the extent to which he or she makes us reassess the art that came before. While we tend to think of artistic influence as a force that only pushes forward, shaping what comes after – El Greco as inspiration to Velázquez, Velázquez to Goya, Goya to Picasso, and so on – in truth, the power of influence is just as strong in the other direction. Time is a myth. The most formidable art alters the past every bit as much as it shapes the future. However mystical it may seem, the work of every great artist leaves palpable traces on the great works that preceded it.[6]

Consider, for instance, the French avant-garde artist Édouard Manet's captivating 1863 portrait of a reclining nude, *Olympia* – an audacious reinterpretation of the Italian Renaissance Titian's 1534 *Venus of Urbino*, which is itself a reinvention of an early painting by the Venetian artist Giorgione. With his fellow French painter Victorine Meurent as his model, Manet scandalously recast the exalted figure of Venus, endlessly idealized in Western culture, in the guise of a prostitute – her eyes fixed unflinchingly forward into ours. Not only does Manet radically revamp the symbolism of Titian's painting, replacing the sleeping toy spaniel at Venus's feet (an emblem of faithfulness) with an erect, saucer-eyed black cat (a symbol of lasciviousness), he daringly inserts into the scene a black woman (rarely featured in Western art) in the role of a maid, standing immediately beside Olympia. Her prominent presence in the work demands that viewers acknowledge the dignified existence of black people in Parisian society, fifteen years after slavery had officially been abolished.[7]

Manet's painting, which caused a stir when it was first exhibited, does not erase or rescind Titian's early painting. It opens up possibilities in it. It rescues it.

As Manet's friend, the writer Émile Zola, explained when contemporary critics condemned the work's reinvention of Titian's masterpiece, *Olympia* is anything but immoral. It rectifies falsehoods that threaten to tarnish the intensity of Titian's work. 'When our artists give us Venuses', Zola explained, 'they correct nature, they lie. Édouard Manet asked himself why lie, why not tell the truth; he introduced us to Olympia, this *fille* of our time, whom you meet on the sidewalks.'[8]

Telling the truth on sidewalks is what Banksy does, too. After beginning his career as a graffiti artist on the streets of Bristol, freestyling outsized tags extemporaneously on the spot, a time-consuming practice that left him vulnerable to arrest, Banksy eventually hit upon the notion of using stencils that could be fashioned ahead of time. The 'epiphany' came, he says, when hiding under a dump truck after being chased by British transport police one night.[9] He had been attempting to emblazon the words 'LATE AGAIN' on a passenger train in huge balloon letters when he was rumbled and chased through a thorny hedge. As the truck leaked oil onto his scratched-up body, he resolved either to find a faster way of working or to throw in the towel. It was then that his eyes fell fortuitously on a sign that had been stencilled onto a fuel tank, suggesting a much more efficient way of imprinting images onto surfaces. It lit a spark. By creating stencils for his works in advance, Banksy could construct far more elaborate, meaningful, and subversive images and spray them onto a wall in a fraction of the time. By the turn of the millennium, Banksy's signature stencil style was allowing him to intervene in iconic works of art in a way that would not have been feasible otherwise.

Was Banksy the first street artist to use stencils for a faster tag and dash, or to glimpse in the approach a greater potential for complex image-making? No. As Banksy himself has freely acknowledged, the now-legendary French graffiti artist known as Blek le Rat, christened by critics 'the grandfather of stencils',[10] began staking claim to the territory in the early 1980s. 'Every time I think I've painted something original,' Banksy has said, 'I find out that Blek le Rat has done it as well, only 20 years earlier.'[11] A recognized pioneer of street art, Blek le Rat (born Xavier Prou in 1952) is credited with helping ignite the world's embrace of the genre, even if relatively few people know his name or could call to mind the contours of a single one of his works.

While Blek le Rat may have started stencilling first, Banksy's independent epiphany beneath that dump truck was no less consequential. In the years that followed, Banksy would succeed in striking a much deeper and more resonant chord, capturing the attention and imagination of people who may otherwise have had little interest in either the genre of graffiti itself or in the history of art generally. What fascinates in the pages that follow is how Banksy does it – how his work manages to capture the world's gaze and to turn it back on itself.

Conversely, what is of little concern is Banksy's real name, or evaluating the conclusions reached by those who have endeavoured to unmask him. Banksy's refusal (to date) to confirm who he is does not hinder the type of assessment of his work that is undertaken here. It is a profound advantage.

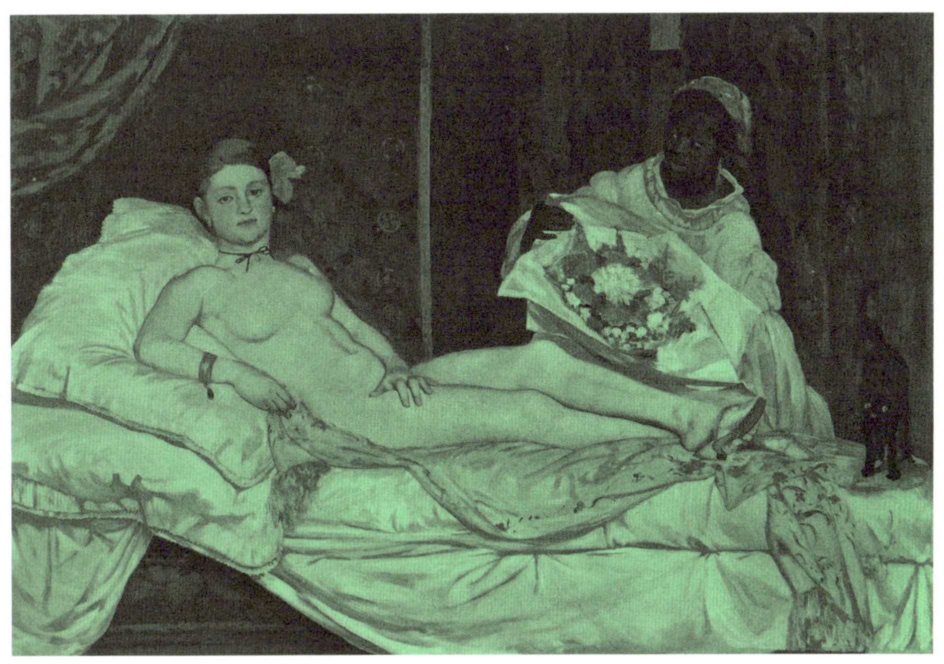

Édouard Manet, *Olympia*, 1863

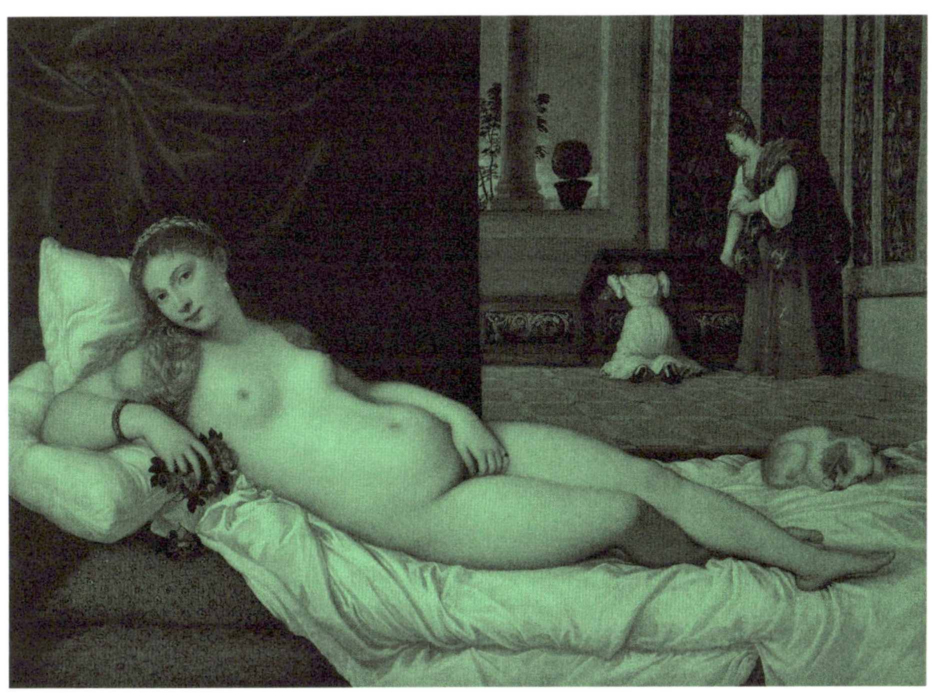

Titian, *Venus of Urbino*, 1534

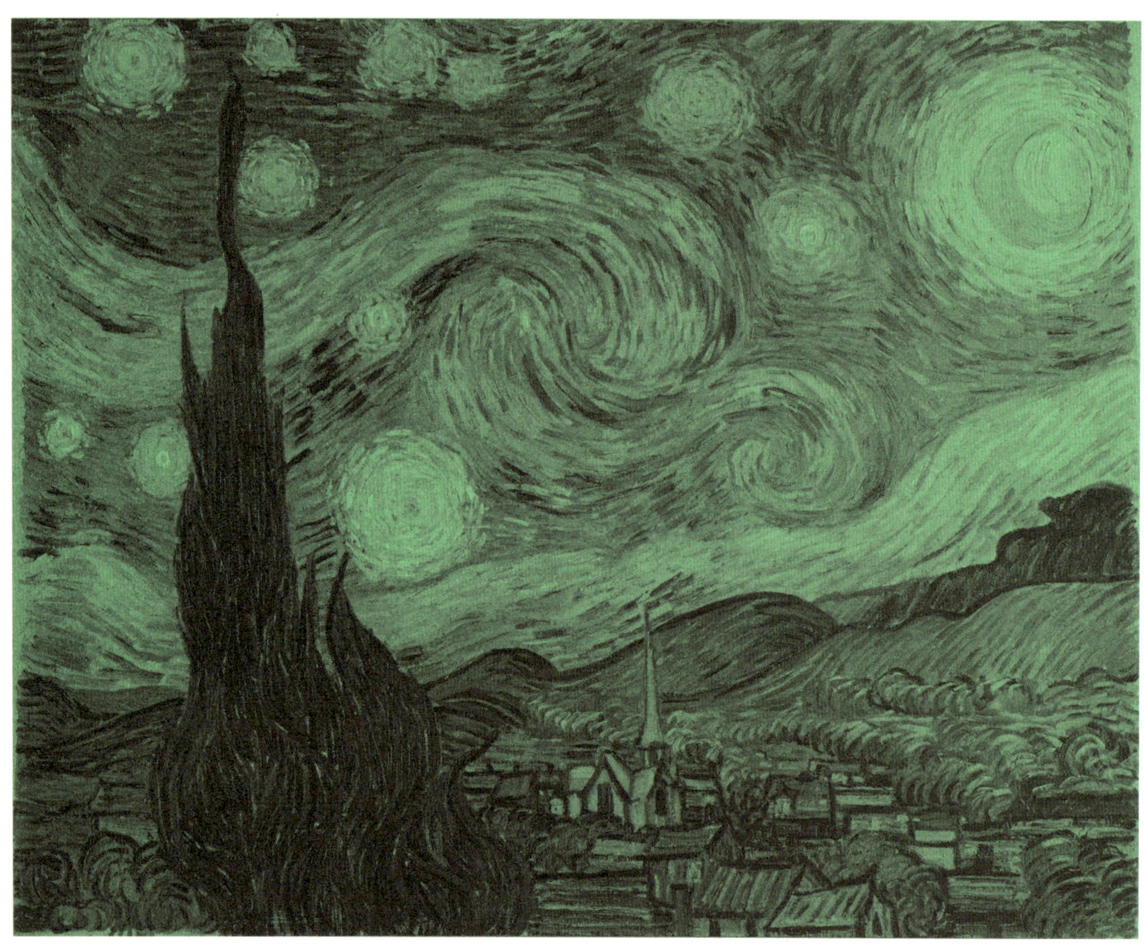

Vincent van Gogh, *The Starry Night*, 1889

Once known, an artist's identity has a way of encrusting itself to the surface of their works, clouding our clear sight of them. The images cease to be pure visual statements and are made to serve instead as illustrations of the artist's journey – the triumphs and tragedies, breakthroughs and breakdowns that define a life. Can you imagine for a moment approaching the turbulent cosmos of Van Gogh's *Starry Night* through a lens wiped clean of any awareness of the tempestuous state of mind the troubled artist was in when he painted it? No, I can't either. The agitated canvas has become less a painting in its own right than a lava lamp of Van Gogh's anguished existence as a patient in the Saint-Paul-de-Mausole asylum in Saint-Rémy-de-Provence, France, where he admitted himself after a breakdown. *How Banksy Saved Art History* isn't interested in catching Banksy out, pinning him down, or using his works to interrogate his upbringing or education, his friendships or fallings-out. What interests us here is how Banksy's work works on us, whoever he might be.

Even when Banksy is not being overtly visual, a covert aesthetic sensibility, steeped in the story of art, is invariably at play. Take, for example, his famous adaptation of a slogan by the Lithuanian-born American political activist, author and revolutionary Emma Goldman: 'If voting changed anything, they'd make it illegal'. Rewriting Goldman to read 'If graffiti changed anything it would be illegal' for a mural unveiled in London in April 2011, Banksy has shown himself to be a dab hand at forging phrases that echo the radical adages and axioms coined by politically-minded predecessors in the art world, such as the anonymous group of feminist artists, the Guerrilla Girls. Their acerbic 1995 poster *Ten Trashy Ideas About the Environment*, which features sardonic statements such as 'I like to use plastic, especially for making art about the environment. After all, art is eternal and so is plastic', is not only in accord with Banksy's temperament – it reveals that Bansky's witty one-line monologues are in fact deft dialogues. They are part of a ceaseless conversation that suggests that art, in truth, never ends.

Taking readers on a journey through the milestones of art history, this book enlists as its irreverent guide a selection of Bansky's most memorable murals, paintings and sculptures that open possibilities in those icons. The result is a provocative re-examination of some of the world's most famous and revered artistic touchstones – from Raphael's *The Mond Crucifixion* to Vincent van Gogh's *Sunflowers*, from Jacques-Louis David's *Napoleon Crossing the Alps* to to Kara Walker's *Virginia Lynch Mob*. It is worth noting that the course this book navigates through Bansky's oeuvre and through art history more broadly is one entirely unauthorized by the artist. Pest Control, the 'parent/ legal guardian' for Banksy, rarely license the artist's images. The reader should therefore be aware that Banksy had no participation in this book. The decision on which Banksy works to include was made entirely by me in consultation with the pub-lisher. The volume before you is, therefore, as it ought to be, one that required no approval or prior restraint by its subject or his studio – one that seeks through unfiltered reflection to provide a map for appreciating one of the most intriguing imaginations of our era.

I'VE LEARNT FROM EXPERIENCE THAT A PAINTING ISN'T FINISHED WHEN YOU PUT DOWN YOUR BRUSH – THAT'S WHEN IT STARTS.[12]

BANKSY

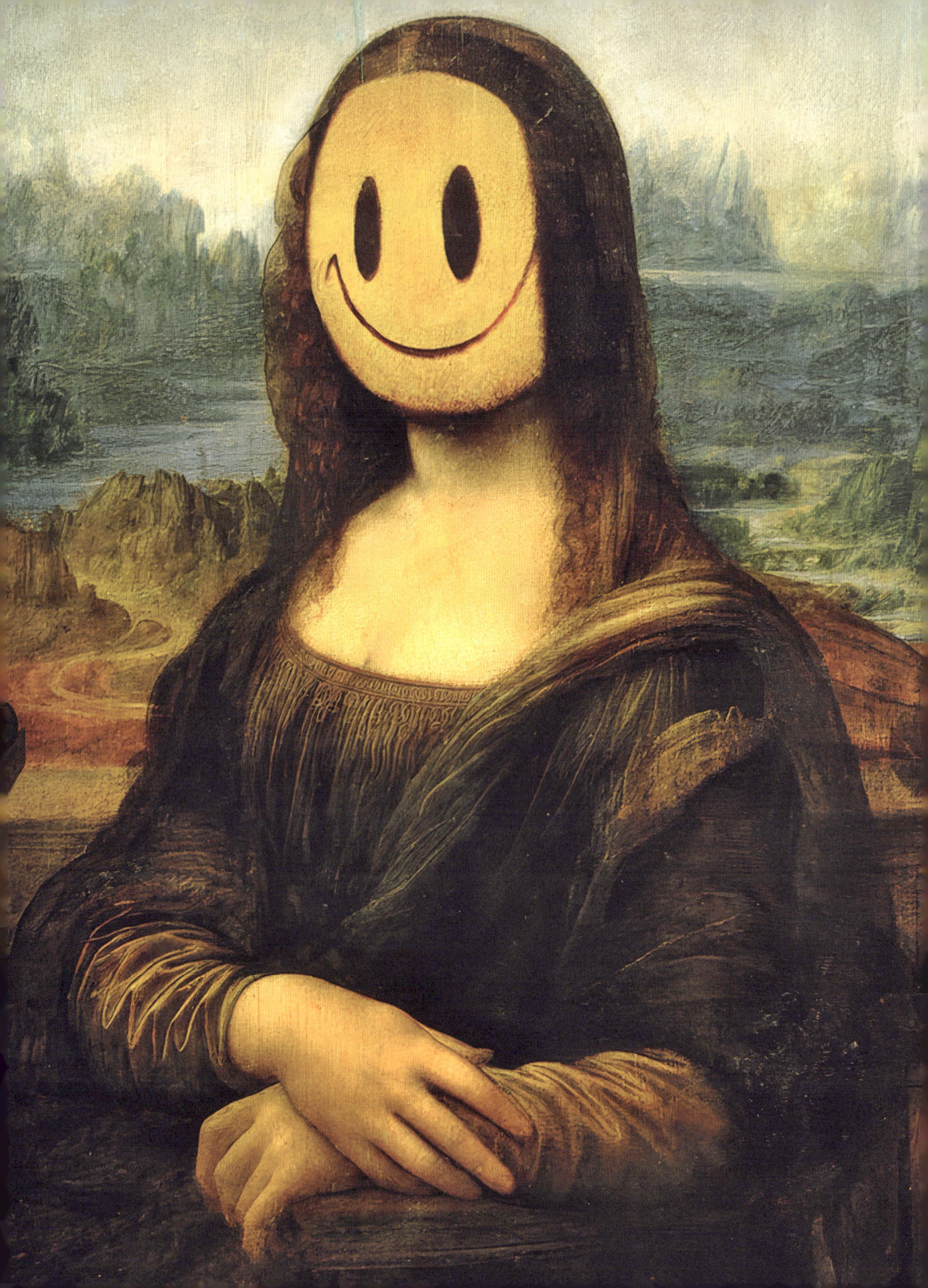

ERASE AND REWIND

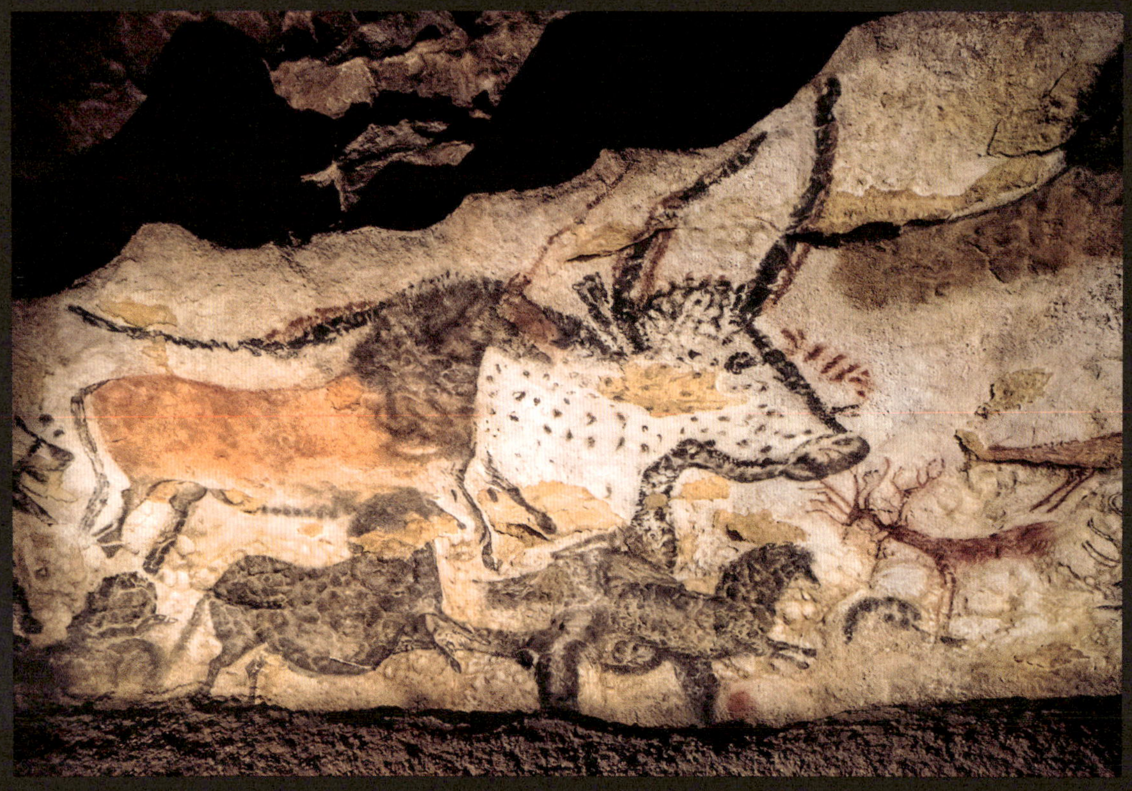

Palaeolithic paintings at the Cave of Lascaux, France, 15,000 BC

W hat is the difference between a damnable act of wanton vandalism and a priceless treasure of incalculable cultural significance? About 17,000 years, apparently. That is among the many messages vibrating back from an elaborate mural that Banksy created in early May 2008 in London's legendary Leake Street Arches – a 300-metre long (985 foot) tunnel in the borough of Lambeth where graffiti is permitted. Hosting what he called his 'Cans Festival' (poking fun at the pretentiously posh 61st Annual Cannes Film Festival that was being held at the same time in the French Riviera), Banksy invited street artists to enshroud with spray paint and stencil the subterranean space that stretches beneath Waterloo Station (formerly occupied by Eurostar).

Banksy's own contribution to the anti-glamorous exhibition was a sprawling mural, which transformed a section of the tunnel's wall, beneath a pair of back-to-back CCTV cameras pointing left and right, into a replica of prehistoric Stone Age drawings of the sort found variously in the Lascaux Cave system near the village of Montignac in the Vézère Valley, in the Dordogne region of southwestern France, and in the so-called Cave of Hands discovered in Santa Cruz, Argentina. Against this compelling collage of rudimentary rock art, Banksy superimposed the figure of a street cleaner holding the long lance of a high-pressure washer. The frozen spray from its ferocious nozzle, precisely the type of weapon wielded by high-vis-wearing municipal minions to expunge the work of street artists from the fabric of city walls, is suspended in the act of erasing forever the sole surviving traces of ancient art.

By equating his own work with that of artists whose vision and skill are now cherished, Banksy asks us to consider the short-sightedness of public officials deputized with deciding which creative expressions are worth keeping and which should be erased. 'Art is not like other culture', Banksy has said of the disparity between the rules that seem to govern the legitimacy of visual enunciations and other forms of creative expression,

> *because its success is not made by its audience. The public fills concert halls and cinemas every day, we read novels by the millions and buy records by the billions. We, the people, affect the making and the quality of most of our culture, but not our art. The Art we look at is made by only a select few. A small group create, promote, purchase, exhibit and decide the success of Art. Only a few hundred people in the world have a real say. When you go to an Art gallery you are simply a tourist looking at a trophy cabinet of a few millionaires.*[13]

By echoing the cave in which humankind first found its artistic voice, Banksy reminds us that art began as a raw, unrestrained impulse, not cordoned off by curators and museum directors. Art was the rough wall beside which we cooked our meals, slept and shat, burnt bones in sacrificial fires, and clubbed each other to death. The good ol' days.

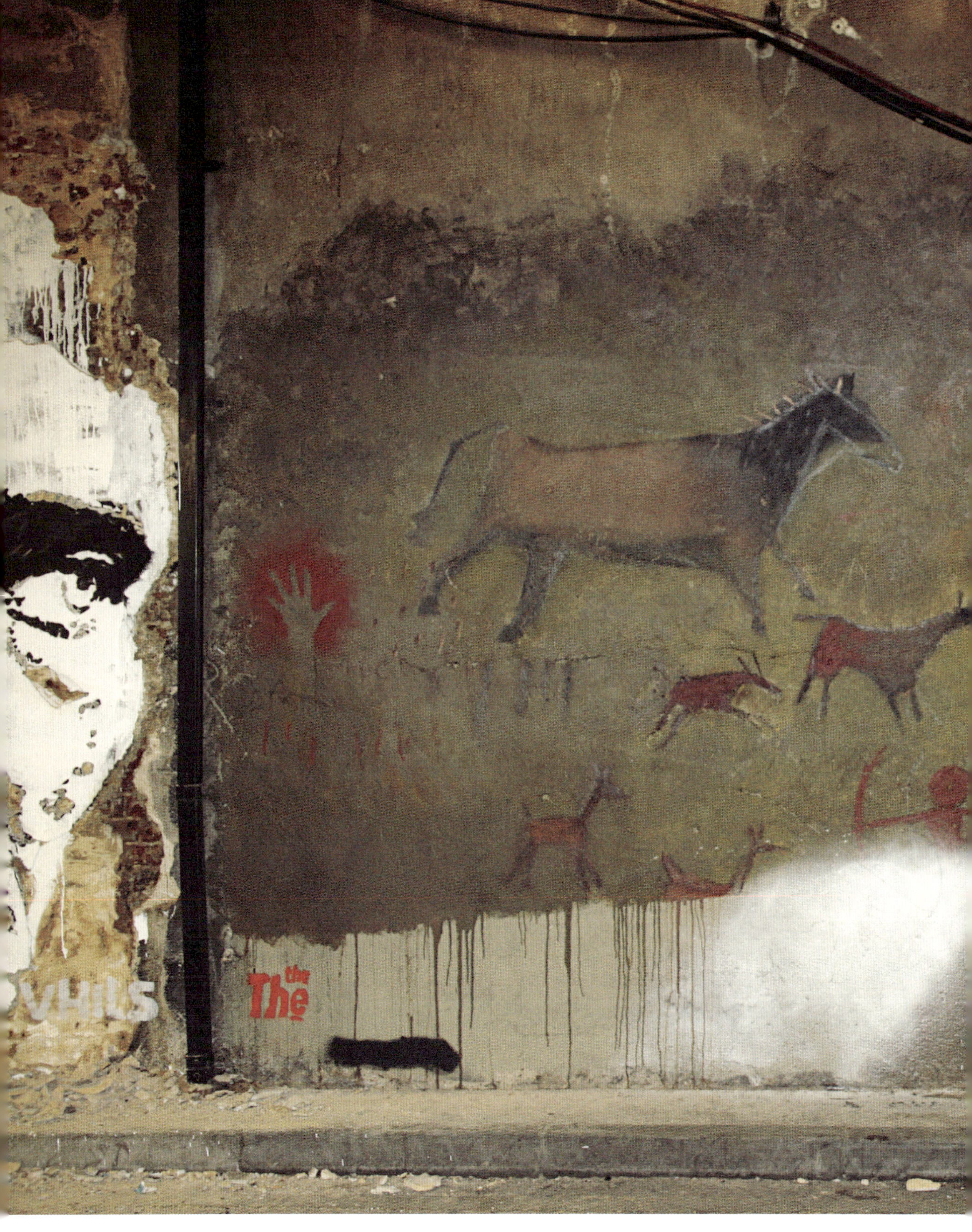
VHILS
The the

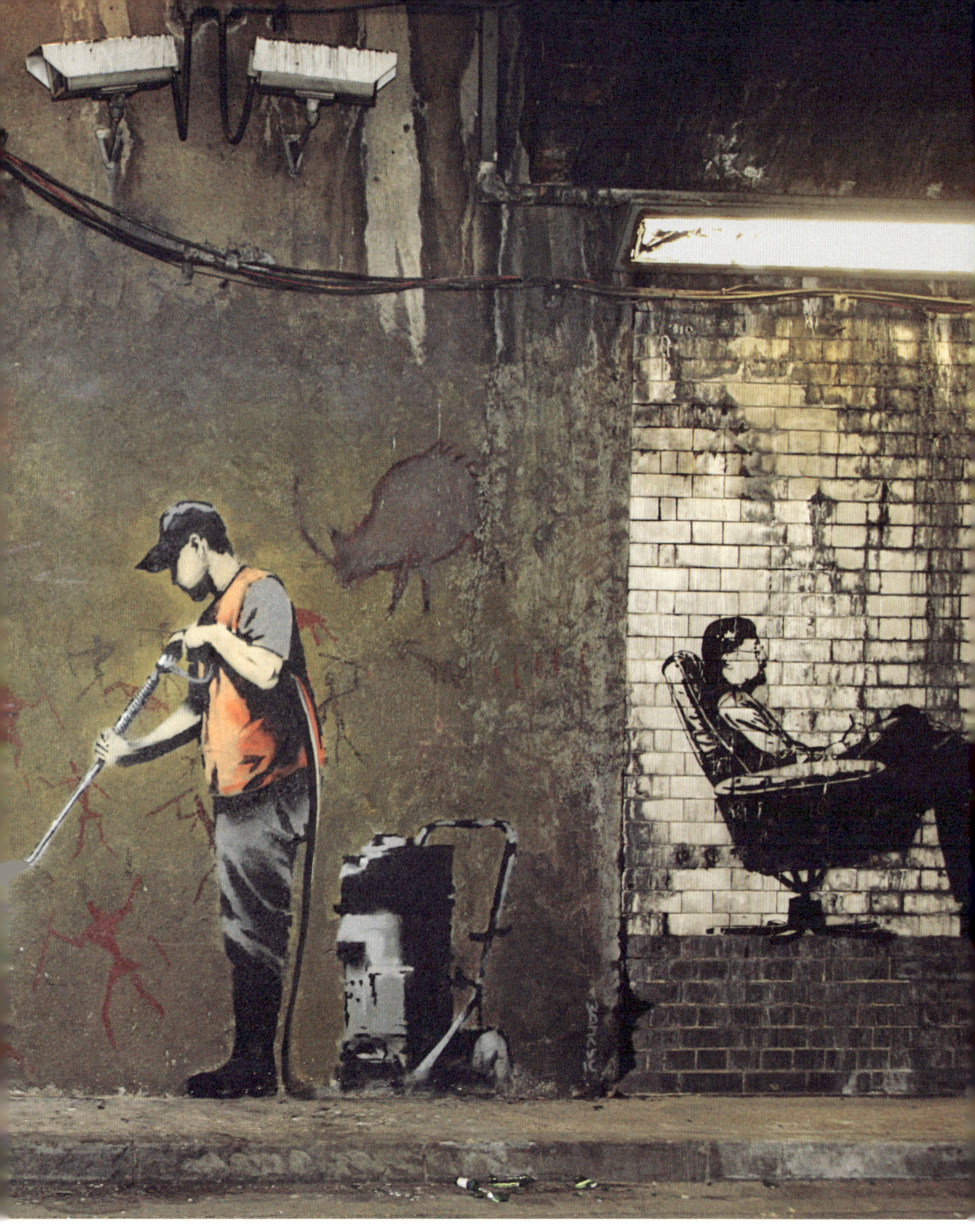

South Bank, London, 2008

GREAT MINDS SPHINX ALIKE

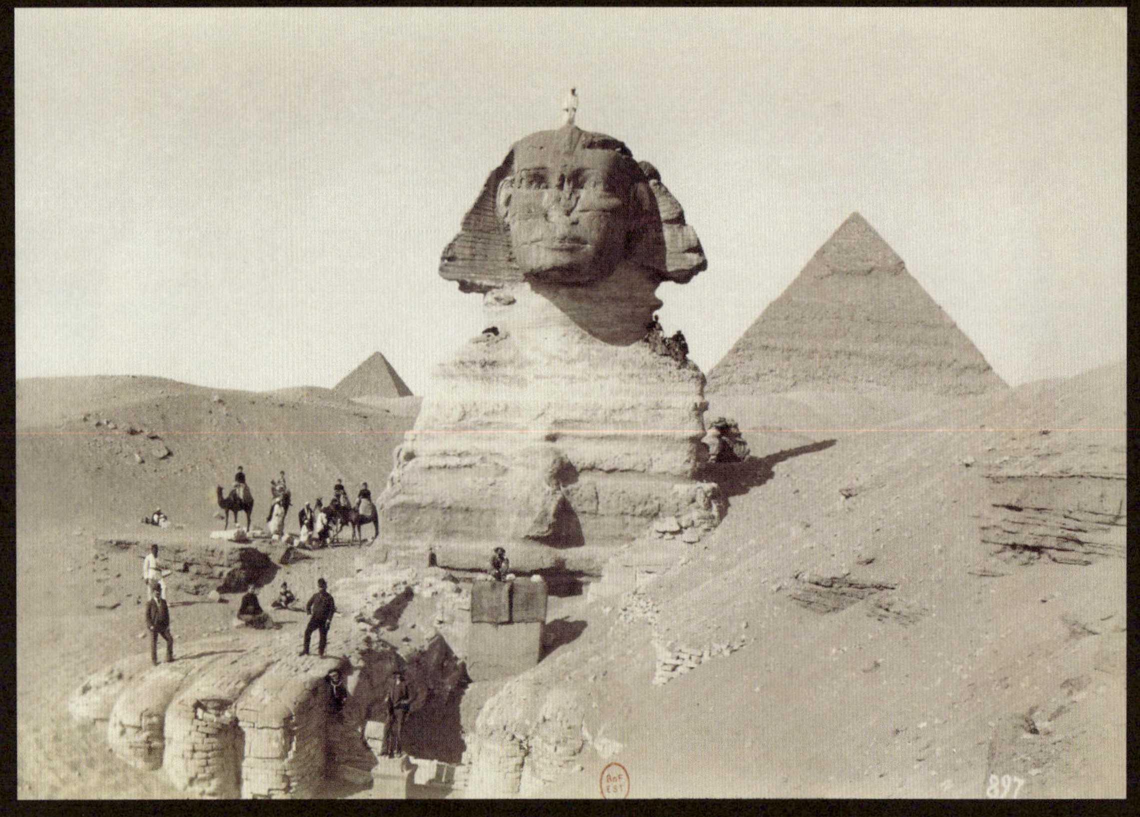

The Great Sphinx of Giza, *c.* 2,500 BC (Photographed by Bernardino Facchinelli, *c.* 1880s)

In October 2013, a miniature version of the Great Sphinx of Giza, fashioned from smashed cinderblocks, was spotted rising from a murky pool of stagnant water on the streets of Queens, New York, as if a pile of abandoned rubble had suddenly assembled itself into something mysterious and strange. The rough-and-ready replica of one of the world's largest, oldest and most enigmatic works of art invested the scrap of urban wasteland with an air of world-weary wonder.

Built from limestone by ancient Egyptians over 4,500 years ago, during the reign of the Old Kingdom pharaoh Khafre, the Great Sphinx is the oldest monumental sculpture in existence and depicts a mythical creature with the body of a lion and the head of a human. Protectively prowling the sands of the necropolis where the great pyramids rise, the work has weathered many defacements over the course of its slow, static slouch across centuries – loss of the vibrant colours in which it was once painted, the addition and removal of a beard, and, most famously, the shabby shattering of its nose (most likely by chisel-wielding vandals in the 14th century, not by Napoleon's army in the 19th). The Sphinx's scrappy survival has become a synecdoche for the invincibility of art and culture generally. We too will endure, we tell ourselves, because it has. Then along came Banksy.

Unlike the ancient icon it echoes, which has gazed across the desert sands of the Nile's west bank for many millennia, Banksy's *Everything but the Kitchen Sphinx* succeeded in staying put for less than a single day before it was hastily dismantled, shoved in the back of a van, and hauled away. A curious caption to the work that Banksy posted to his website and on Instagram left little doubt, however, that the scruffy sculpture was anything but slight or slapdash in its meaning. 'No turn unstoned', Banksy cryptically quipped, 'you're advised not to drink the replica Arab spring water'.

On one level, the warning is an allusion to the wave of protests for reform that swept the Arab world between 2011 and 2014, widely referred to in the media as the Arab Spring. But the remark is also a bitter and recurring rebuke of the appalling prevalence of polluted water in much of the world. 'There's an elephant in the room', Banksy wrote on a flyer six years earlier for his exhibition 'Barely Legal':

> *There's a problem we never talk about. The fact is that life isn't getting any fairer. 1.7 billion people have no access to clean drinking water. 20 billion people live below the poverty line. Every day hundreds of people are made to physically be sick by morons at art shows telling them how bad the world is but never actually doing something about it. Anybody want a free glass of wine?*

Whether *Everything but the Kitchen Sphinx* – the 22nd work Banksy unveiled during his month-long residency in New York in October 2013 – was intended to show solidarity with the uprisings or to sound a sage note of caution in believing that the revolutions would secure lasting change is anyone's guess. After all, the power of Banksy, like that of the Sphinx, relies on inscrutability.

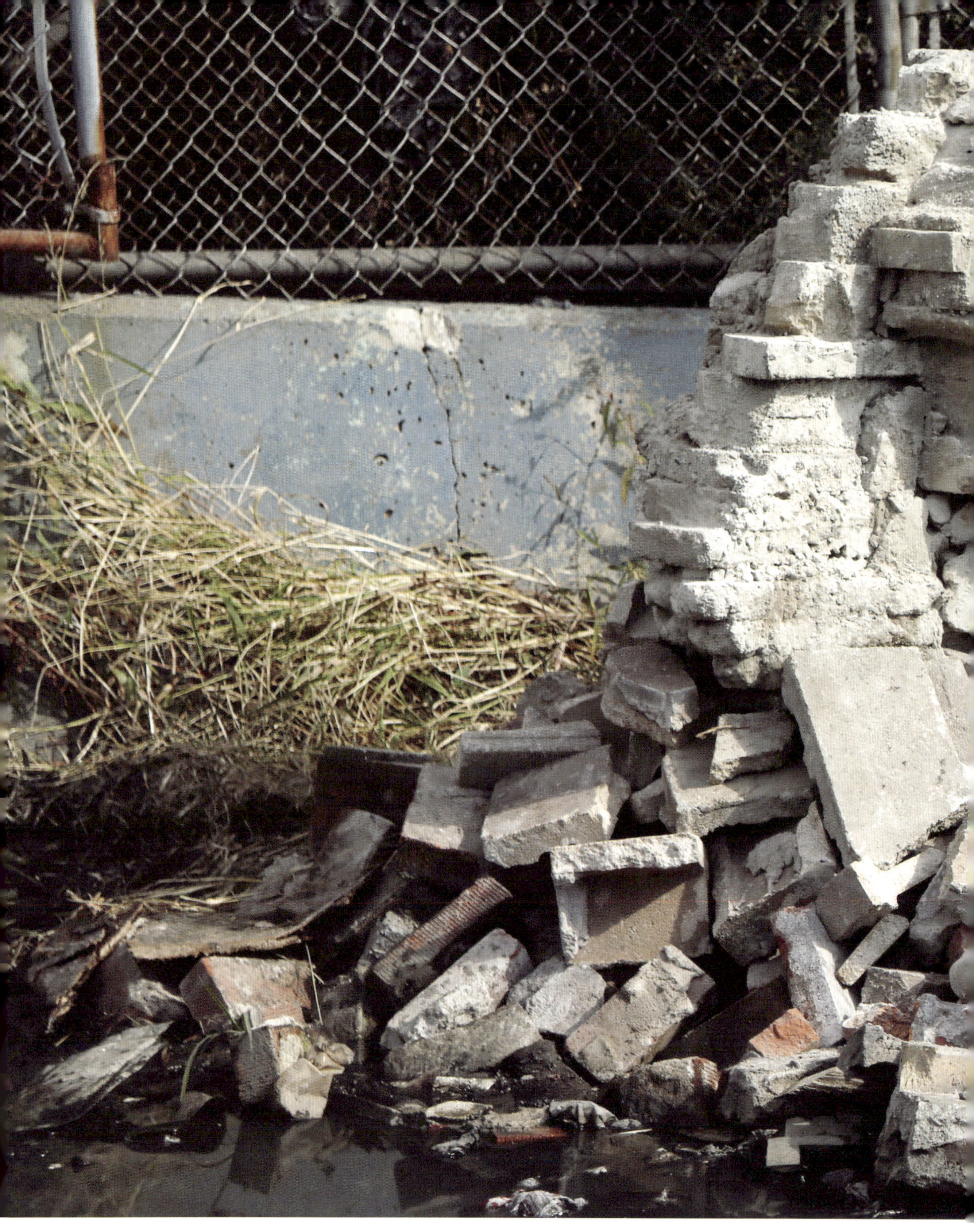

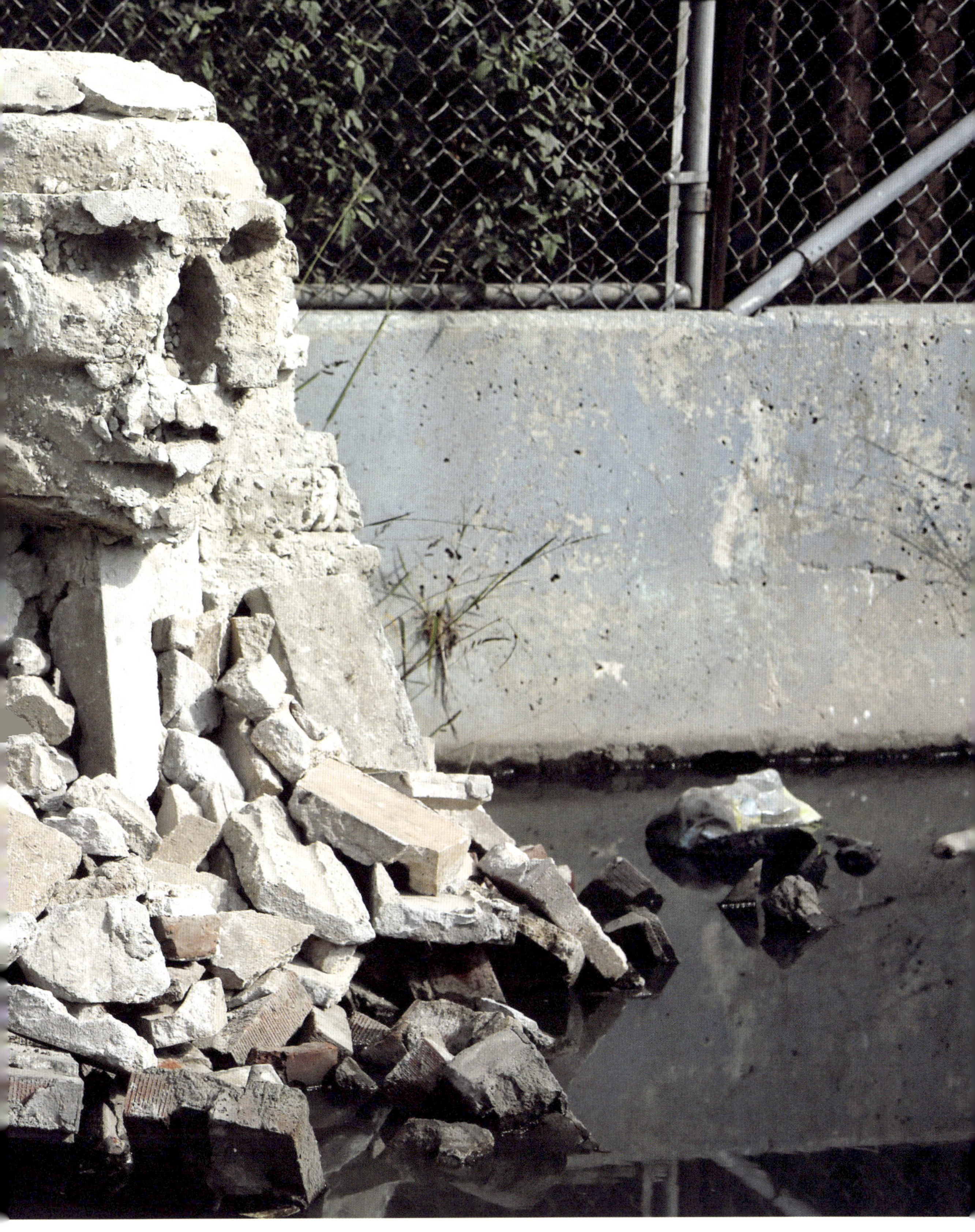

Everything but the Kitchen Sphinx, 2013

FLOWER
POWER

An intensely focused figure, fashioned from darkest shadow, shifts his weight to his back foot as he prepares to leverage the full elastic force of his body's frame to unleash what is clenched in his cocked fist. His taut posture and tense concentration are as compelling as they are at odds with the imagined fragrance of the fragile flowers he's clutching.

No, I'm not talking about Banksy's famous *Love is in the Air*, a powerfully poignant portrait of a masked protestor on the verge of hurling a bouquet of brightly coloured blossoms. The figure (or figurine) that I have in mind, a votive statue of the Phoenician god Melqart, prefigures by some fourteen centuries the fully flexed physique of Banksy's pseudo-self-portrait, which appeared in 2003 in a Palestinian town near Bethlehem, a stone's throw from the wall that separates Israel from the West Bank territories of Palestine.

According to myths current in the ancient civilization to the north of Palestine, Melqart, founder of the city-state of Tyre, was charged both with ruling the underworld and with protecting the Universe – holding dominion over both the living and the dead. To convey Melqart's hybrid nature, he was typically depicted brandishing both a battle axe and a lotus flower, an ancient symbol of hope and rebirth. Look closely at the pocked and tarnished bronze statue of the god that stands forever poised to strike in the collection of Seville's Archaeological Museum and you'll see that time has roughly frisked him, confiscating his symbolic props, leaving him looking a little out of sorts – more flailing than fearsome – cutting plaintive shapes in the stale gallery air.

With Melqart rendered empty-handed, we're left to speculate about which fist gripped the axe and which the flowers. It seems logical, of course, that the arm raised above his head, steadying for thrust, was likely the one that wielded the sharpened weapon. But I can't help hoping, imagining in my mind's eye, that it's the other way around – that Melqart is waving across millennia with his right hand a big, beautiful lotus blossom to his distant descendant, the flower thrower. All I can say for sure is this: I'd rather be hit in the face with a bouquet of painted flowers hurled by a masked silhouette than watch with bleeding eyes the horrors of war unfold before us.

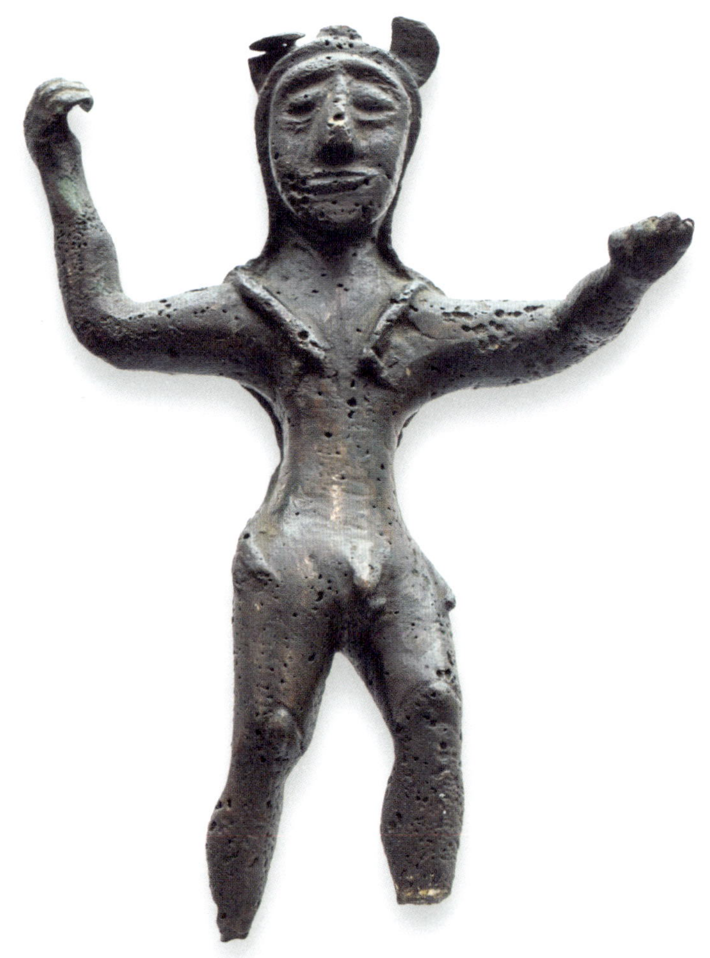

Bronze figurine of Melqart, 7th century BC

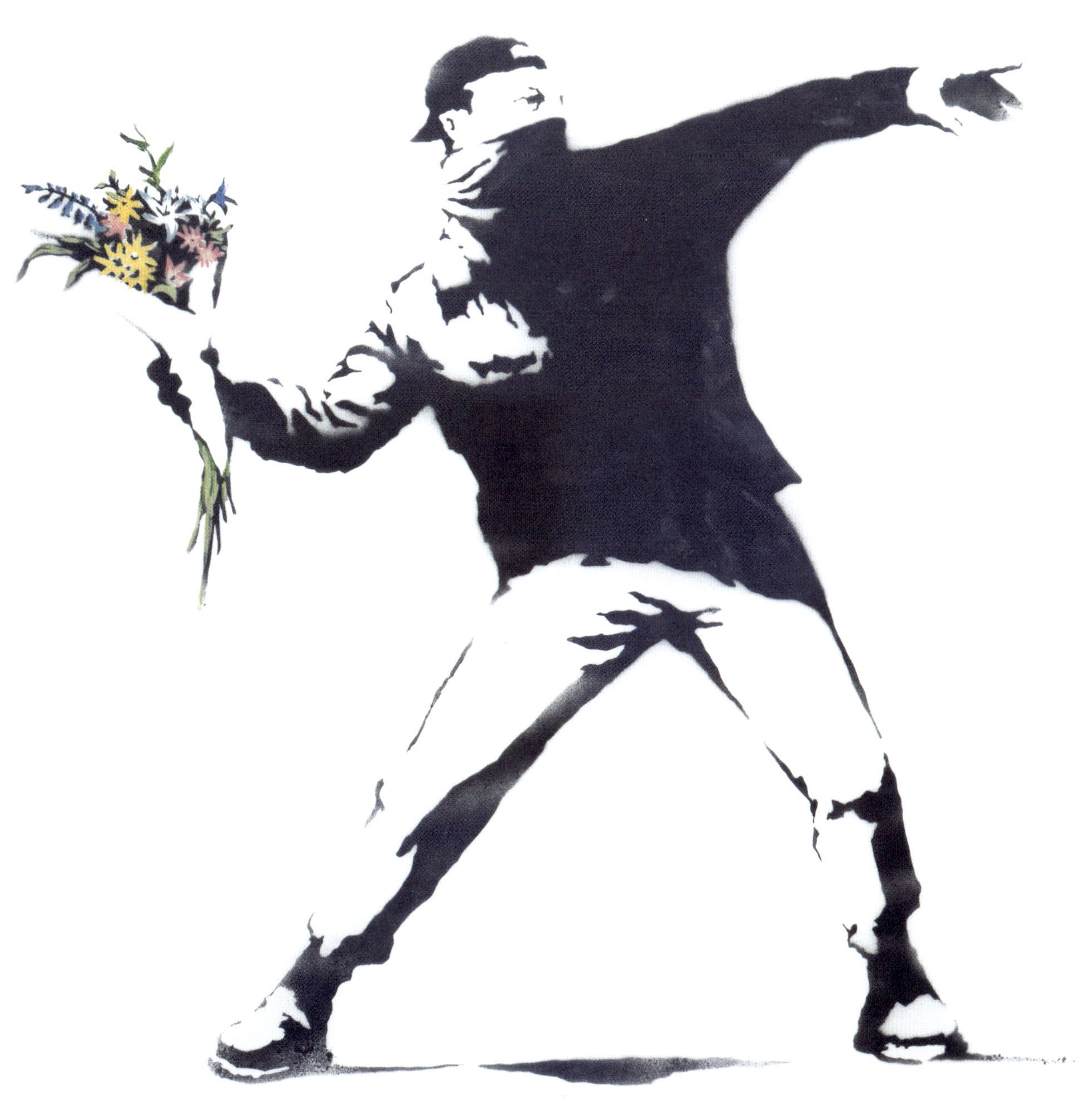

Love is in the Air, 2003

COPY

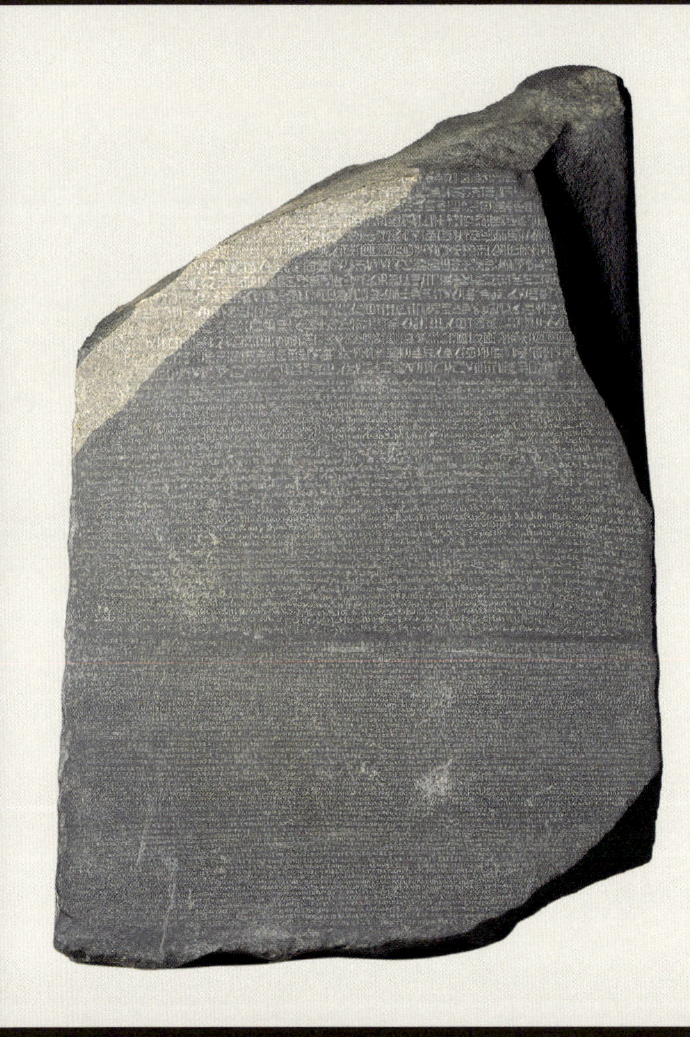

The Rosetta Stone, 196 BC

Want to solve a complex problem? What you need is a Rosetta Stone. Though the actual archaeological artefact to which that famous appellation attaches is a fragment of a large stone monument from the 2nd century BC, the term has metaphorically been applied to any object that is key to cracking a code, to unlocking a mystery. The enormous chunk of grey granodiorite, discovered in Rashid ('Rosetta'), Egypt, in 1799 by Napoleon's army as it tried to gain control of the East Mediterranean, proved indispensable in translating ancient Egyptian hieroglyphs – one of the three scripts in which the stone repeats the same decree that its readers hail Ptolemy V, 'the god who makes himself manifest, whose deeds are beautiful'. In recent decades, the human genome, finally sequenced in 2003, has been exalted as the 'Rosetta Stone' for comprehending human biology. In physics, the Higgs boson particle, observed in 2012 after much speculation, has been called a 'Rosetta Stone' for understanding the forces of nature.

But what about in art? Has any object or enunciation ever been uncovered that helps us penetrate into the essence of creative genius? In 2009, Banksy, with characteristic audacity and misdirection, proposed one. On a crude slab of marble whose ragged shape recalls the contours of the Rosetta Stone, Banksy chiselled a famous quote often credited to Pablo Picasso: 'The bad artists imitate, the great artists steal.' As if to prove the point in real time, and right before our very eyes, Banksy violently crosses out Picasso's byline and replaces it with his own. As an insight into the nature of artistic ingenuity, the simple assertion that originality is never original but deceptively derivative is both incisive and, well, not very original. When Mark Twain had the idea that 'there is no such thing as a new idea',[14] it wasn't a new idea. Four centuries earlier, Shakespeare began his 59th sonnet by observing that 'there be nothing new', and that our 'brains' spend their time 'labouring for invention' in vain. Nothing new there either, as Shakespeare was merely pilfering with impunity from Ecclesiastes, which says 'there is nothing new under the sun' (1:9). What is interesting about Banksy's fearless grift of Picasso's unoriginal statement about the unoriginality of originality, however, is that it wasn't even Picasso who wasn't being original when Banksy unoriginally stole his unoriginality – it was T. S. Eliot. In *The Sacred Wood* (1920), Eliot rehearses the recycled contention and in doing so, ironically, manages to cast original light on Banksy's own original achievement. Inexperienced poets, Eliot says, are clumsy mimes. Mature ones, on the other hand, are more artful. They shamelessly steal. They cover their tracks by transforming their thefts into something fresh and new.[15] That's exactly what Banksy does, time and time over, and I feel very original in pointing that out, whether I am or not.

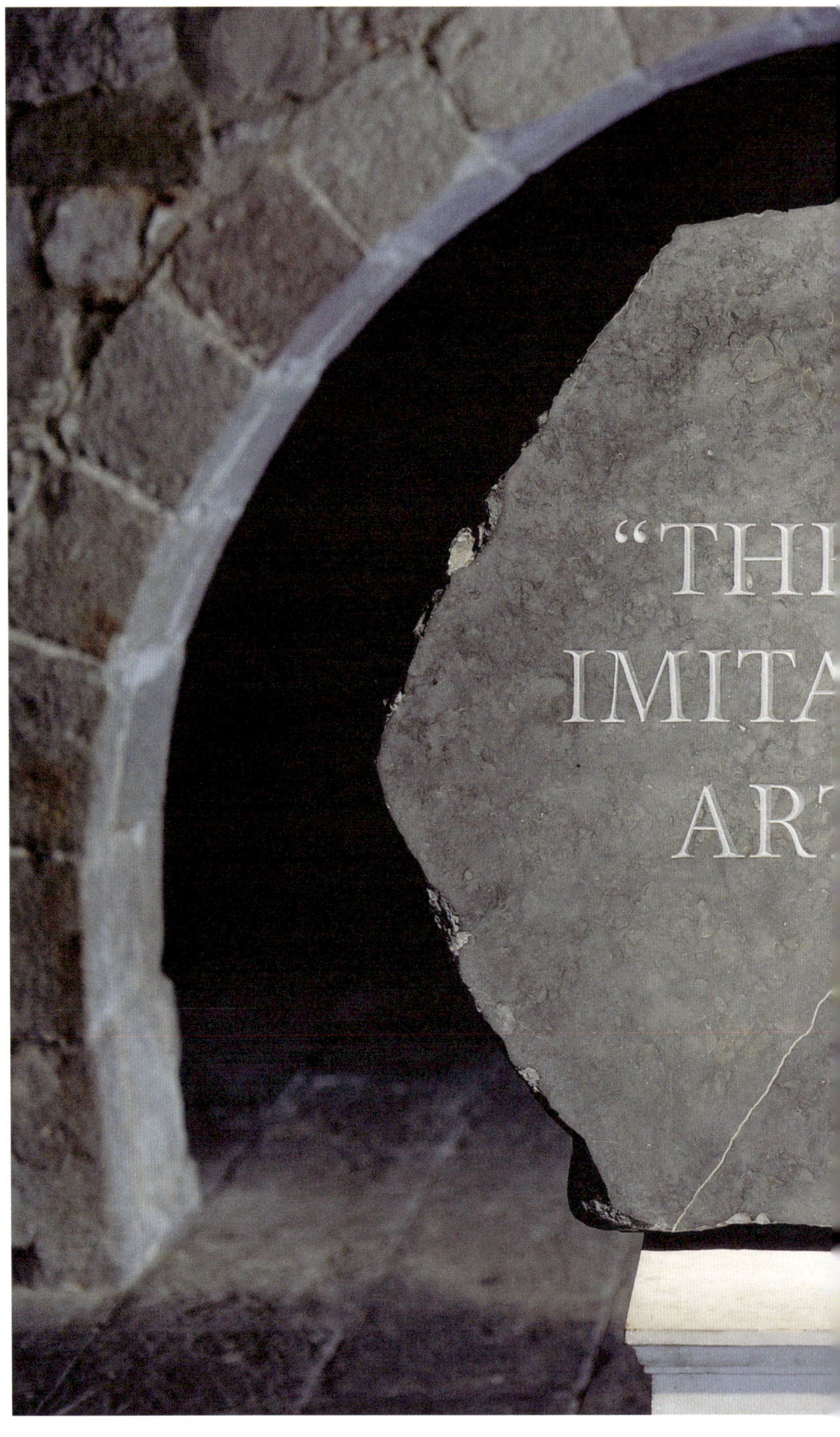
"THE
IMITA
ART

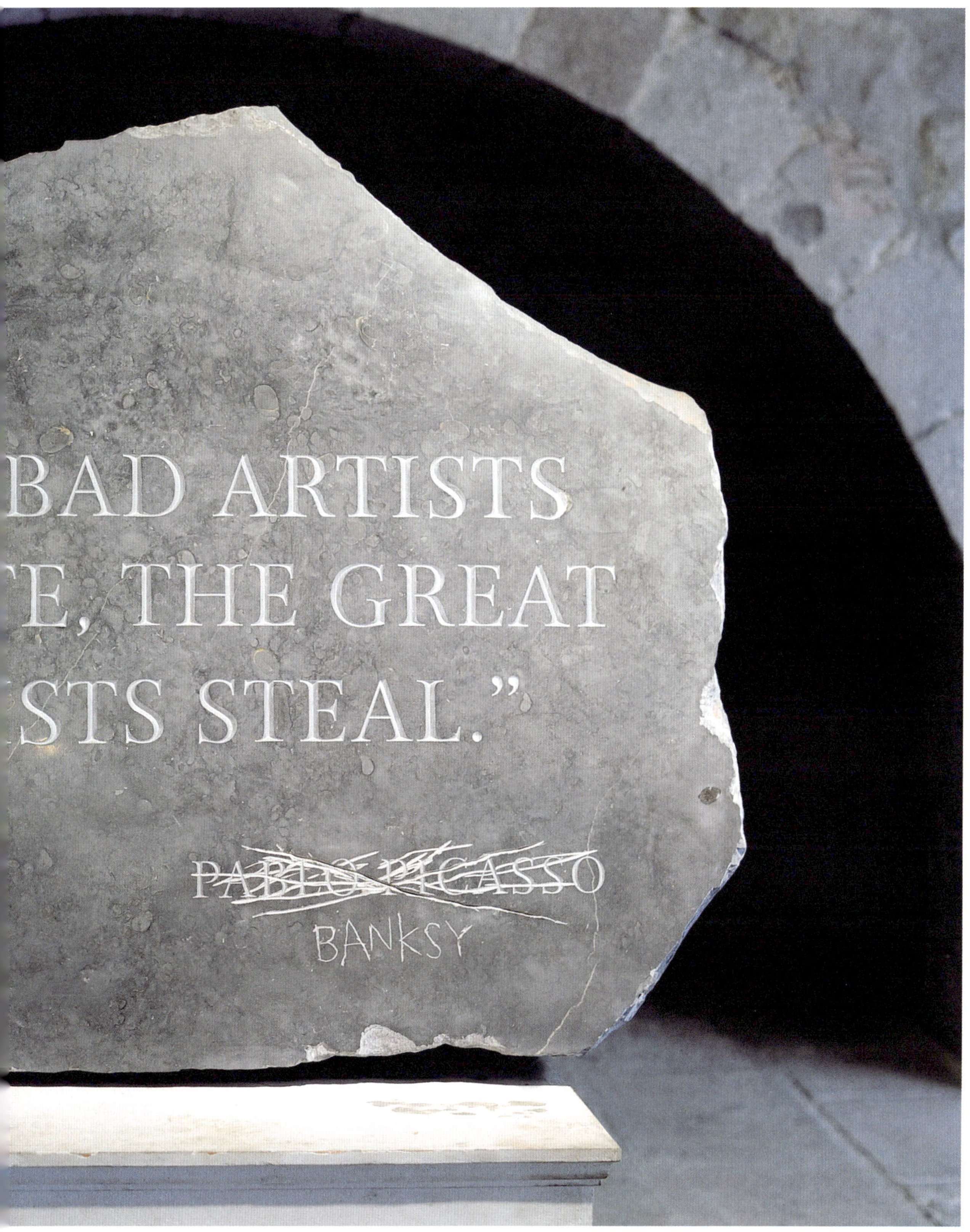

The Bad Artists Imitate, 2009

OFF YOUR TROLLEY

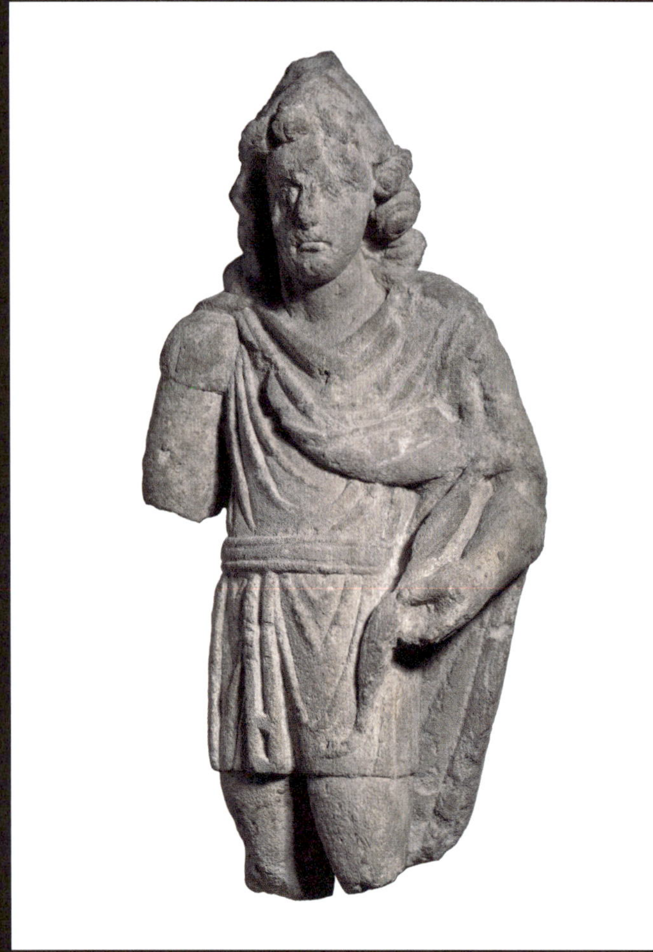

Figure of a hunter god, 2nd century AD

It's now the stuff of legend: a dishevelled man shuffles into the Roman Britain rooms of the British Museum in May 2005 carrying a plastic bag that is stretched out of shape by the weight of what's inside it. Wearing a fake beard and long coat, he is hoping to fit in unnoticed – just another dowdy academic, killing time before a lecture. But rather than taking an interest in the displays, this visitor reaches inside his shabby bag and fetches instead a hunk of stone he has brought with him, one already fitted with strips of strong adhesive tape. Unheeded, he fixes the contraband fragment to the wall, just below the broken marble effigy of a curly-haired young hunter god who happens to be missing his lower right arm and both legs below the knees. Happy with his illicit instalment, the visitor grabs from the bag one last thing: a carefully composed placard. 'This finely preserved example of primitive art dates from the Post-Catatonic era', the sign read, 'and is thought to depict early man venturing towards the out-of-town hunting grounds. The artist responsible is known to have created a substantial body of work across South East of England under the moniker Banksymus Maximus but little else is known about him. Most art of this type has unfortunately not survived. The majority is destroyed by zealous municipal officials who fail to recognise the artistic merit and historical value of daubing on walls.'

Just how long, exactly, this rogue, ragged stone – on which a caveman pushes a shopping trolley – remained undiscovered by museum officials in Room 49 of the British Museum is the source of some debate. The museum itself insists it was no more than two days, but legend has it that it lasted a week. 'It was the cause of considerable embarrassment for the museum at the time', according to one of the museum's curators, 'and when Banksy asked for it back we were only too pleased to oblige.'[16] Apart from the sheer joy it brought to the institution's sober walls, what was Banksy trying to achieve with the piece? The geographer Luke Dickens took a stab when he wrote in 2008: 'the rock was intended to poke fun at the consumption habits of modern Britain, promote the work and name of an artist, assert the artistic and historical value of work of this type, and berate the purveyors and enforcers of "zero-tolerance" urban policy.'[17]

Okay, sure. But it also seems likely, given the 'consumption habits' of the museum into which the object was smuggled – namely the habit of hoarding priceless treasures from other cultures that has come under accelerating scrutiny – that Banksy was making a bigger point. Who decides what gets flung into the vast trolley of culture? Who is watching to see if it all gets scanned at checkout? Did you pay for that bag? There's something unexpectedly poignant, too, about the spot that Banksy chose to display the piece – about the sad, stony stare of that hobbled hunter. Side by side with Banksy's *Peckham Rock*, his crumbling physique is suddenly whisked back into action by the speed lines whizzing off the back of the postmodern hunter god pushing his trolley. He's reimagined. Made anew.

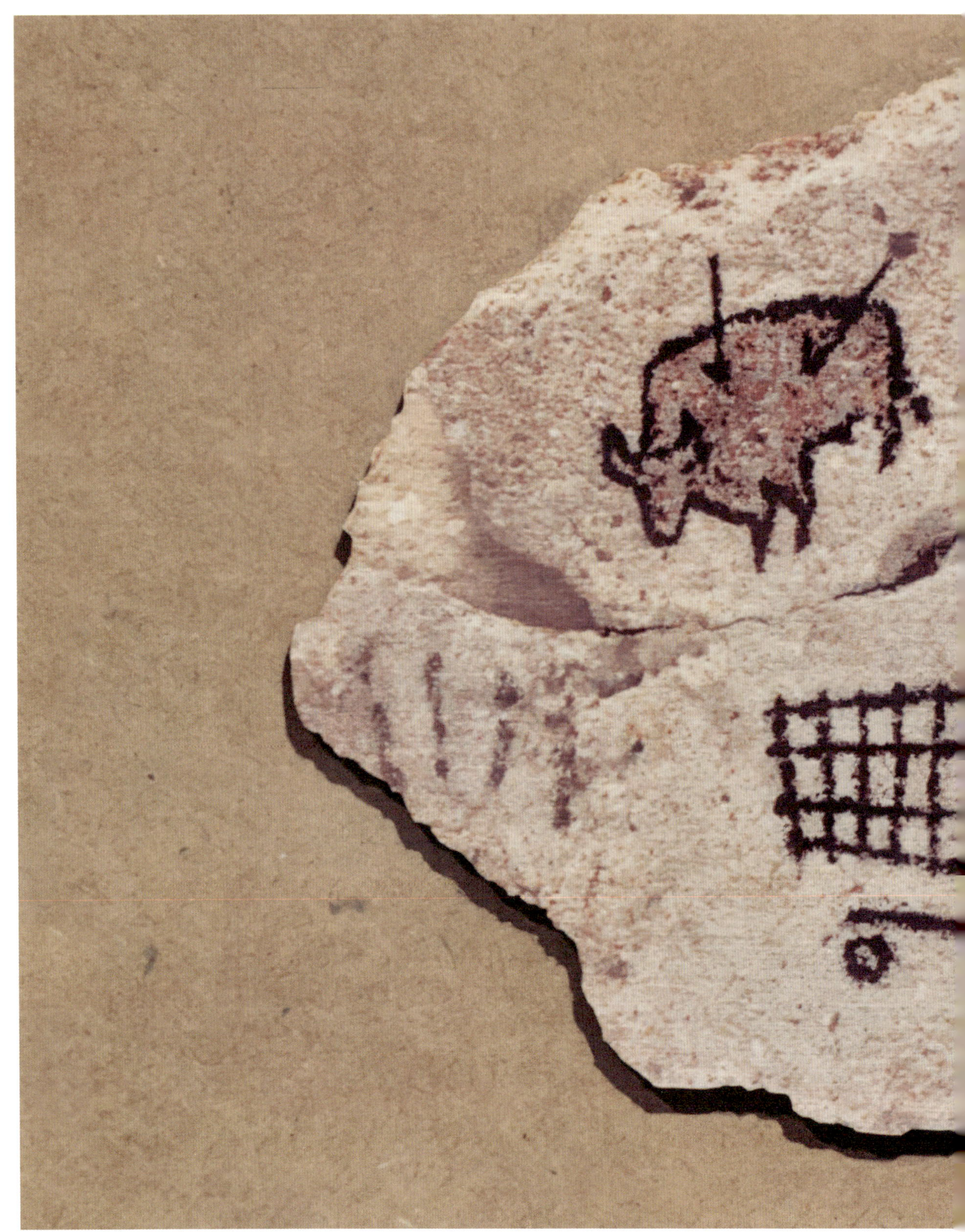

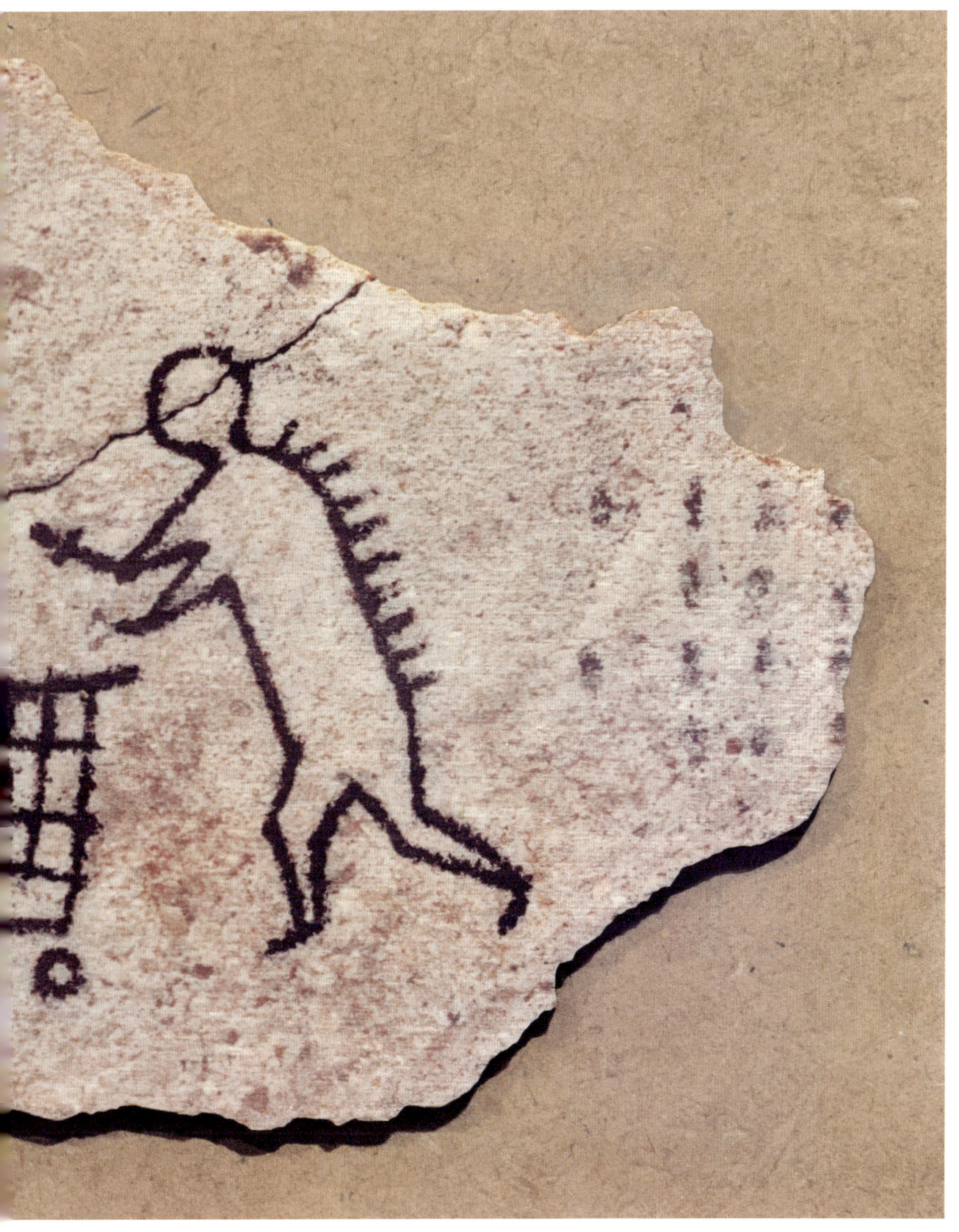

Peckham Rock, retitled *Wall Art*, 2005

NAKED TRUTHS

Which is more absurd: striding buck naked into mortal combat with a fearsome sword-wielding giant who is clad in impenetrable armour, or facing that same foe while wearing a state-of-the-art protective vest? Judging from reactions to Banksy's 2006 sculpture *Bullet-Proof David* – a satirical take on Michelangelo's famous sculpture of the biblical underdog who defeated the physically more powerful Philistine titan Goliath with a simple slingshot and stone in the Book of Samuel – there is no contest. By flippantly fitting the young shepherd, harpist and future king of Israel with a snazzy, if risibly anachronistic, ballistic waistcoat, Banksy dares us to look again at a work that is so familiar we hardly ever look at it at all.

Immediately upon its unveiling in 1504, Michelangelo's *David* was a hit. 'To be sure, anyone who sees this statue', insisted Giorgio Vasari, the celebrated historian and contemporary of the artist, 'need not be concerned with seeing any other piece of sculpture done in our times or in any other period by any other artist.'[18] Michelangelo was himself a young man in his early twenties at the time that he chiselled free the famous physique of David from a massive block of marble – a hulking chunk of rock so awkward and uneven in its contours that it had defeated the talents of several more experienced sculptors before him.

Installed not on the roof of the Florence Cathedral, as initially planned, but in the Piazza della Signoria, the epicentre of civic life, the unwieldy 90-tonne work was seen, according to Vasari, 'as a symbol of the Palace ... just as David had defended his people and governed them with justice, so, too, those who governed this city [Florence] should courageously defend it and govern it with justice.'[19] Unfortunately, David proved unable even to defend himself. The first five decades of the sculpture's existence alone saw a string of brutal attacks on the work. It was stoned by youths in 1504, struck by lightning at its base in 1512, and had its arm shattered in three places during an anti-Medici riot in 1527. For four centuries, beginning in 1550, David was forced to wear a ludicrous and uncomfortable copper garland over his unconvincingly small genitals. The abuse continued. In 1991, the second toe of David's left foot was hammered to pieces by a vandal who bizarrely insisted that a model for the 16th-century Venetian painter Veronese had instructed him to do so. Needless to say, a little protective wear was long overdue.

It would be easy, of course, to see the interjection of a 21st-century bulletproof vest in a work created in the Italian Renaissance as an allusion to the frequent appearance of that garment in the news in the months and years leading up to Banksy's satirical sculpture. Long before the British rapper Stormzy took to the stage wearing a stab-proof vest designed by Banksy in 2019, ballistic vests were everywhere in reports from the front line in the Iraq War, which began in 2003, and in coverage of the war on terror. Is Banksy's David doubling as a member of the security services, who many believed had begun to surveil us from every vantage point? Or perhaps Banksy just wants to make us snigger again at the pulsing veins of a work whose disproportionately outsized head and foreshortened penis are already hardwired with humour.

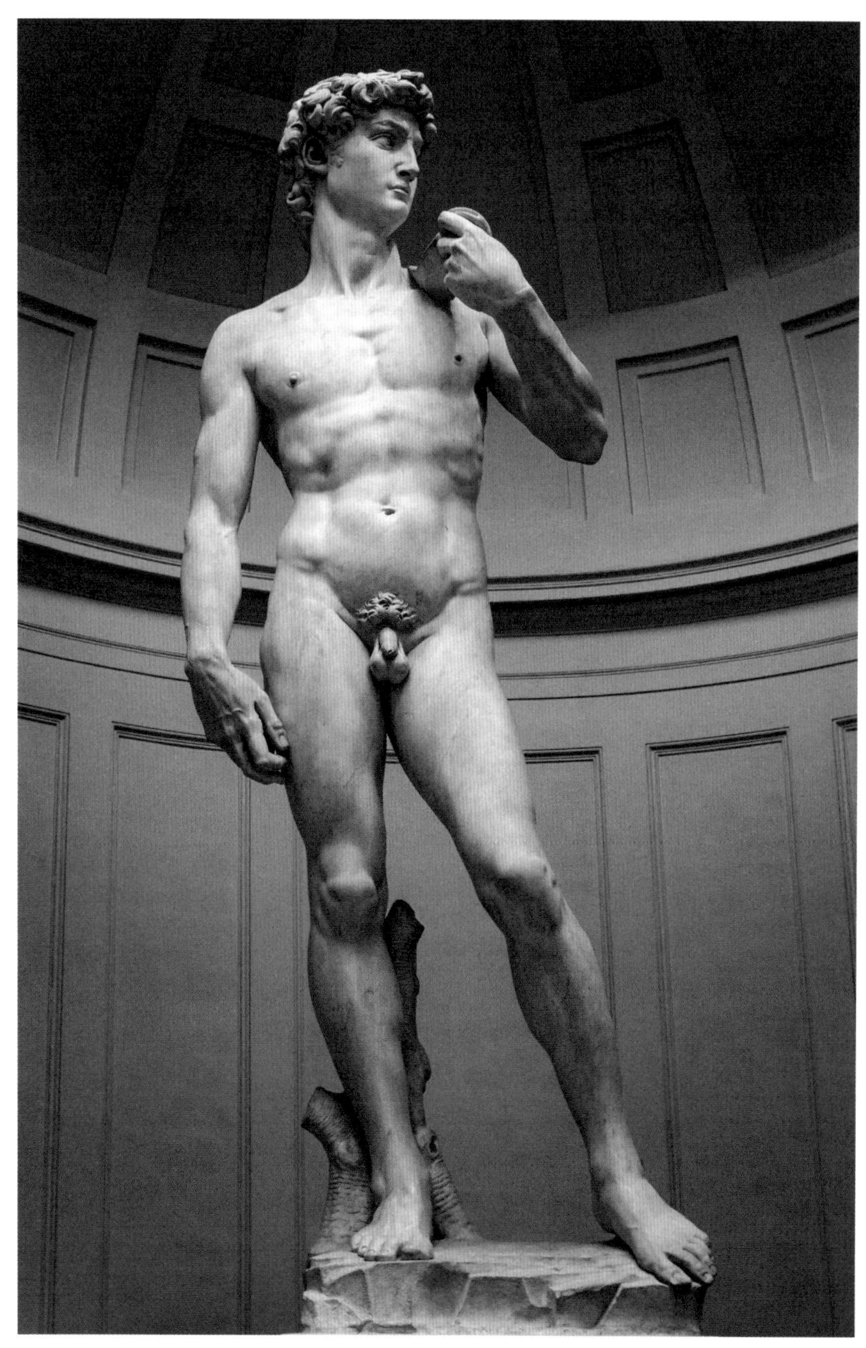

Michelangelo, *David*, 1501–4

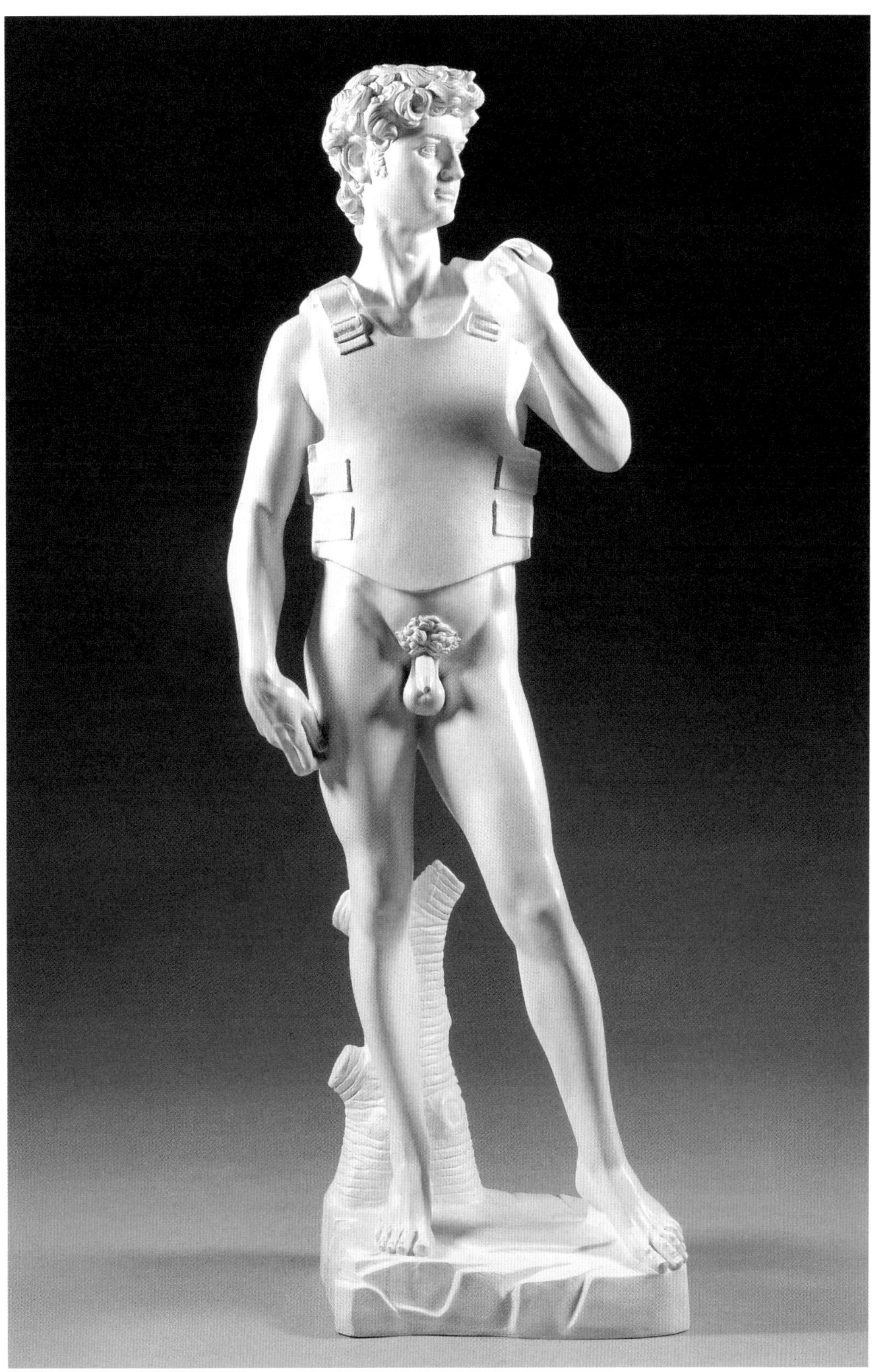

Bullet-Proof David, 2006

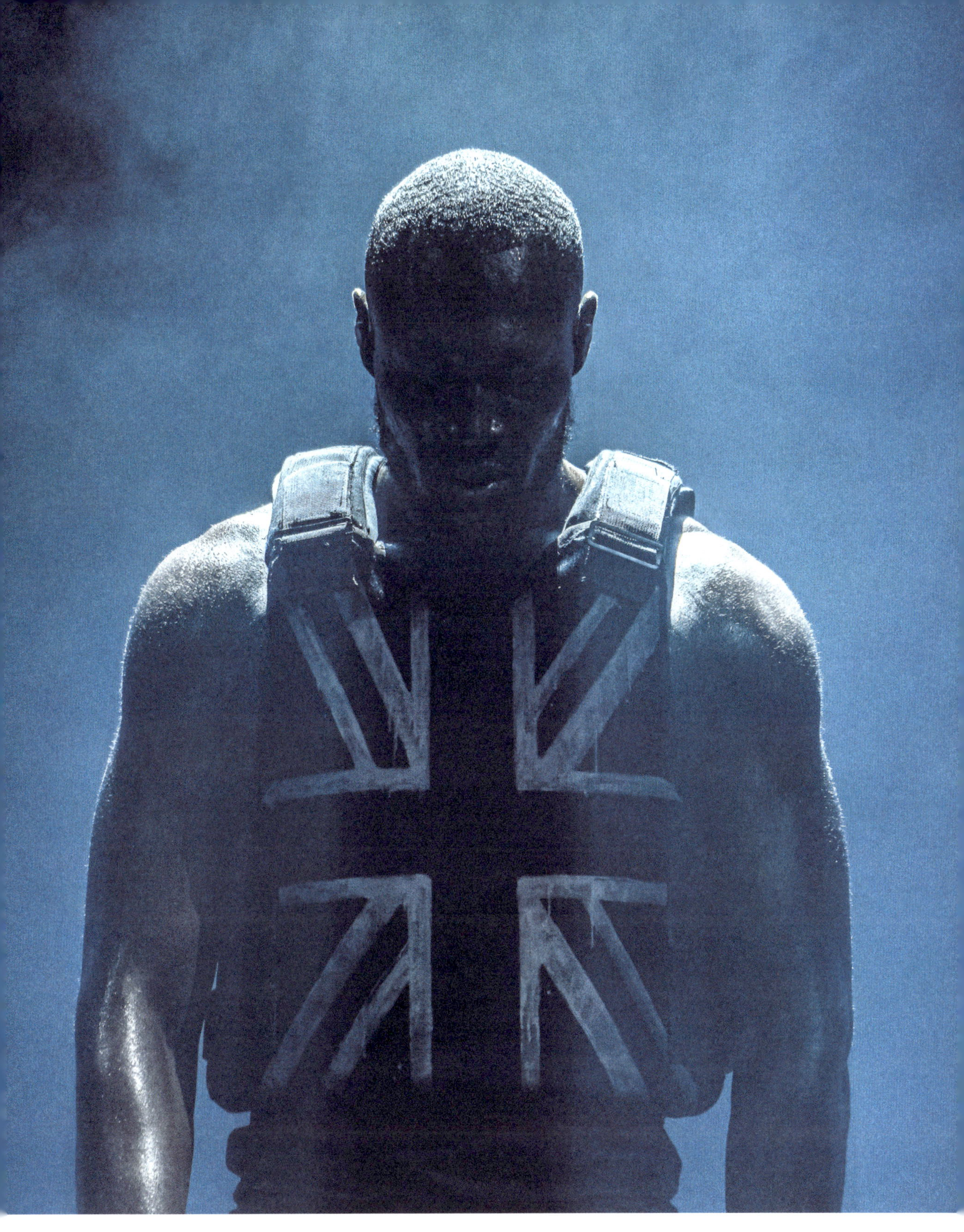

Stab-proof vest designed by Banksy for Stormzy's headline performance at Glastonbury, 2019

CLOSING DOWN SOUL

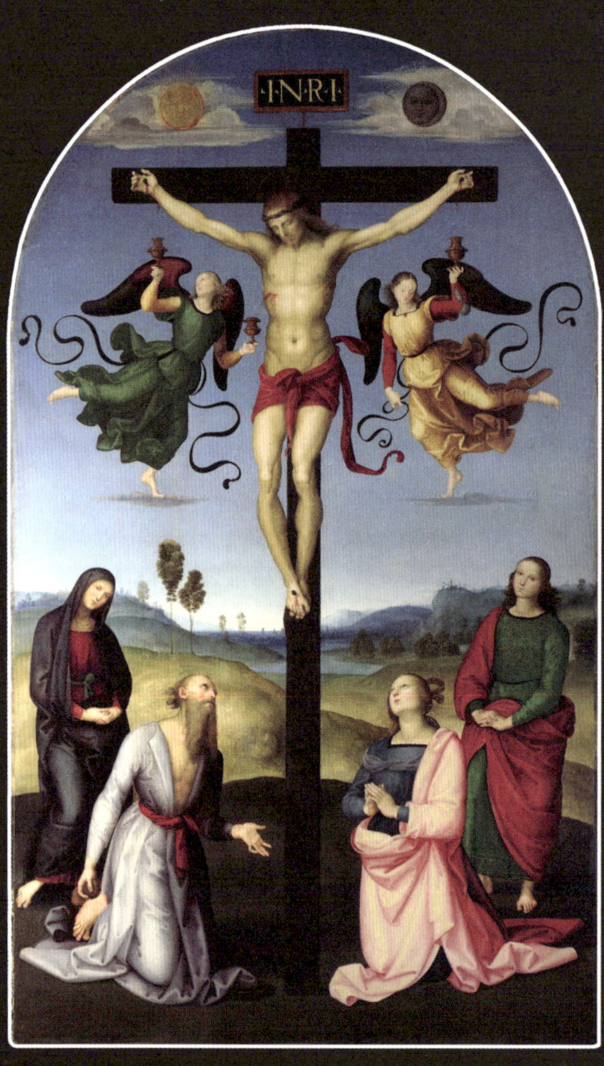

Raphael, *The Mond Crucifixion*, 1503

The sheer scale of Banksy's spare and sprawling oil-on-canvas painting *Sale Ends Today*, which stretches to over 4 metres (13 feet) in length and over 2 metres (6½ feet) high, commands from viewers a depth of contemplation that goes beyond its surface swipe at our age's reverence for retail discounts that results each year in bruising Black Friday brawls. On closer inspection, *Sale Ends Today*, which blurs the boundary between spontaneous street art and hefty museum masterpiece, provides a profound comment on one of the most cherished themes in Western art history, the crucifixion of Christ – a subject tackled by everyone from Giotto to Salvador Dalí. Raphael's early masterpiece *The Mond Crucifixion*, completed the same year that Da Vinci began work on the *Mona Lisa*, is among the most revered examples of the tradition. Commissioned by the wealthy Italian banker and wool merchant Domenico Gavari to adorn his own burial chapel in the church of San Domenico in Città di Castello, Umbria, the oil-on-poplar painting is exemplary of the countless works whose meaning is unexpectedly sharpened by Banksy's seemingly irreverent intervention.

One might be surprised to discover that the everyday consumer term 'savings', meaning a reduction in the price paid for a good or service, and the much older theological concept of 'saving', as in the spiritual deliverance of one's soul from eternal punishment, are closely related. They can both be traced back to the Latin *salvus* and its root, *sol*, meaning 'whole'. While many of us today may not be in the habit of reflecting on the economics of redemption, the connection between something for sale and one's salvation was once of paramount importance for wealthy patrons of the Church, desperate to see an eternal return on the investment of the monies they managed to amass in this world. In addition to the explicit sale of 'indulgences', a kind of cosmic get-out-of-purgatory-early deed that well-to-do parishioners were invited to purchase from the Church from the late 11th century through the 16th, it was made abundantly clear to the congregation that any financial contribution to the Church's coffers, including to the decoration of church interiors, would be factored in by the eternal bookkeeper in making his final determination about where one's soul was headed. Potential patrons were aware that, while salvation itself might be eternal, its sale was for a limited time only. The offer was always about to expire. In the Middle Ages, life expectancy in Europe was a mere thirty-three years,[20] the same short span that Christ himself had reached when he was crucified. The opportunity to secure a place in heaven could lapse at any moment; the 'sale' might well 'end today'. In such a context, every crucifixion scene was implicitly a 'Salvation Ends Today' sign – a warning to act now, while supplies last.

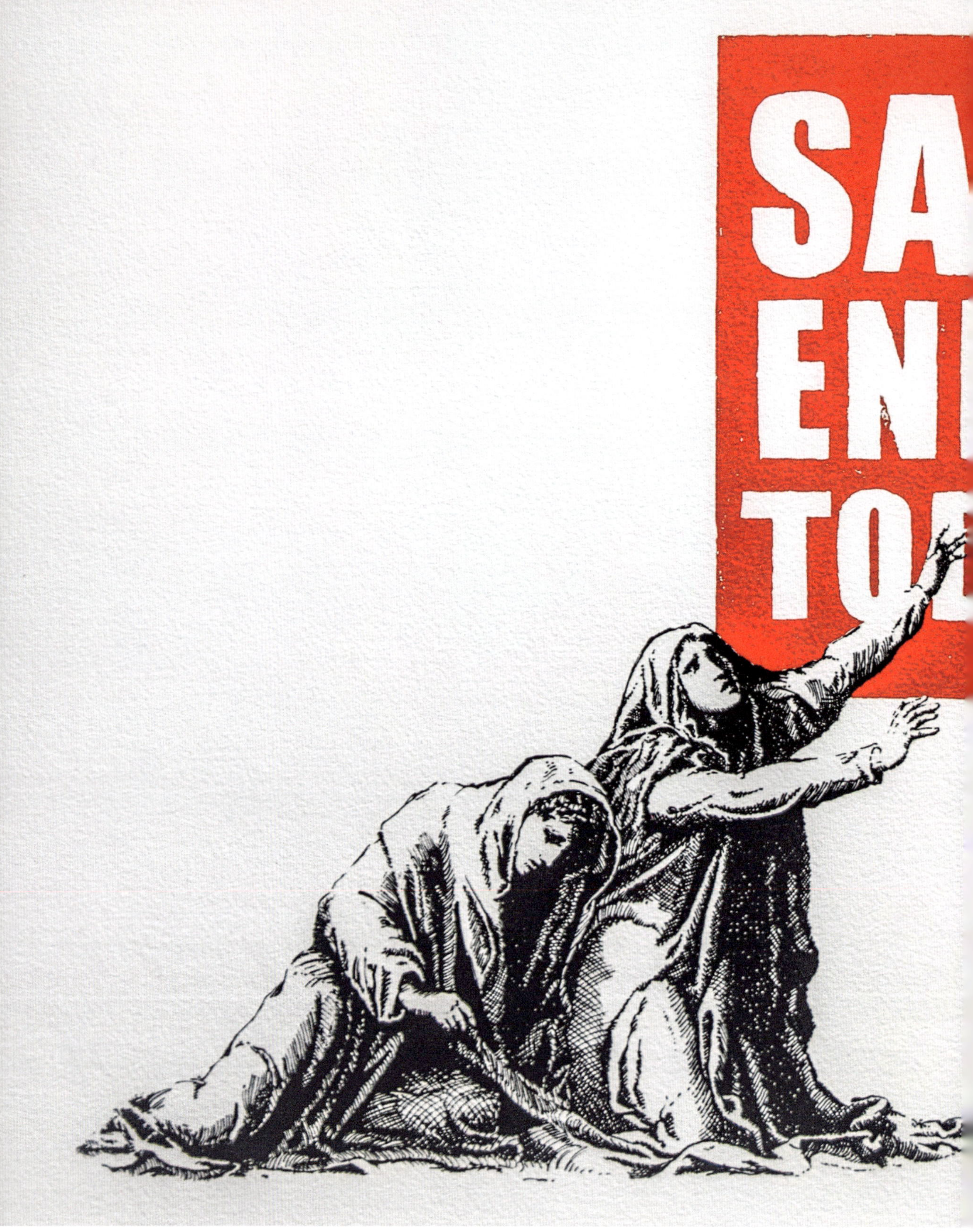
SA
EN
TOD

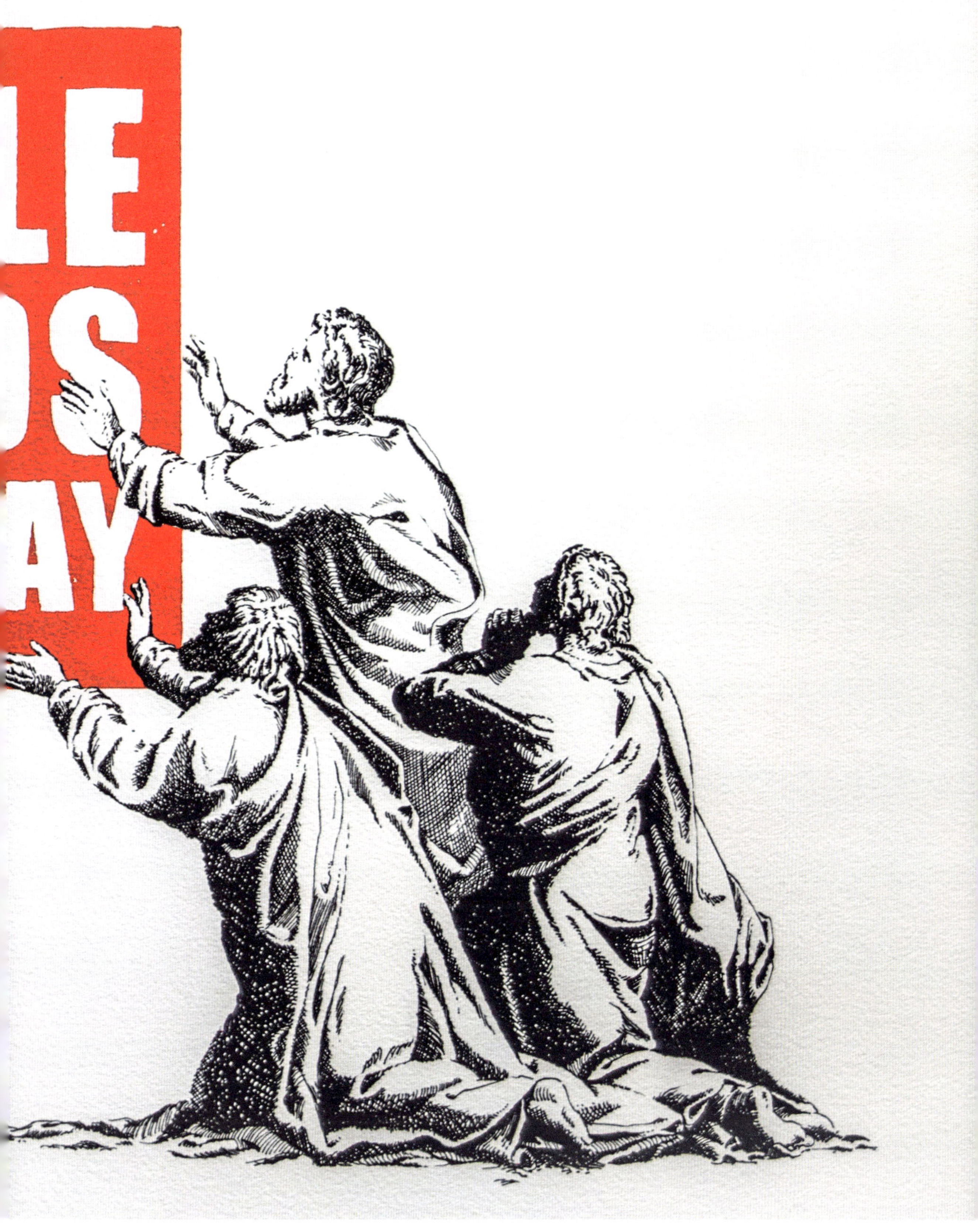

Sale Ends Today, 2006

TRIGGER HAPPY

Push something, or someone, far enough and it will eventually snap. Has anything ever been pushed around more than the *Mona Lisa*? Over the past half a millennium, since Leonardo da Vinci began work in 1503 on the portrait of the 16th-century Florentine noblewoman Lisa del Giocondo, it has been dragged across Europe, stalked and stolen, assaulted with rocks, teacups and cake, poked, prodded, scraped and X-rayed for secret messages, shoved inside a claustrophobic, bullet-proof case, and, worst of all, forced into international celebrity.

No wonder Mona emerged in 2000, locked and loaded, brandishing an Avtomat Kalashnikova gas-operated assault rifle (or AK47 for short). Whether it was Banksy who kidnapped and groomed her, Patty Hearst-style, into his elite urban guerilla army, or she who volunteered, after centuries of cultural trafficking, it hardly matters. She's his now. If you're lazy, you'll call this spray-paint-stencil-on-board work a parody and liken it pretentiously to Marcel Duchamp's 1919 readymade gag, in which the French Surrealist fitted a faded postcard reproduction of the *Mona Lisa* with a silly Menjou moustache and gave the impromptu piece a puerile name, *L.H.O.O.Q.* (initials which, when read phonetically, form the sentence *Elle a chaud au cul*, 'She has a hot ass').

But in Banksy's hands, the joke isn't on her. That red dot that stares out unblinkingly from the middle of her forehead like a bloodshot third eye? It was put there by those who ceaselessly target her with stares that aren't really stares at all, but interrogation and greed – by those who would like to see what more they can squeeze out of her. The portentous pupil that Banksy has imprinted on Mona Lisa's forehead makes an unexpectedly profound point: that the penetration of looking is never one-way. She has us in her crosshairs too. The longevity of Da Vinci's work in our cultural consciousness is not down to the new layers scholars discover endlessly, generation after generation, in his painting, but the new layers, generation after generation, she discovers in us. The more scholars and critics gaze and scrape at Mona Lisa, it is clear it is she, not they, who controls the silent conversation. However desperately they may try to fix her in time and space, in the snipe scope of their looking – to pin down her biography and locate the precise coordinates of the mythic landscape in which she timelessly sits – they are far more vulnerable to her mysterious marksmanship than she is to theirs. It is she who has them in her sights, not the other way around.

By ripping Mona Lisa from the privileged space of the museum – not to mention the misty terrain that shimmers behind her in Da Vinci's original poplar panel – Banksy has forged an audacious avatar to which most of us can actually relate. Like us, she's tired of being looked through and interrogated. Banksy's Mona Lisa is trapped, on the edge, and disinclined to take prisoners – a hair-trigger away from ending it all. Look at that inscrutable smile. Those eyes. She's crazy enough, she just might do it.

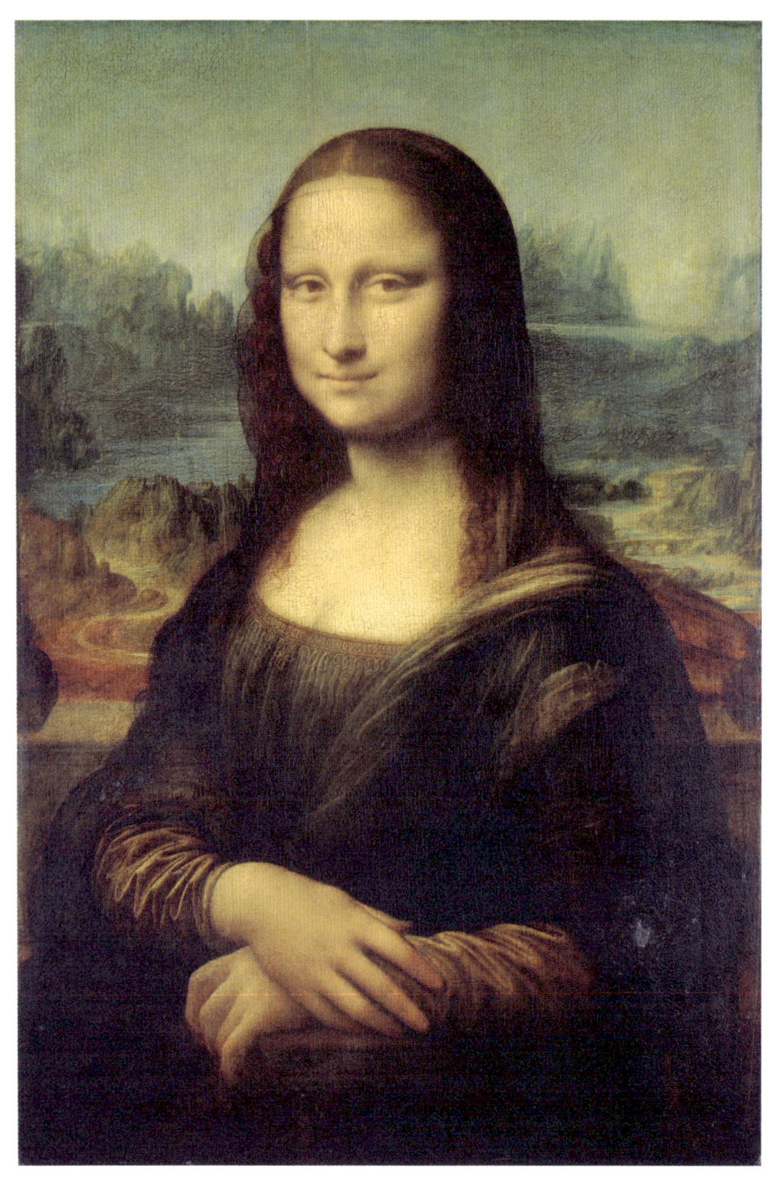

Leonardo da Vinci, *Mona Lisa*, 1503–6

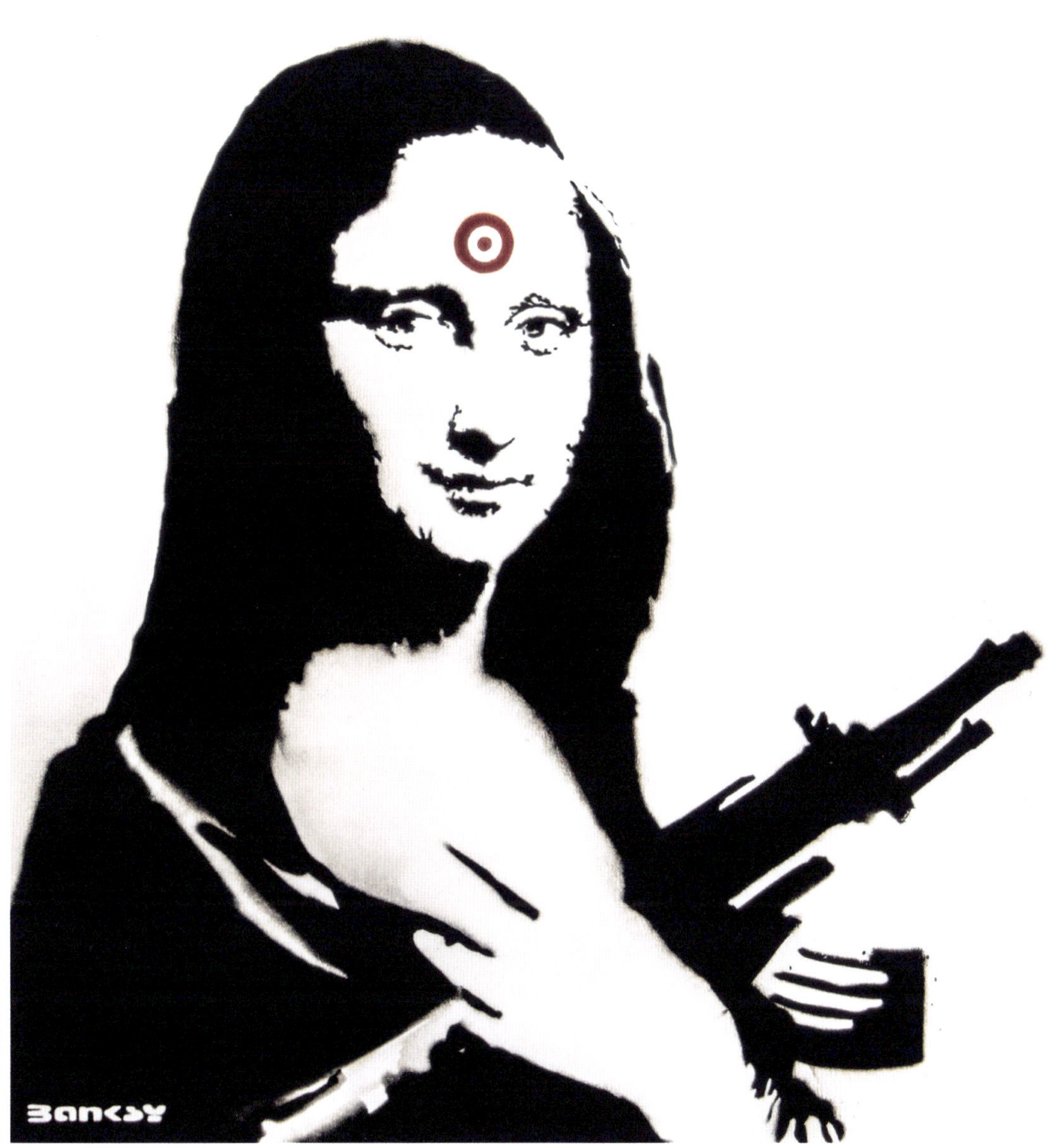

Mona Lisa with AK47, 2000

DEATH BECOMES YOU

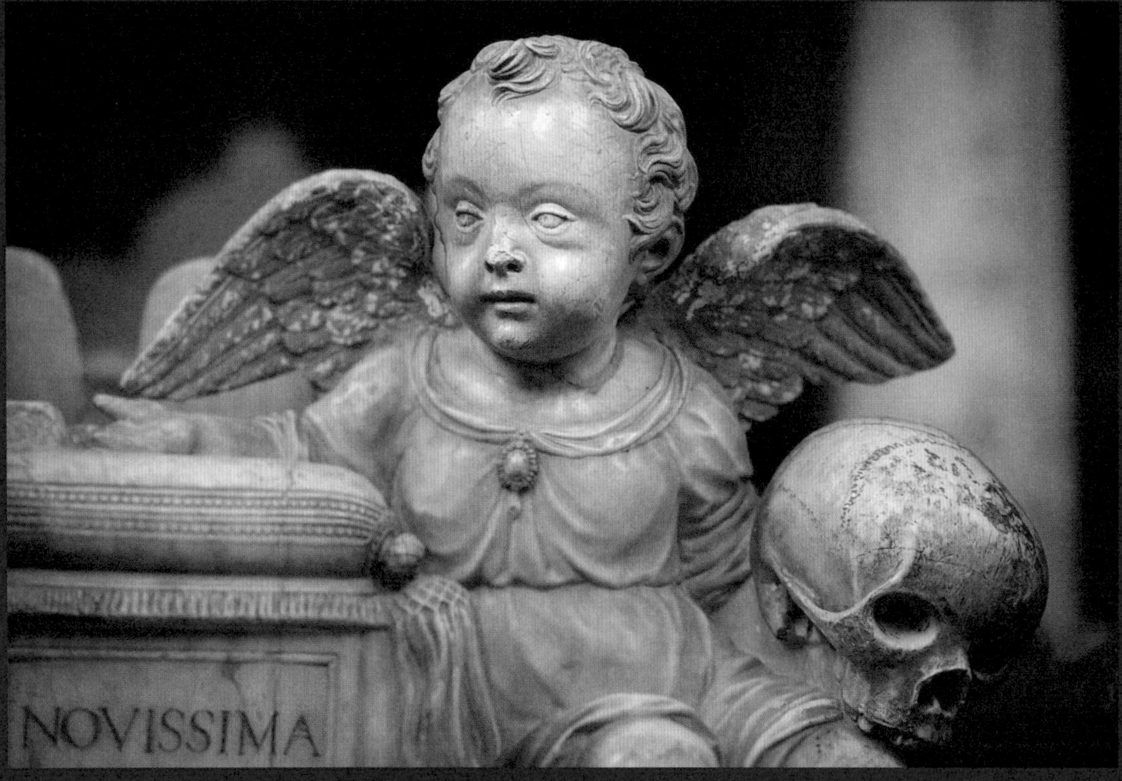

Statue of an angel in Uppsala Cathedral, Sweden, 16th century

The history of art is riddled with skulls – morbid reminders that death, your death, is always just around the corner. For centuries, artists and architects skilfully scattered skulls around their works, tucking them into the corners of paintings and chapels, sculptures and cemeteries. Among the creepier incarnations of *memento mori*, as the tradition is known (meaning, in Latin, 'remember you must die'), are the countless crania that fall into the innocent hands of winged cherubs and angelic infants, who are found cradling them like cuddly toys, napping on the awkward curve of their fleshless pates, or gazing inscrutably into their sightless sockets. The jarring juxtaposition of tender youth and the jawless decay of mankind's mortal remains was intended to jolt observers into a perpetual state of petrified piety. But the soul-shaking shock that the macabre convention (especially popular between the 15th and 19th centuries) may once have been capable of eliciting doubtless dulled around the gazillionth time that parishioners encountered it. In 2007, Banksy seized upon the moribund tradition of the *memento mori* for a moving mural he created in Shoreditch, London. In doing so, he managed to resurrect and revamp an affecting trope that had long since ceased to unsettle us.

A pair of chubby-cheeked cherubs lolling at the feet of a crowded alabaster mausoleum in Uppsala Cathedral that contains the remains not only of Gustav Vasa, King of Sweden, but also two or three of his wives, is indicative of the tradition. Sculpted by the Swedish artist Willem Boy soon after Gustav's death in 1560, the eternal attendants to the monarch's repose are equipped, respectively, with an hourglass (emblematic of the swift elapse of life) and a gnarled skull (symbolizing what happens when the sand runs out). Boy's boys are just the sort of eerie effigies Banksy appears to have had in mind when he created his emotionally and politically charged memorial for a fellow graffiti writer. On 12 January 2007, twenty-one-year-old Bradley Chapman and his friend, nineteen-year-old father-of-one Dan Elgar, were fatally struck by a London Underground train while fleeing from police who had spotted them, and two others, illegally adorning the tube station's walls with their monikers.

As it happens, Banksy had, himself, been the target of such 'tagging' by Chapman months earlier. A stencilled parody of a scene from the film *Pulp Fiction*, in which Banksy swapped the pistols held by John Travolta and Samuel L. Jackson with farcically flaccid bananas, had been obliterated ('completely dogged', as Banksy later put it) by Chapman, who covered the work with an oversized signature of his handle, 'Ozone', promising 'If it's better next time I'll leave it.' Following the tragic news of Ozone's death, Banksy created an elegant, complex eulogy for his respected rival by portraying a downcast angel, protected by a bullet-proof vest, staring at a skull wearing a backwards baseball cap. In recent years, the sight of flak jackets in the proximity of an Underground station has brought to mind images of security services chasing suspects through the cramped tunnels of public transport. By fitting a seemingly serene angel, an age-old emblem of protection, with protective ballistic gear, Banksy fuses allegories of spirituality and terror, and manages to forge a suitably riddling and angst-riddled emblem for an age that feels forever on edge.

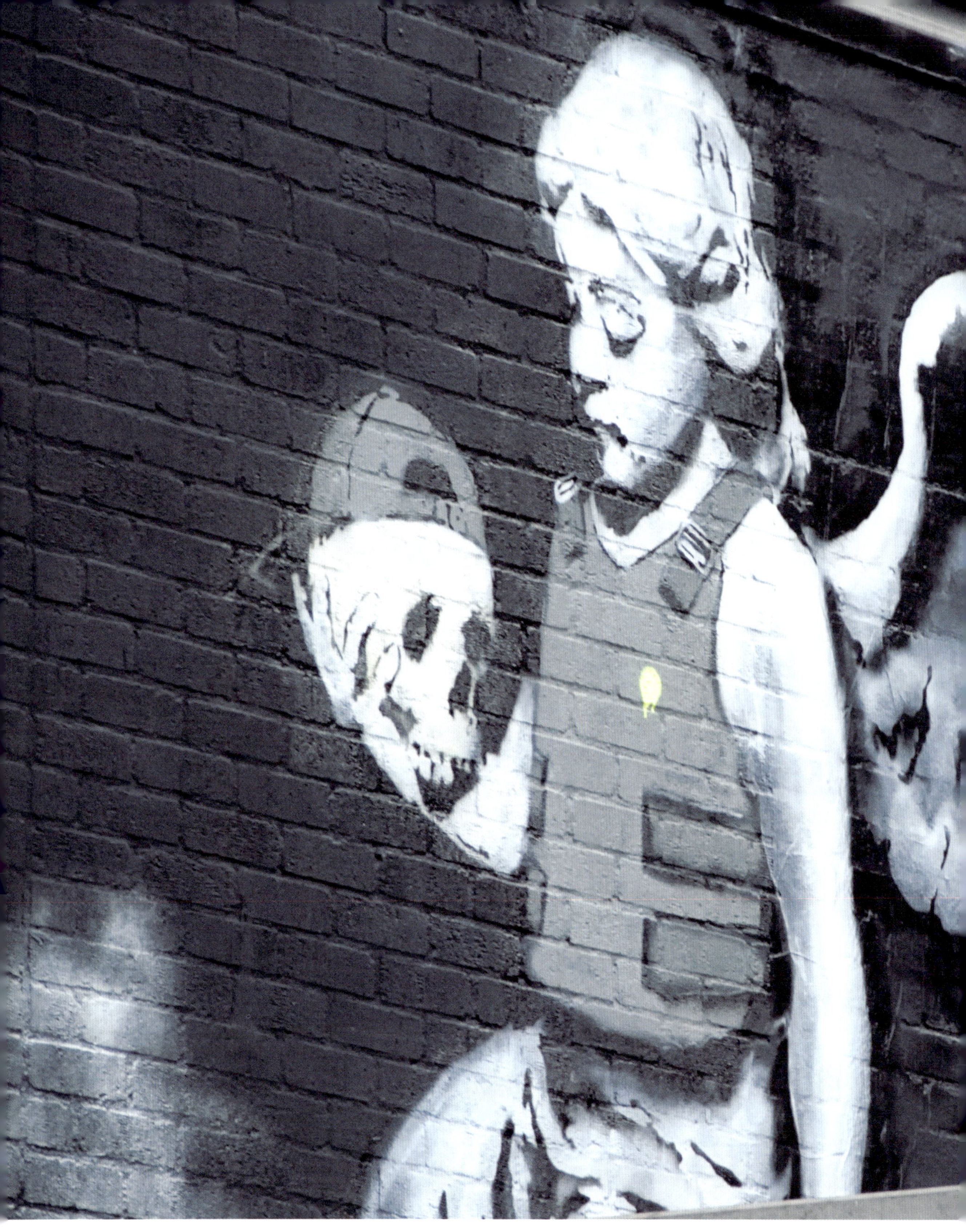

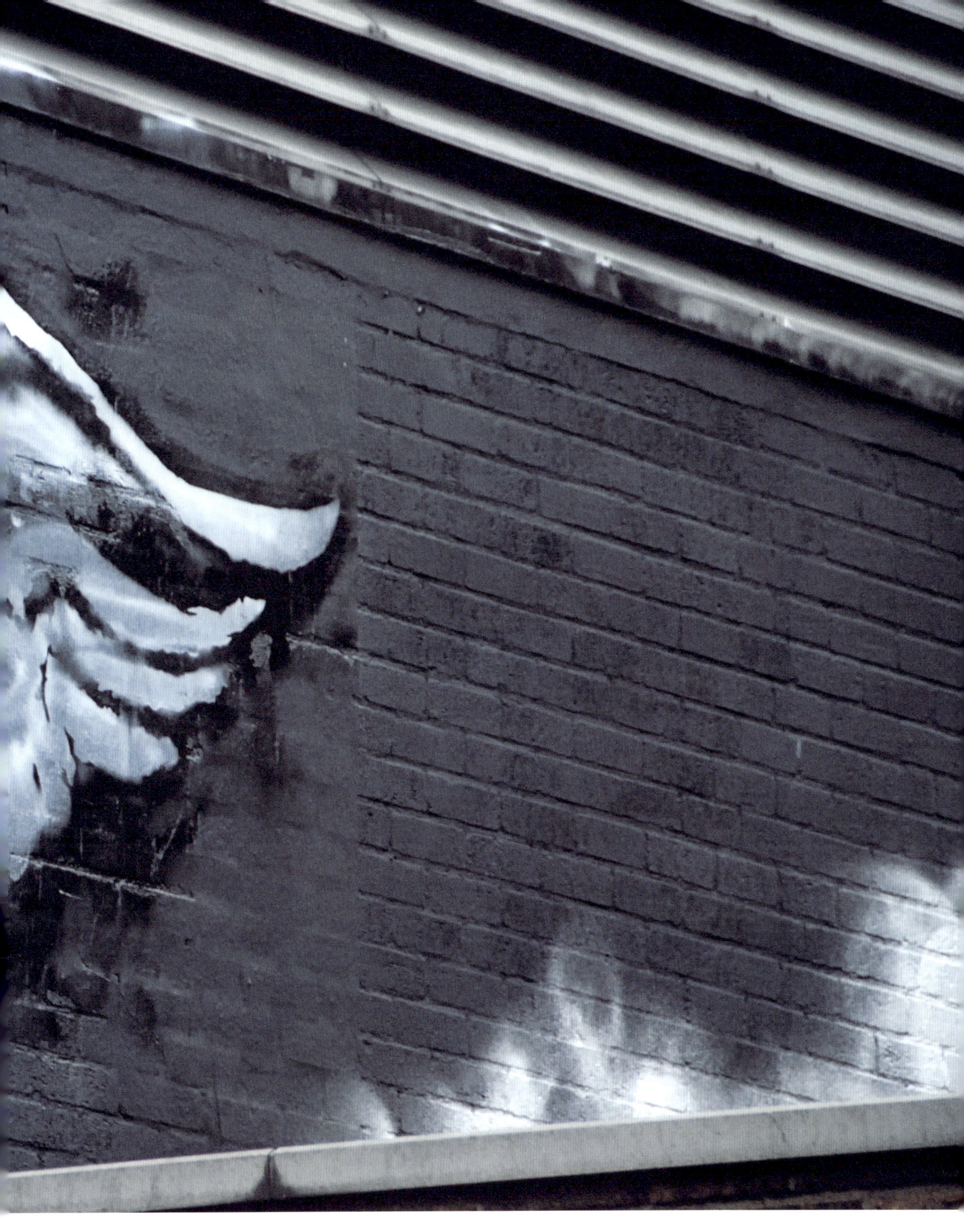

Shoreditch, London, 2007

CROSS PURPOSES

Nobody gets Banksy. Take his limited-edition screen print *Christ with Shopping Bags*, of which a mere eighty-two signed copies were produced in 2004. The wickedly witty print depicts a crucified Christ in the style of a Renaissance or Baroque altar panel, interrupted by the irreverent interposition of garish shopping bags stuffed with holiday goodies and gifts. For his work to resonate with any intensity, Banksy relies on some level of cultural acquaintance with crucifixion scenes, such as the 16th-century German painter Matthias Grünewald's gruelling portrayal of Christ's taunted and tortured body in *The Small Crucifixion* (c. 1511/20) or the exquisitely excruciating crucifixion painted sometime later that same century by Plautilla Nelli, one of the earliest, if not the earliest female Florentine Renaissance painter. Banksy's work only works, in other words, if there is some initial acknowledgment and appreciation of the human poignancy of such ghastly suffering. In that sense, his and Nelli's works arise ironically from something of the same anxiety: that our eyes and minds have become numb to the visceral horror at the heart of the Christian story. Both works seek to resensitize us to the appalling pain that pulses through the crux of Christianity.

Without exception, interpretations of Banksy's print have reduced the image to little more than a comment on the corrosive effect consumerism has had on the observance of Christmas (note the crook of the candy cane curling out of the gift bag in the far left of the print). But is Banksy's image really just a grumpy comment on capitalism of the sort snorted by sullen shoppers stuck in queues on Boxing Day? Look closer, and the livid pink slash on the upper left side of Christ's chest, adjacent to his heart – the only part of the broken body that Banksy has chosen to accent with colour, connecting it to the ribbons and bows of the gifts he lifts aloft – is an ingenious, if easily overlooked, detail in the work. According to the scriptural account of Christ's crucifixion in the Gospel of John, it was only after an unnamed Roman centurion pierced Christ's side with a long spear and watched his still heart spill 'water and blood' that those who had gathered at the foot of the cross knew for certain that Christ was dead. Breaking his legs, as the soldiers were preparing to do and was customary to hasten the death of those being crucified, was no longer necessary.

So, in the logic of Banksy's image, the flaccid physique of Christ, unsupported by the cruel armature of the wooden cross, which has vanished from the image, or the nails that had stapled his hands and feet in place (also gone), manages mystically to levitate not in spite of the heavy gift bags filled with bottles of champagne, stuffed Mickey Mouse toys, and wrapped presents, but because of them. Rampant consumerism, in other words, hasn't killed Christmas; its vapidity is what keeps it afloat. Those drips we see falling from Christ's feet are lines of propulsion as he lifts weightlessly into the air. Take away the emptiness of getting-and-spending that distracts us from suffering, and Christ (and by extension Christmas) would collapse like a lead balloon. Ours is a world in which shopping has become a salve – a superficial salvation. Or, as Banksy himself wryly remarked, 'we can't do anything to change the world until capitalism crumbles. In the meantime we should all go shopping to console ourselves.'[21]

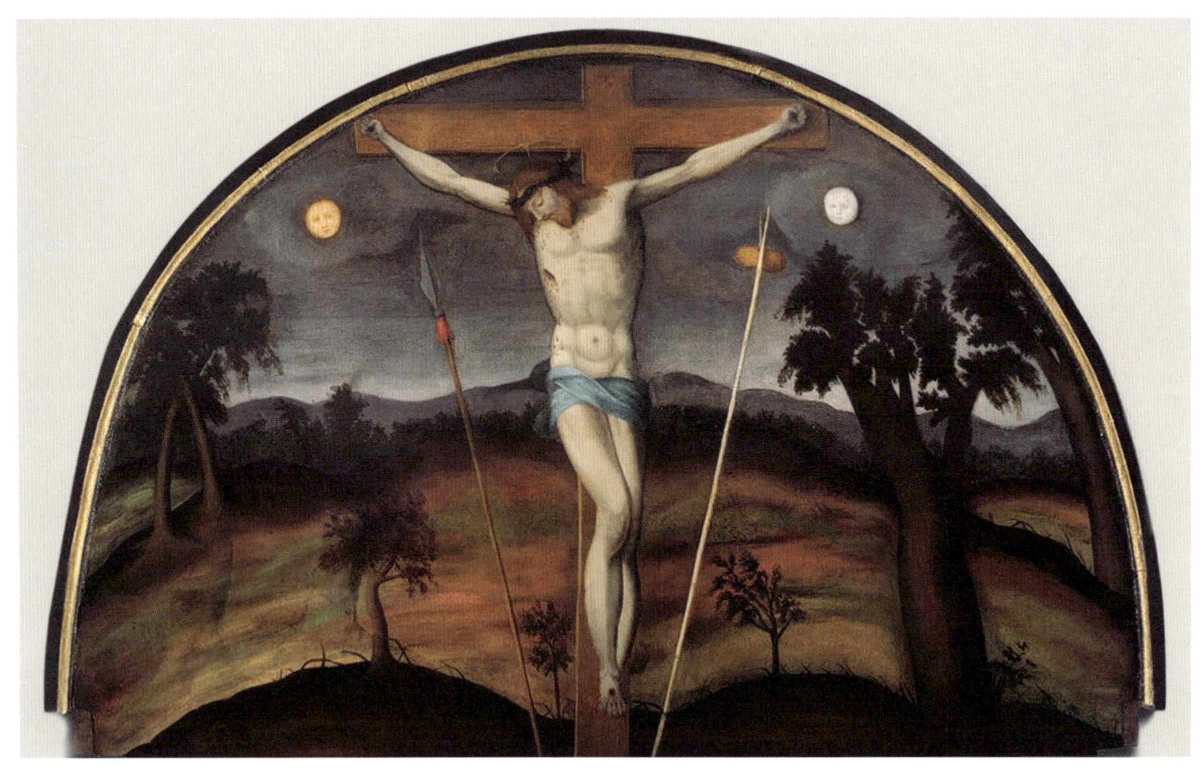

Plautilla Nelli, *The Crucifixion*, 16th century

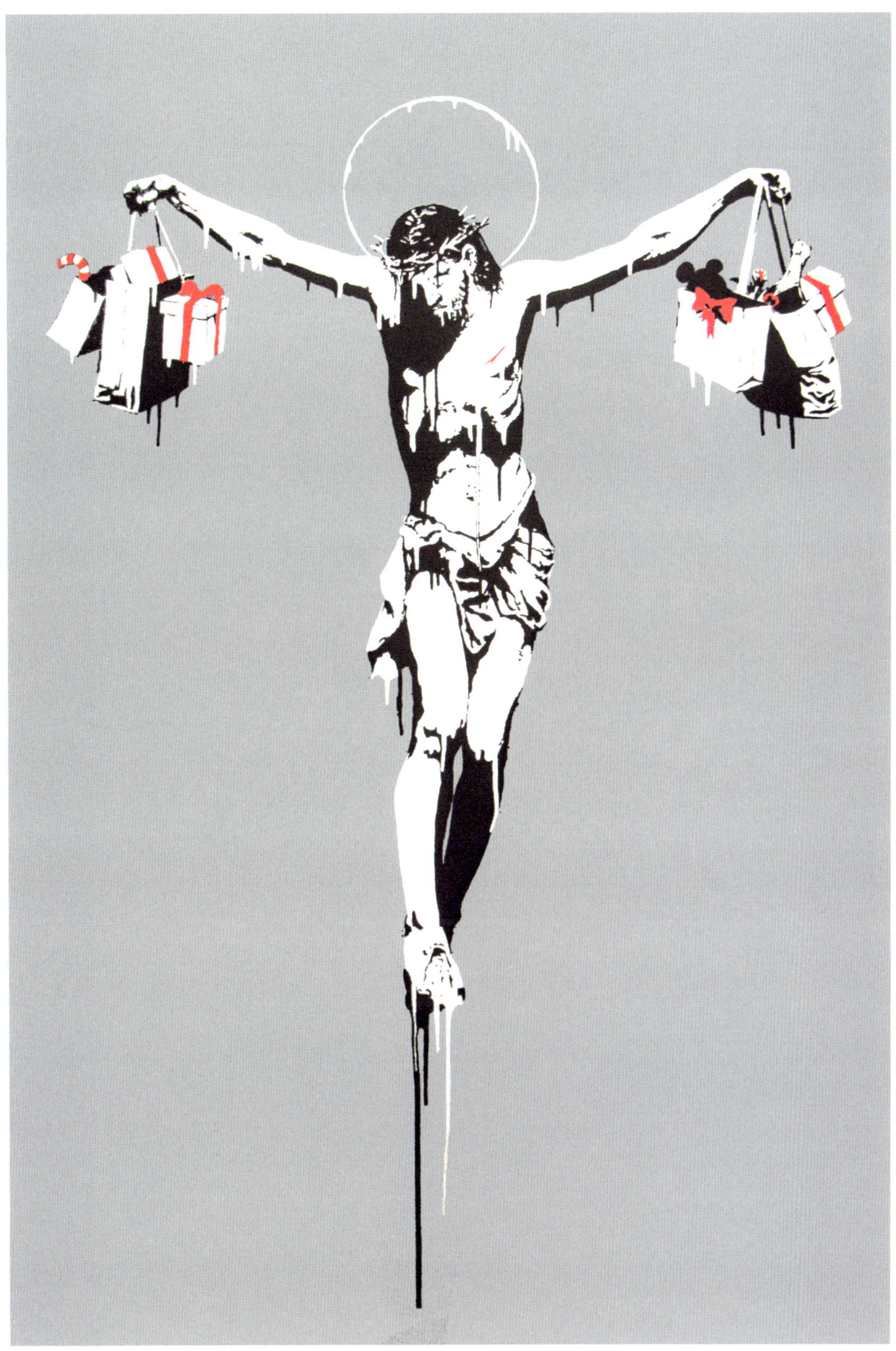

Christ with Shopping Bags, 2004

POISON
CONTROL

It's shocking on many levels. At its most visceral and immediate, Banksy's 2003 limited-edition print *Toxic Mary* is an alarming subversion of that most fundamental of human bonds, the one that connects a loving mother with the vulnerable child she adoringly nurses. By enlisting the woman most exalted in Western culture as the epitome of motherhood, the Virgin Mary, and replacing the vital nourishment of her breast milk with a bottle that bears a sinister skull-and-crossbones label, Banksy interrupts the quintessential paradigm of that foundational relationship. He poisons it.

At first glance, *Toxic Mary*'s message may seem straightforward enough: that organized religion, and Christianity in particular, is a venomous force, and one that has had a pernicious influence on history and culture. That sentiment is in accord with the contemporaneous writings of several prominent academics and intellectuals in the United Kingdom and America, such as Richard Dawkins, Christopher Hitchens, Sam Harris and Daniel Dennett, whose insistence that children should not be indoctrinated with religious belief came to be called the New Atheism. In *A Devil's Chaplain*, a collection of essays published the same year that Banksy's print appeared, Dawkins is also drawn to the language of 'labels' in his criticism of religious ideology. 'Religion', Dawkins says, 'is the most inflammatory enemy-labelling device in history .... My point is not that religion itself is the motivation for wars, murders and terrorist attacks, but that religion is the principal label, and the most dangerous one, by which a "they" as opposed to a "we" can be identified at all.'[22]

But *Toxic Mary* is not nearly as simplistic or unambiguous in its meaning as it might first seem. Banksy's works never are. It isn't enough to say, simply, that Christianity is corrosive. In the complex grammar of the actual image that Banksy has created, Jesus Christ himself is, after all, a helpless victim, not the perpetrator. Echoing familiar Old Master portrayals of the Virgin Mary breast-feeding the infant Christ – a tradition that extended from the late Middle Age to the 17th century and was known variously as *Virgo Lactans* ('The Lactating Virgin') or *Madonna del Latte* ('My Lady of Milk') – Banksy taps intrepidly into a vein of theological thought that seeks to trace the source of Christ's spiritual authority. His outrageous work reminds us that the conventional portrayals of the Mother and Child are anything but simple or straightforward depictions of pure maternal love. They're audacious maps of cosmic power. Banksy dares us to disentangle an archetype of affection from dangerous dogma.

In Banksy's print, the infant Christ has not yet latched onto the suspensefully suspended poisoned bottle. There is still time to save him. In that small but momentous space between the synthetic silicone teat that Mary tilts towards the innocent child and his expectant lips – a gap that recalls the one between the outstretched fingers of God and Adam in the central fresco of Michelangelo's Sistine Chapel – the whole history of Western culture spreads dazzlingly wide. Dripping paint at its edges, as if it were on the verge of being washed away, the irreverent image is surprisingly poignant, as if painted by centuries of tears. Oh, and it's devilishly funny.

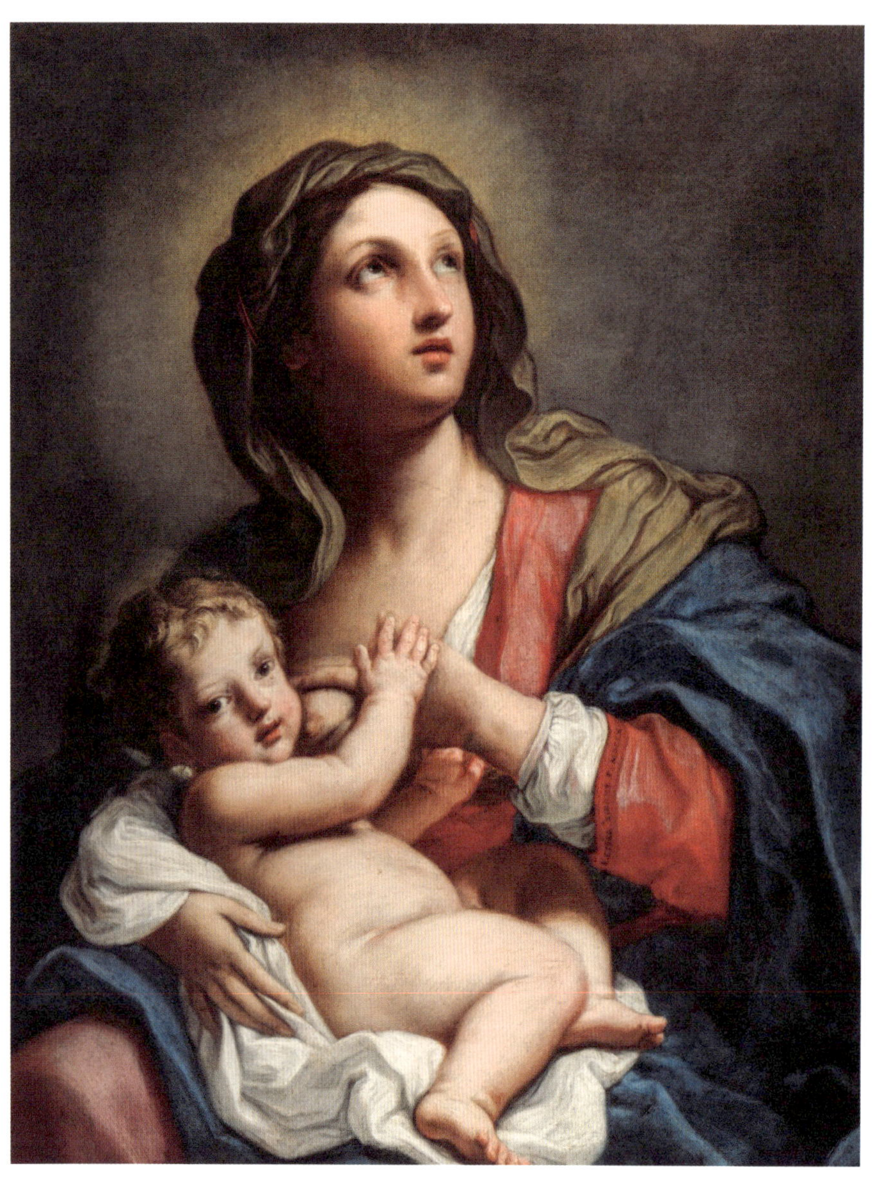

Elisabetta Sirani, *Nursing Madonna*, 1663

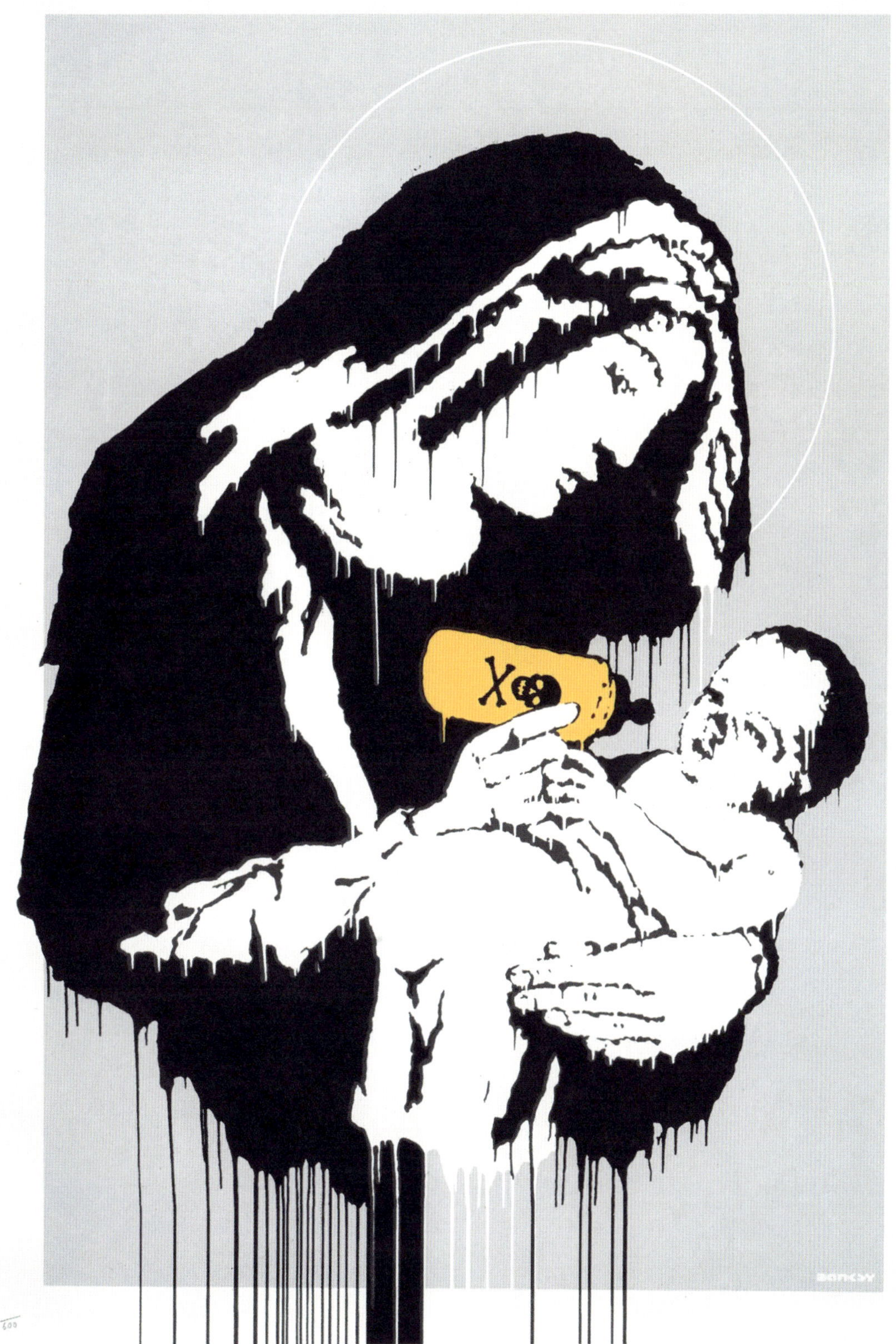

Toxic Mary, 2003

EAR SPLITTING

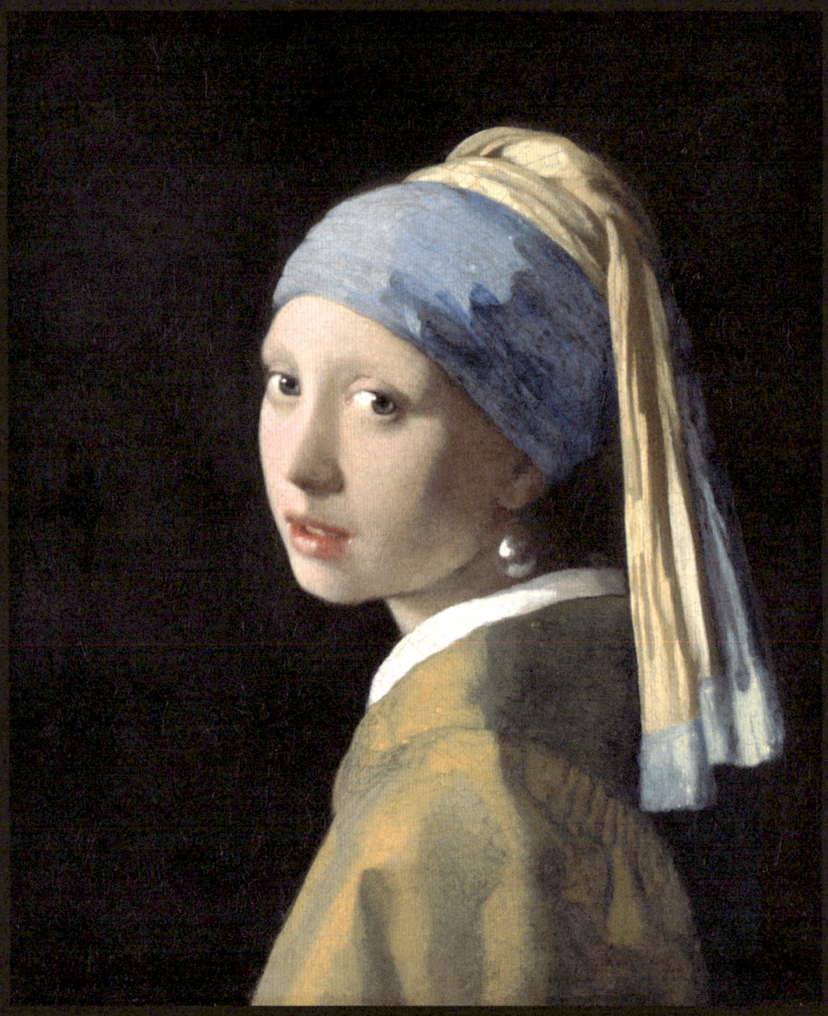

Johannes Vermeer, *Girl with a Pearl Earring*, 1665

Some works of art are so famous, we no longer really see them. Their familiarity has become a kind of defect that repels our stares. Over time, they've gradually imploded into crass avatars of their former grandeur. Sure, queues form outside their native institutions to catch a glimpse. But the urge is less to see them than to have seen them. They're empty as the unticked boxes on a bucket list.

Take Johannes Vermeer's preposterously popular *Girl with a Pearl Earring* (1665), which Banksy memorably lampooned in 2014. In his illicit vision, conjured from gunmetal greys against a backdrop of white bricks on the side of a building in Albion Docks in Bristol's Hanover Place, the outsized head of a young woman with parted, pouting lips turns to meet our gaze. We know her kitschy cheeks and inscrutable stare from a thousand tacky dorm-room posters and discarded diaries. Or do we?

Look closer and we soon realize that here, in Banksy's scruffy send-up, the girl's eyes aren't really searching for us at all, but are chasing the mute, mind-splitting whinge of an outdoor security alarm. The mural bleats in our imagination – an irresistible metaphor for the thousand thrumming distractions that disrupt every second of our daily lives. Flash back to Vermeer's original, and it is difficult to silence the squeal of Banksy's caricature. Yes, the 17th-century Dutch master has managed to coax a kind of mystery from the eternal darkness out of which the girl's startled countenance looms. And Vermeer's skill in teasing soft, supple features from a mere insinuation of inflected shadow is duly noted.

But in the insolent light of Banksy's raw reinvention, Vermeer's image regains something it lost long ago – an energy that was sapped every time its soul was sold, licensed to a disposable knick-knack or slapped like Goofy or Donald Duck onto a calendar or coffee mug. Created in the mid-1660s as an archetypal character study, or 'tronie', Vermeer's painting was likely never intended to be seen as the portrait of a particular person, but to capture instead an essential aspect of what it means to be alive. The girl's timeless costuming – her shimmering silk gown and 'exotic' turban (sculpted from ultra-expensive ultramarine) and the weightless heft of her outlandishly outsized earring – amplifies her eternal allure. But excessive exploitation and ceaseless commodification of the painting have dimmed its seemingly irrepressible lustre. It lost itself in the deepening gloom of its own incessant celebrity. To save it, the painting needed to be destroyed and created again, this time with a thicker skin.

The dishevelled drips of paint that propel Banksy's parody into orbit have left an indelible mark on the better-behaved original. We can't unsee them. By transforming the ginormous gem that swims beneath the girl's ear like an undiscovered planet into a screeching plastic eyesore that the privileged install to protect their junk, Banksy strips away the veneer of self-satisfied significance that has come to encrust Vermeer's painting. Slap-dash and sleeping rough, Banksy's girl is not the kind you take home to meet your parents or that can be hung in the dry, dull air of an art museum. Thank goodness for that.

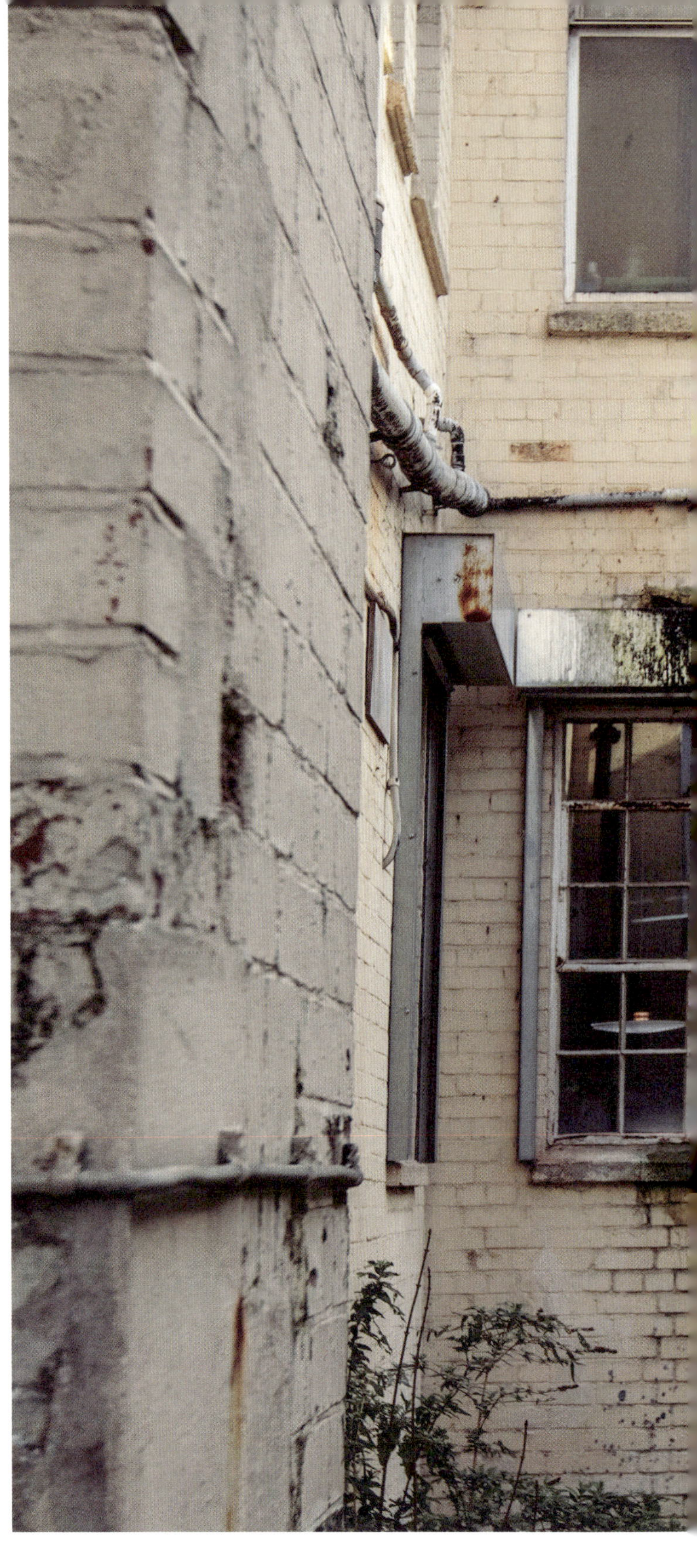

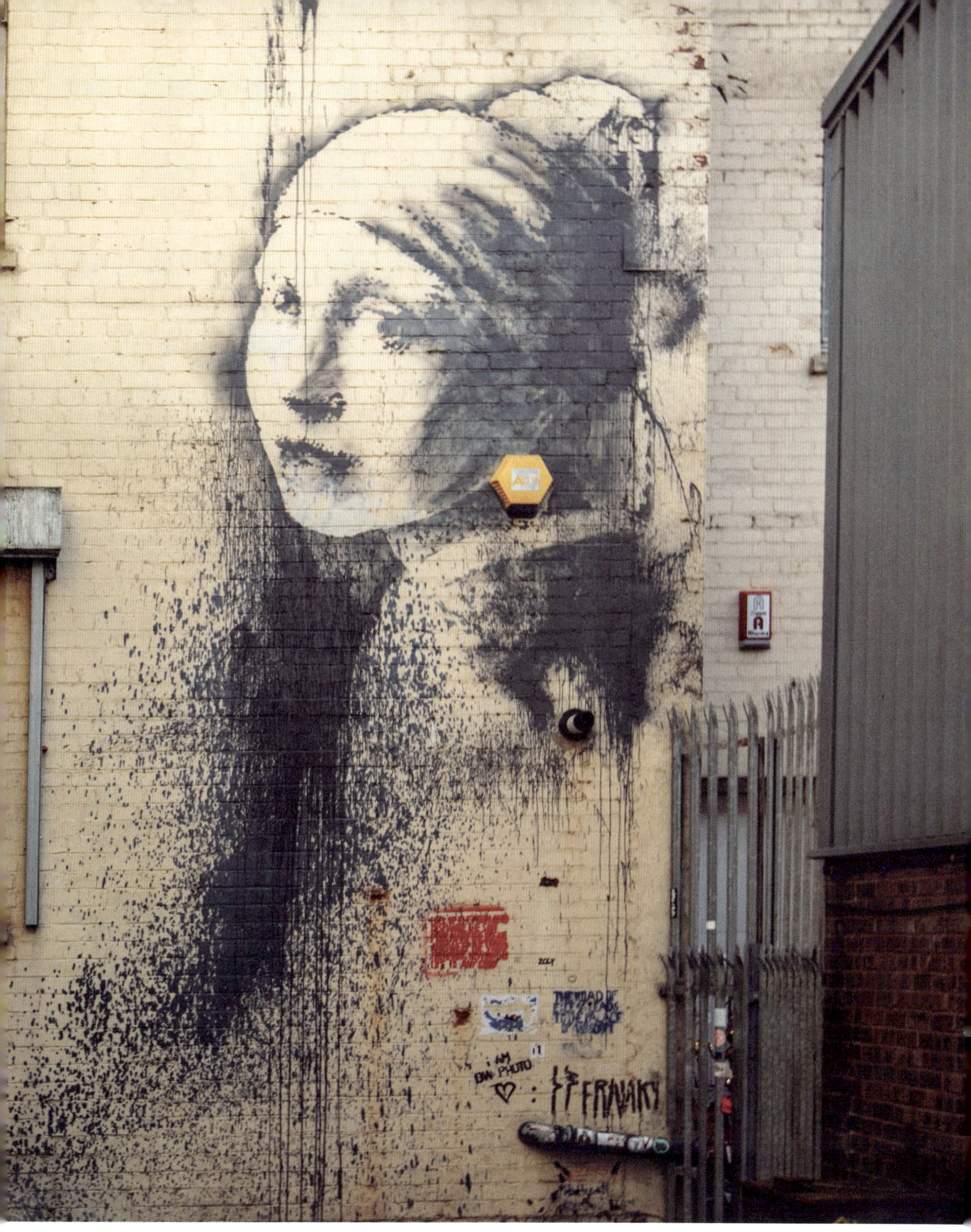

Bristol, 2014

ON THE BLINK

Rembrandt saw seeing differently. His eyes are revolutionary. According to research undertaken at the University of British Columbia and published in 2010, the Dutch master mastered the art of conducting the gaze of his paintings' observers around canvases by luring them first into the eyes of the sitter, which he depicted with unprecedented precision. Once hypnotized by the poignancy and pathos of the subject's uncanny stare and delicate area around the eyes, observers are then 'guided' through the 'narrative' of the painting by carefully constructed 'edges' and 'flows'.[23] The subliminal sequence of cues and clues that spins our pupils around the canvas like a pinball bouncing from bumper to bumper has a double effect. Directed by the portrait's eyes, we feel the subject is not merely sentient but omniscient. At the same time, we feel an intense emotional and psychological connection with the subject. Though admirers of Rembrandt have long suspected that his grasp of gazing, both towards and from within his work, is key to understanding his portraits' power, the 2010 study was the first to propose a scientific explanation for how the phenomenon functioned. The genius of Rembrandt's carefully calculated captaincy of seeing around his canvases is its ability to make us comprehend the entire world the artist has conjured. His eyes make our eyes at home.

As if anticipating the upshot of the intriguing study, Banksy, a year before the research was published, likewise drew our eyes to Rembrandt's in his send-up of the Dutch artist's *Self-Portrait at the Age of 63* (1669). In doing so, he forged a fitting, if facetious, portrait of our own boggle-eyed, pupil-popping, image-addled age.

In the two years before Banksy unveiled his subversion of Rembrandt's self-portrait, onto which he affixed a protruding pair of plastic 'googly' gag eyes, the multinational technology company Google passed a few truly extraordinary milestones in its emergence as an information giant. In 2007, Google unveiled a universal search that allowed users access to simultaneous search results across all content types, including images, videos and news. The following year, the company launched not only its own smartphone, allowing users to carry the full sweep of its sweeping technology with them at all times, but also a bespoke browser, Chrome (whose logo resembles an all-seeing chromatic eye with a popping blue pupil at its centre), which would soon eclipse its rivals.

By the time Banksy revealed his googly-eyed rendition of Rembrandt's self-portrait, the whole world was wearing Google goggles when it came to seeing, well, everything. 'If it isn't on Google', as the founder of Wikipedia put it, 'it doesn't exist'.[24] Fully fixated on the small screens of our smartphones, the scope of society's seeing has altered irrevocably. If Rembrandt's original portraits, with their innovative verve of vision, are emblematic of an age that sought to see deeper and further, Banksy's slapstick riff captures instead an era whose eyes are caught in the shrinking blue light of their own self-involvement.

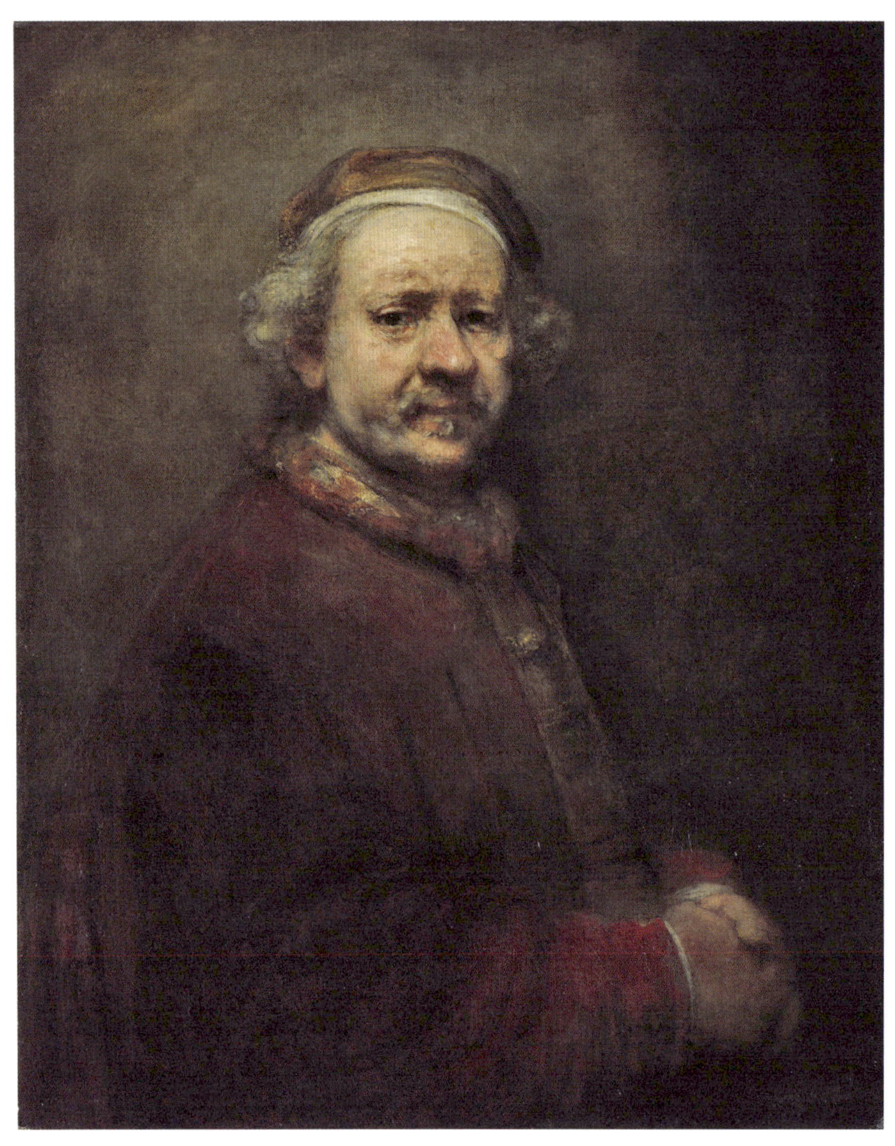

Rembrandt van Rijn, *Self-Portrait at the Age of 63*, 1669

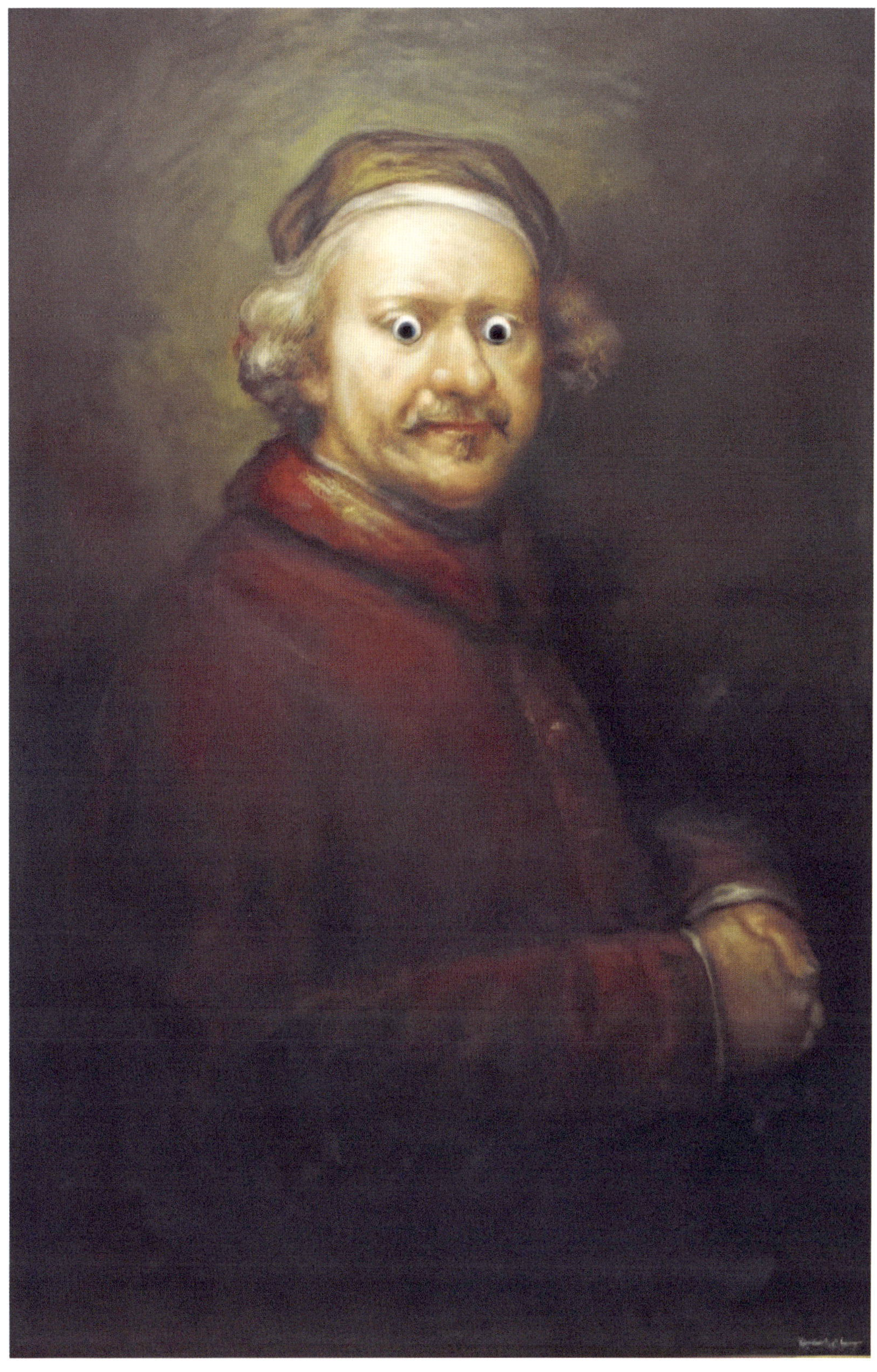

Rembrandt, 2009

HORSE
PLAY

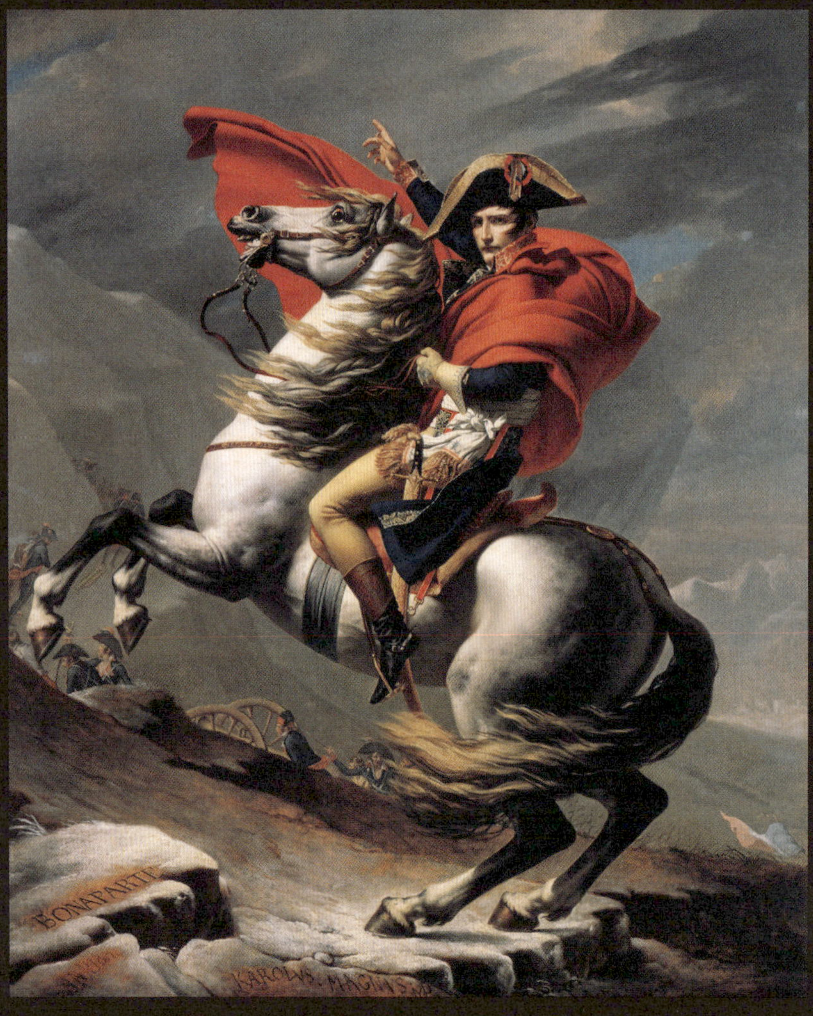

Jacques-Louis David, *Napoleon Crossing the Alps*, 1801–5

Question: What do you call a sitter who refuses to sit? Answer: Napoleon Bonaparte. That at least is what the celebrated French Neoclassical painter Jacques-Louis David discovered in 1801, when the King of Spain commissioned him to create a portrait of Bonaparte as a gift to the formidable French commander, who had recently taken control of France and led an army across the Alps to reassert control of Italy. Keen to capture an accurate likeness of Bonaparte in an equestrian pose, David requested an audience with him, but the famously fidgety general refused to play along. 'Sit?' Bonaparte fired back at the artist, 'What's the point? Do you believe that the great men of antiquity whose image we have sat?' Bonaparte insisted that the portrait should be considered from the first not a convincing depiction of his actual physical appearance, but a compelling metaphor for his irrepressible power. 'It's not the exactness of the features, a little pea-sized wart on the nose, that makes the resemblance. It is the character of the physiognomy that animates it.' 'It is enough', he maintained, 'that their genius lives there.'[25] Spurred on, David determined to make an entrancing avatar of commanding genius and, by all accounts, succeeded handsomely. The resulting portrait, untethered from the contours of reality, was an immediate hit and quickly became the era's most reproduced image, not of Bonaparte himself exactly – how could it be? – but of galloping gusto, unbridled zeal and egregious ego. It became, in other words, the perfect fodder for an eventual Banksy send up.

In June 2018, just as the international press was frantically shuttling its cameras' shutters back and forth between coverage of the unwearable fashions mincing up and down runways during Paris's Fashion Week and the deepening migrant crisis in Calais, Banksy treated Parisians strolling the city's streets to a series of subversive murals. Among his most powerful was an irreverent riff on David's brash rider, only in Banksy's reinvention of the famous alpine scene the winds of imperial destiny have shifted. The turbulent red cloak that boldly billows around the imagined portrait of Bonaparte has blown back and wrapped itself tightly around the rider's face and torso. The formidable leader has been reduced to a kind of captive, a blinded prisoner charging headlong into an unknown future. Attaching to his work the satirical phrase '*Liberté, égalité, cable TV*' – mocking France's national motto '*Liberté, égalité, fraternité*' (popularized by the radical political figure Maximilien Robespierre in the early years of the French Revolution) – Banksy suggests that the civic ideal of an outreaching fellowship of mankind has been replaced by a more insular and socially suffocating obsession with media. It isn't just our leaders who have covered their eyes and are charging off blindly into oblivion. You might not have sat for the portrait either, but we're all under the red cloak now.

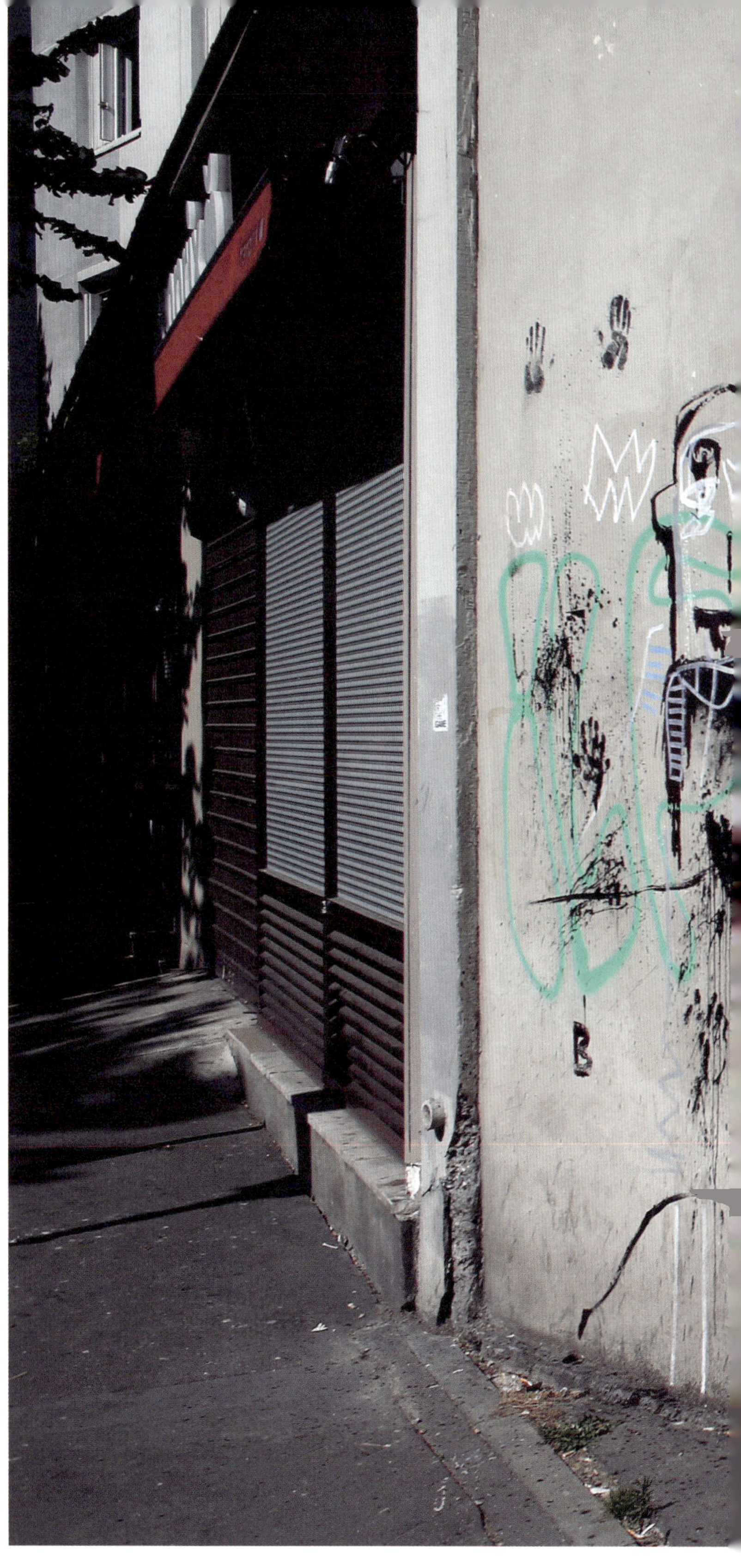

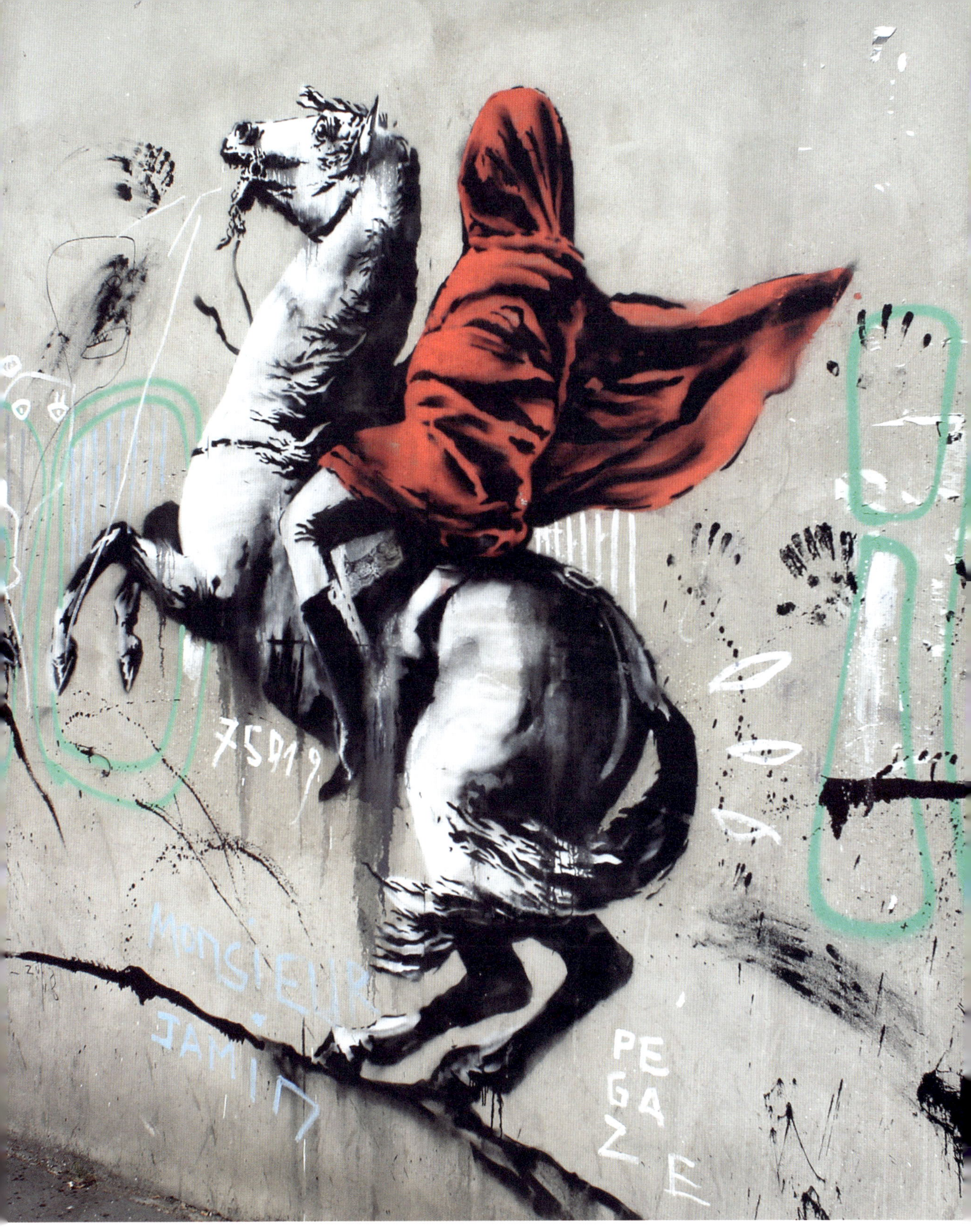

Paris, 2018

HAMMER TIME

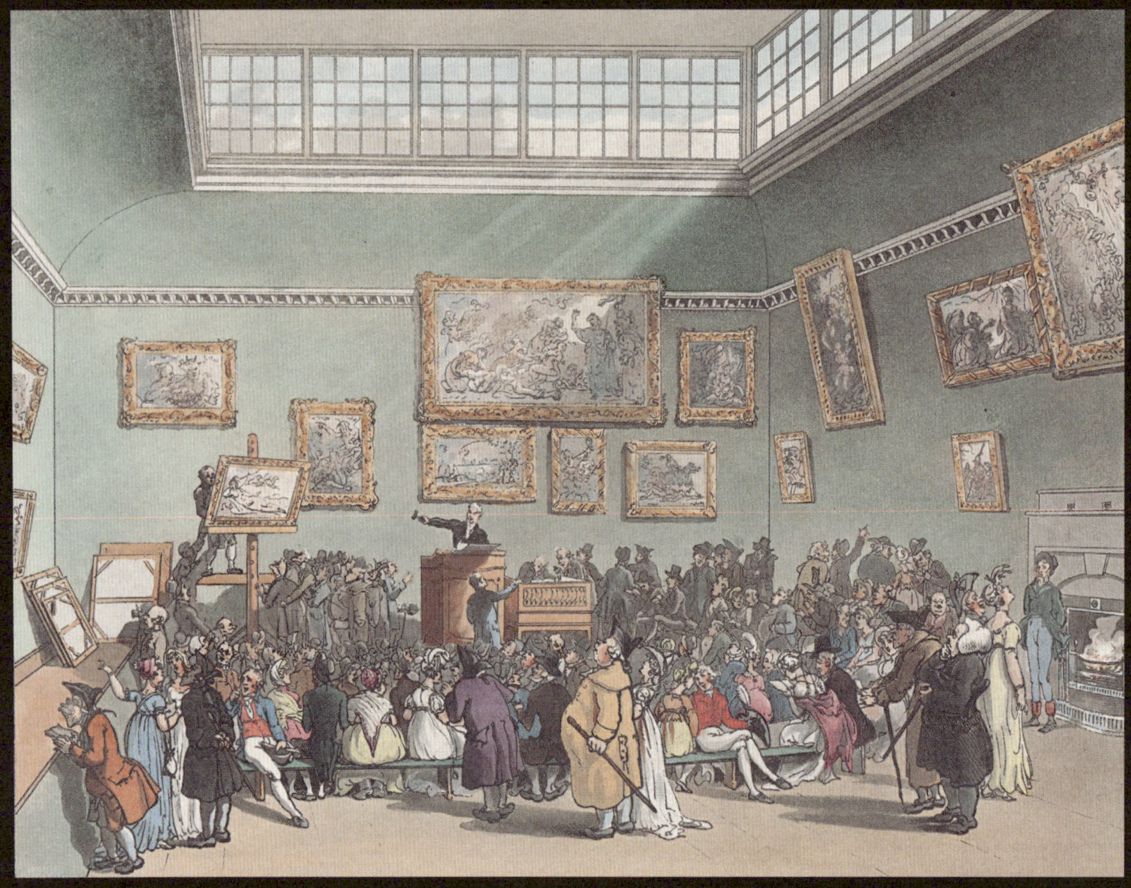

Thomas Rowlandson, *Christie's Auction Rooms*, 1808

'I am so clever', the protagonist of Oscar Wilde's fairytale 'The Remarkable Rocket' dryly boasts, 'that sometimes I don't understand a single word of what I'm saying.'[26] The tradition of self-deprecation in art is, ironically, a rather proud one. Painters inclined towards self-portraiture have proved especially adept at delineating its contours. Rembrandt's unflinching transcription of his own slowly slackening flesh comes to mind. Then there are those whose faces were the butt of the jokes. The 18th-century French nobleman and artist Joseph Ducreux, for instance, was fond of capturing himself in a series of farcically unflattering poses – now yawning, now shushing the viewer, now seemingly surprised, caught off guard by his own penetrating gaze. Salvador Dalí, who was famously full of himself, was also capable of producing deliciously self-derisory canvases, such as his 1941 *Soft Self-Portrait with Fried Bacon*.

A subspecies of the tradition of self-deprecation was popular with artists and cartoonists of the later 18th and early 19th centuries, who delighted in the disdainful depiction of art collectors gathering to admire and purchase the very pictures and prints that they themselves made a living from creating and selling. Among the most unflinchingly fearless of those happy to bite the hand that fed them was the British caricaturist Thomas Rowlandson, whose 1808 aquatint *Christie's Auction Rooms* questions the moral turpitude of those attending an art auction. As prices for works of art have soared exponentially in recent decades, it is hardly surprising that the practice of insulting one's potential buyers by calling into doubt their judgment, let alone their decency, has fallen out of favour with most artists. But Banksy isn't most artists.

Look closely at Rowlandson's claustrophobic tableau and there is something insalubrious about the sweaty scrum of old men leering at the reclining nude that the auctioneer has put under his hammer. The lewd air is hardly lightened by the portrayal of these same doddering and lecherous fogeys cosying up to much younger girls in this orgy of ogling. The seedy scene lays bare the motivations behind one's engagement with the art world and doesn't appear to be afraid to do so. Did Banksy have in mind Rowlandson's caustic caricature when, in 2007, he created his own bitterly biting print *Morons*, which likewise showcases a crush of pretentious art collectors presided over by an eager auctioneer as they stare at a work whose explicit message mocks their very existence: 'I can't believe you morons actually buy this shit'? Who can say. What we do know is that immediately behind Banksy's print is a press photograph taken in 1987 at Christie's auction house in London on a landmark evening in modern art. It was on that occasion that one of Vincent van Gogh's series of *Sunflowers* still lifes, created in 1888 – a painting that Banksy reworked in 2005 – sold for nearly $40 million (£22.5 million), making it, for the moment, the most expensive work of art ever to sell at auction. The sale of *Sunflowers* (the painting that Banksy has discreetly replaced with his indignant indictment both of those who buy art and the art he makes himself) has widely been seen as a watershed in the runaway inflation of art prices that has defined our era. Banksy's willingness to undermine the value of his own work and interrogate the motivations of those who collect it has, ironically, only added to his and its value.

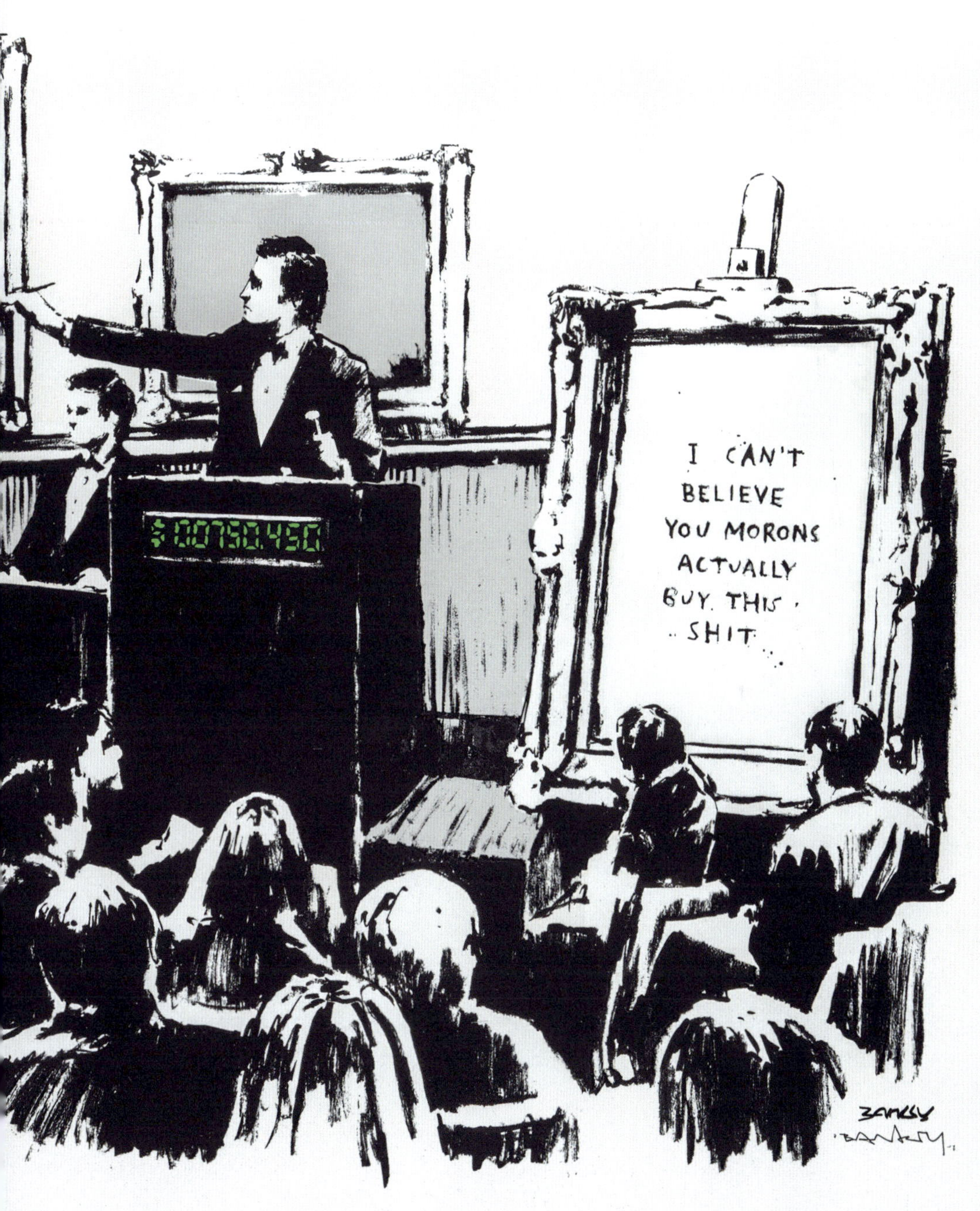
$007SD.4SD
I CAN'T
BELIEVE
YOU MORONS
ACTUALLY
BUY. THIS.
.SHIT.
BANKSY

Morons, 2007

NOT WAVING BUT SYNCING

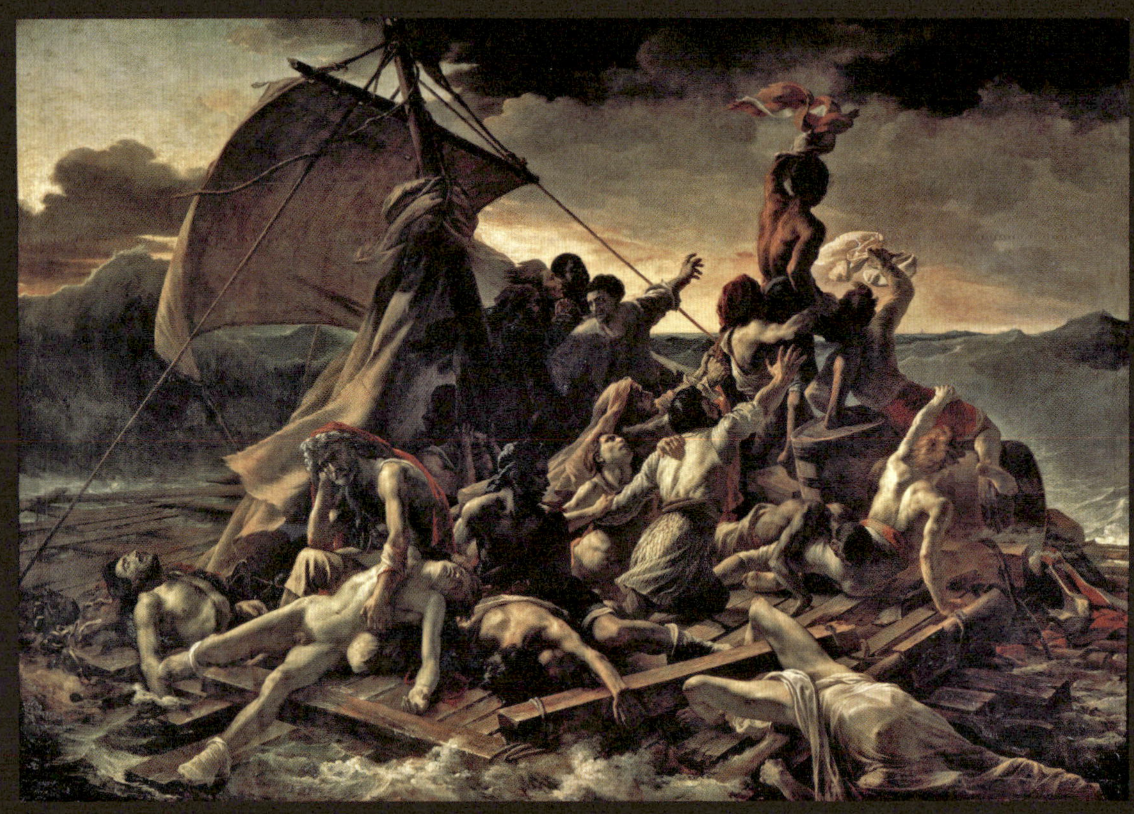

Théodore Géricault, *The Raft of the Medusa*, 1818–19

In 2015, shocking images of migrants stranded in 'The Jungle' – the disquieting handle by which a squalid and overcrowded refugee encampment in
Calais, France, came to be known – scandalized both France and the United
Kingdom, where most of the refugees were trying to reach. To focus attention
on what many perceived to be the shameful abandonment of these migrants
by wealthy nations that could afford to do more to assist those languishing
inside, Banksy undertook to rejuvenate for contemporary eyes one of the
most powerful rebukes to human callousness in all of art history: Théodore
Géricault's tragic seascape *The Raft of the Medusa* (1818–19).

Géricault's absorbing canvas imagines the moment when the few survivors of a shipwreck off the coast of Mauritania in 1816, clinging desperately
to a makeshift raft for two weeks without sustenance or supplies, manage to
attract the attention of the *Argus* – a brig passing by chance in the distance.
As no effort had been made by anyone on land to search for or to rescue the
passengers and crew of the ill-fated French frigate the *Méduse*, 132 of the raft's
147 passengers perished in unconscionable agony – many having resorted to
cannibalism in vain efforts to live.

With withering wit that manages not to diminish the gravity of his message, Banksy intervenes in Géricault's work by replacing the tiny silhouette of
the distant *Argus* – barely visible at the vanishing point of the original painting – with a much larger outline of a luxury yacht (complete with helipad and
private chopper), whizzing by obliviously on the much-nearer horizon line
of Banksy's mural. To make clear the true target of his unflinching lampoon,
Banksy attached to his mural the droll tagline 'we're not all in the same boat'.

The relative speed, if not haste, with which Banksy installed his work with
the aid of stencils and spray-can is in remarkable contrast to the patience
Géricault showed in creating the original. Convinced the canvas would propel
him into prominence, Géricault took his time constructing a life-size model of
the doomed raft and even purloined human remains from nearby morgues to
help him capture the textures and tones of decomposing flesh. When finally
unveiled at the Paris Salon in 1819, the painting caused a stir and quickly
established itself as one of the most arresting works of the age. Though its
edgy geometry and central surge of distress are familiar to many of us today,
how many can recall the contours of its backstory? Banksy's intercession into
Géricault's canvas reinvigorates the relevance of a once era-defining painting –
a masterpiece whose urgency had begun to fade.

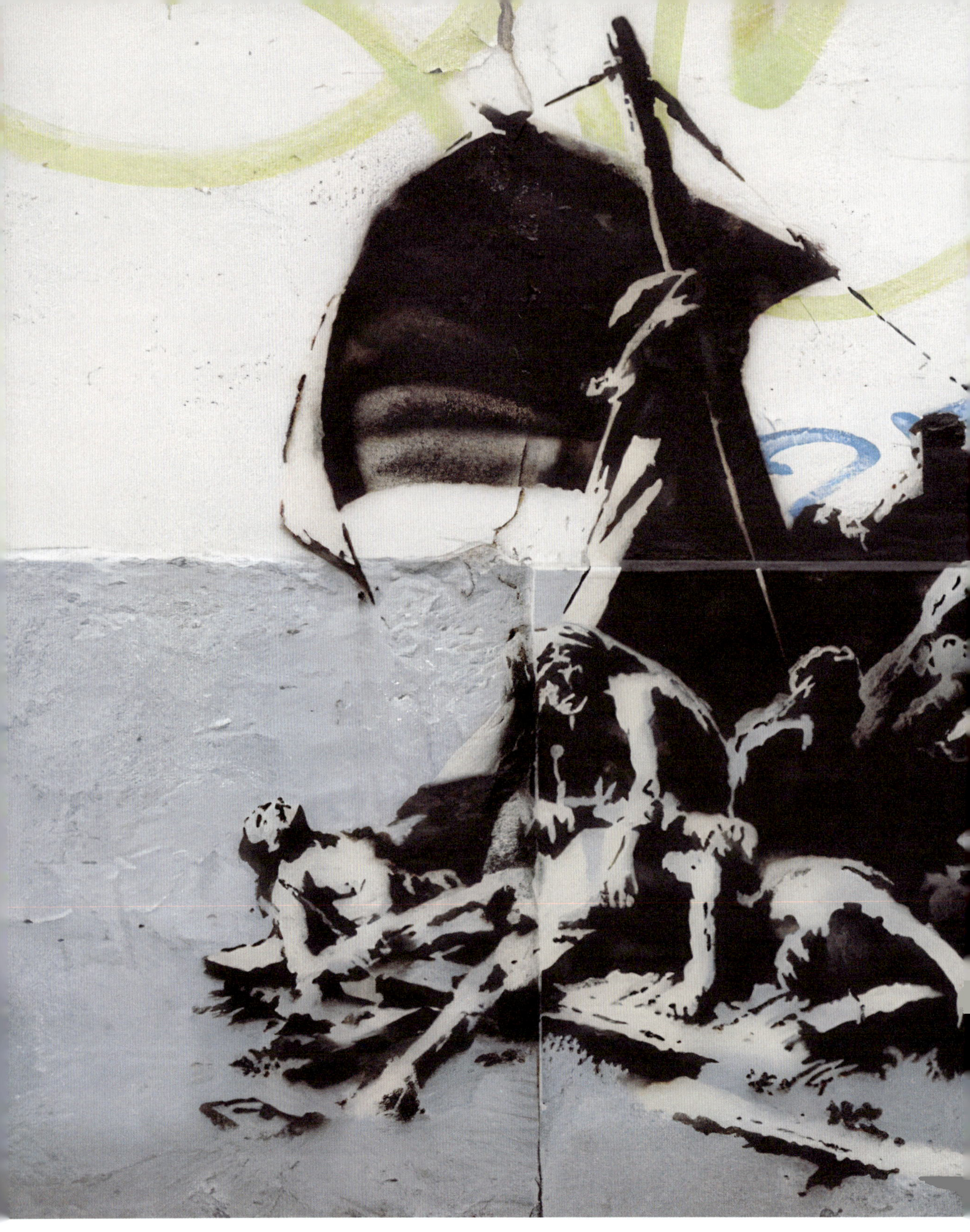

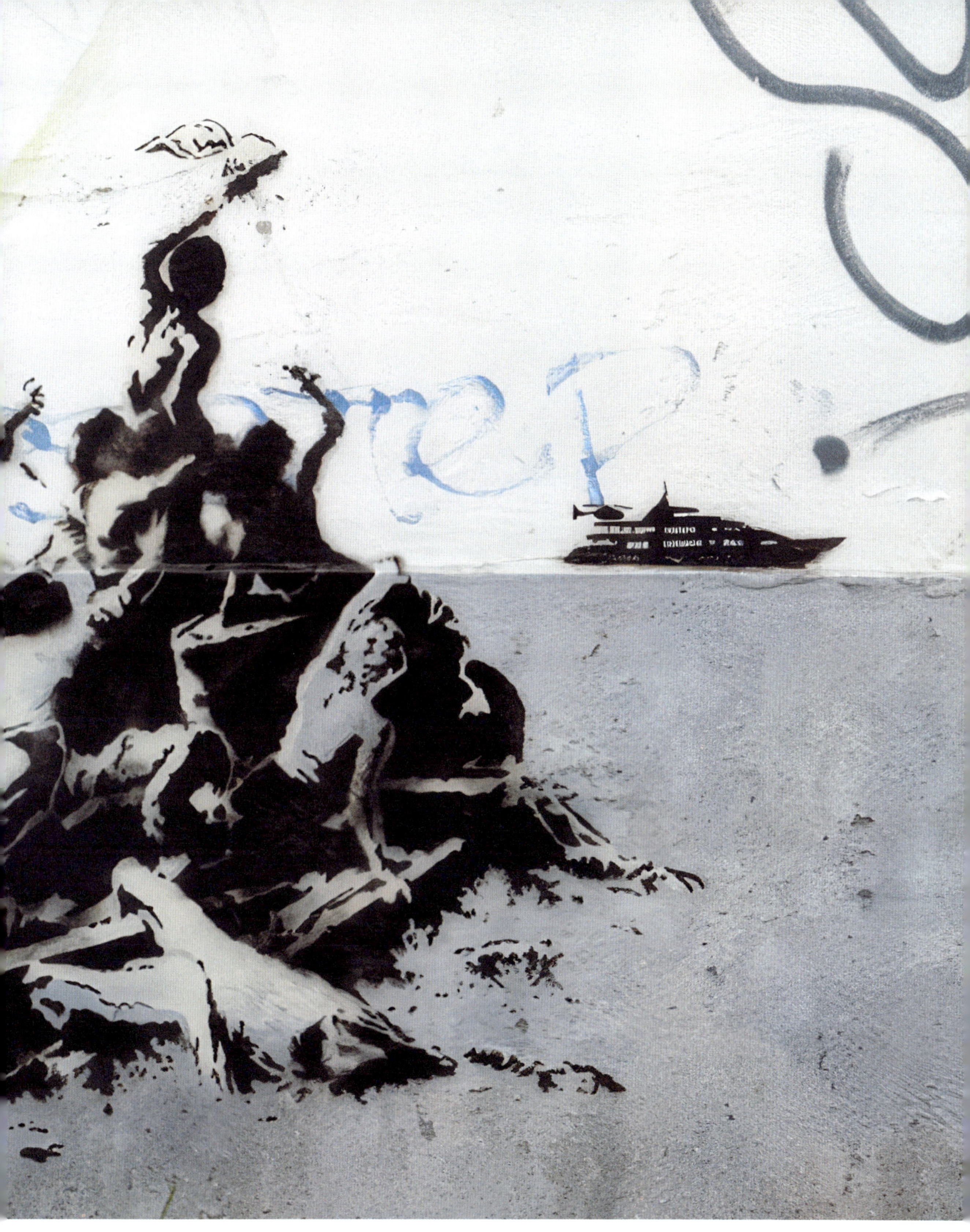

Calais, 2015

GOT A LIGHT?

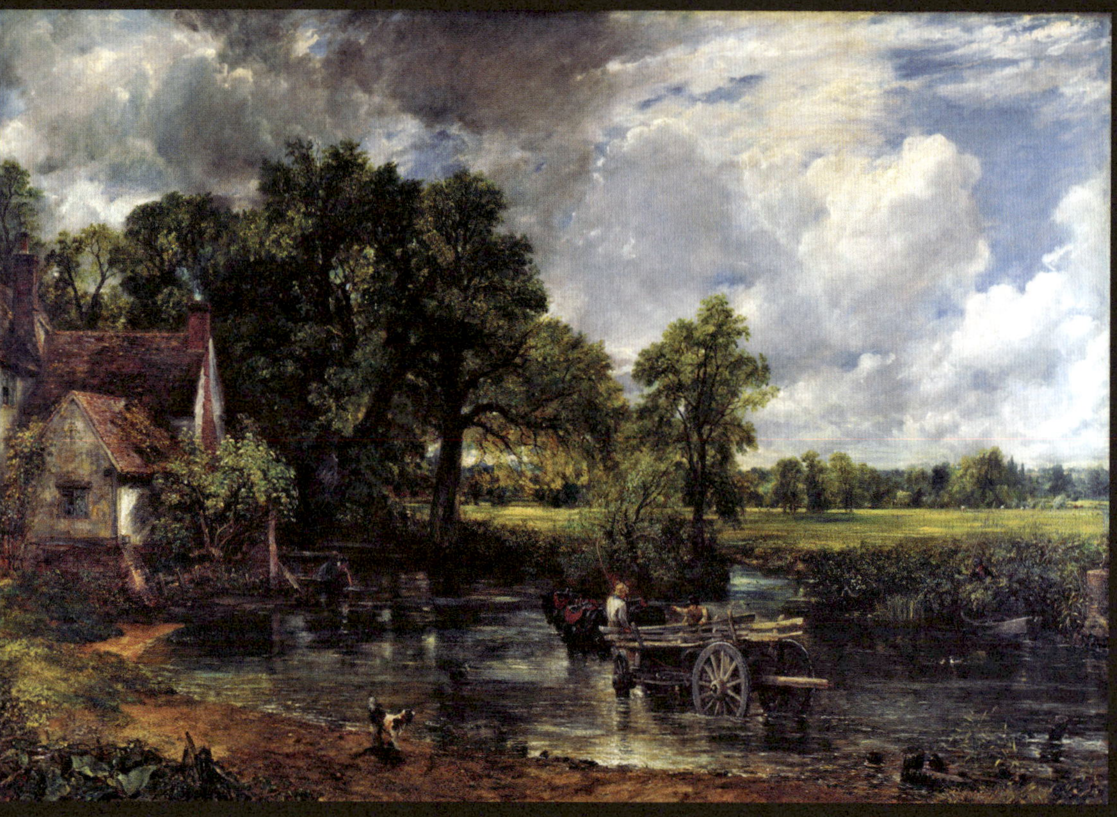

John Constable, *The Hay Wain*, 1821

You can spend your time feeling bad, measuring your blighted opportunities against some distant, gleaming, out-of-reach ideal of a fabled past and striving in vain to attain what generations who came before us allegedly enjoyed: mile after mile of lush, unspoilt countryside, pristine air, streams rippling with unpolluted water, and innocent sunshine so soft it wouldn't dream of damaging your skin. Or, you can follow the example Banksy sets in his incendiary send-up of a saccharine scene whose idyllic dapples and bucolic breeze recall the halcyon hooey of John Constable's deceptively simplistic depiction of rural life, *The Hay Wain*: douse the vision with petrol, strike a match and burn the mother down.

In *Crude Oil Jerry*, Banksy appears to reveal the 'con' in Constable. He superimposes on the pastiche pastoral of a recycled canvas the figure of the indomitable mouse from the cartoon duo Tom and Jerry, perched upon a leafy limb, holding a can dripping with flammable fuel in one hand and a lit match in the other. But Jerry's destructive presence only makes sense if Tom, the hapless cat, is chasing after him. Where is he? Perhaps Tom is us, peeping in from outside the frame, and Banksy is Jerry, about to torch the place. A statement read out by a representative for Banksy around the time the piece was made, presumably written by the artist himself, makes clear that his is a scorched-earth policy. 'The vandalized paintings reflect life as it is now. We don't live in a world like Constable's *Hay Wain* anymore, and if you do, there's probably a traveller's camp on the other side of the hill. The real damage to our environment is not done by graffiti writers and drunken teenagers but by big business and lazy architects, exactly the people who put gold-framed pictures of landscapes on their walls and try and tell the rest of us how to behave.'[27]

What is so shrewd about Banksy's work, and his comments regarding it, is how he weaves *The Hay Wain* into a combustible straw man – just as Constable himself had done two centuries ago when he painted the masterpiece. Like Banksy, Constable was alarmed at the accelerating loss of unpolluted rural life. *The Hay Wain*, which imagines a view of the millpond at Flatford, where Constable's family had owned and operated a corn-grinding mill for many generations, is not a celebration of how things were at the moment he painted it, but an ode to a vanishing world under threat by rapid industrialization and the rise of factories and locomotives (if not the unsightly scars of police cordons and CCTV cameras that Banksy inserts in comparable canvases). Constable created his work in the solitude of his studio, recalling the scene from his childhood – a scene that, for all intents and purposes, had already disappeared, gone up in flames and smoke when someone struck the match that lit the wick of our modern world.

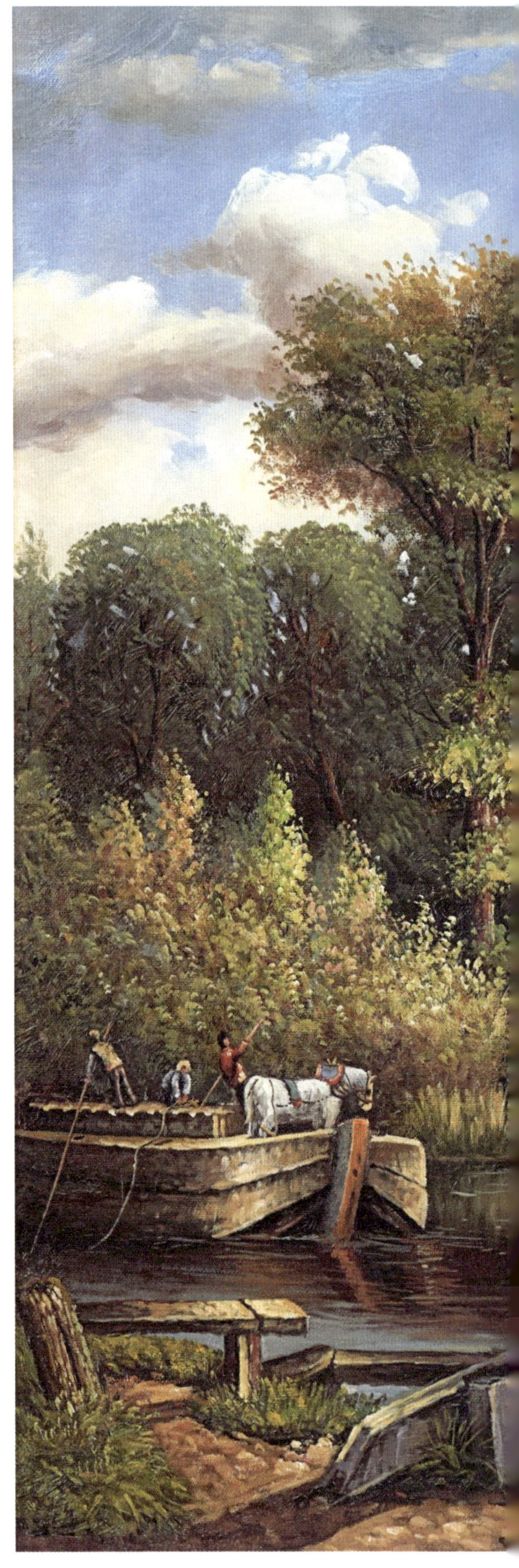

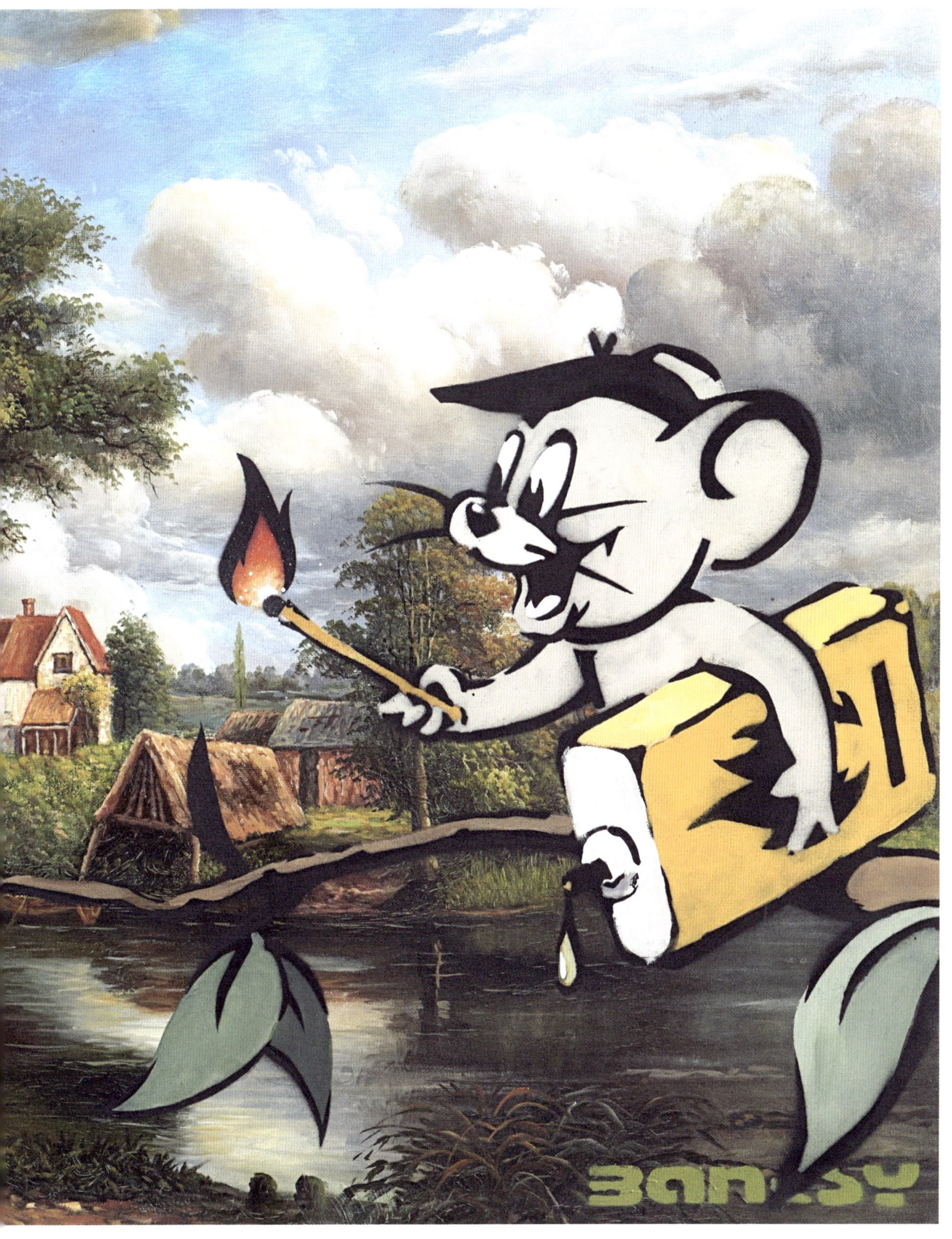

Crude Oil Jerry, 2003

THAT SINKING FEELING

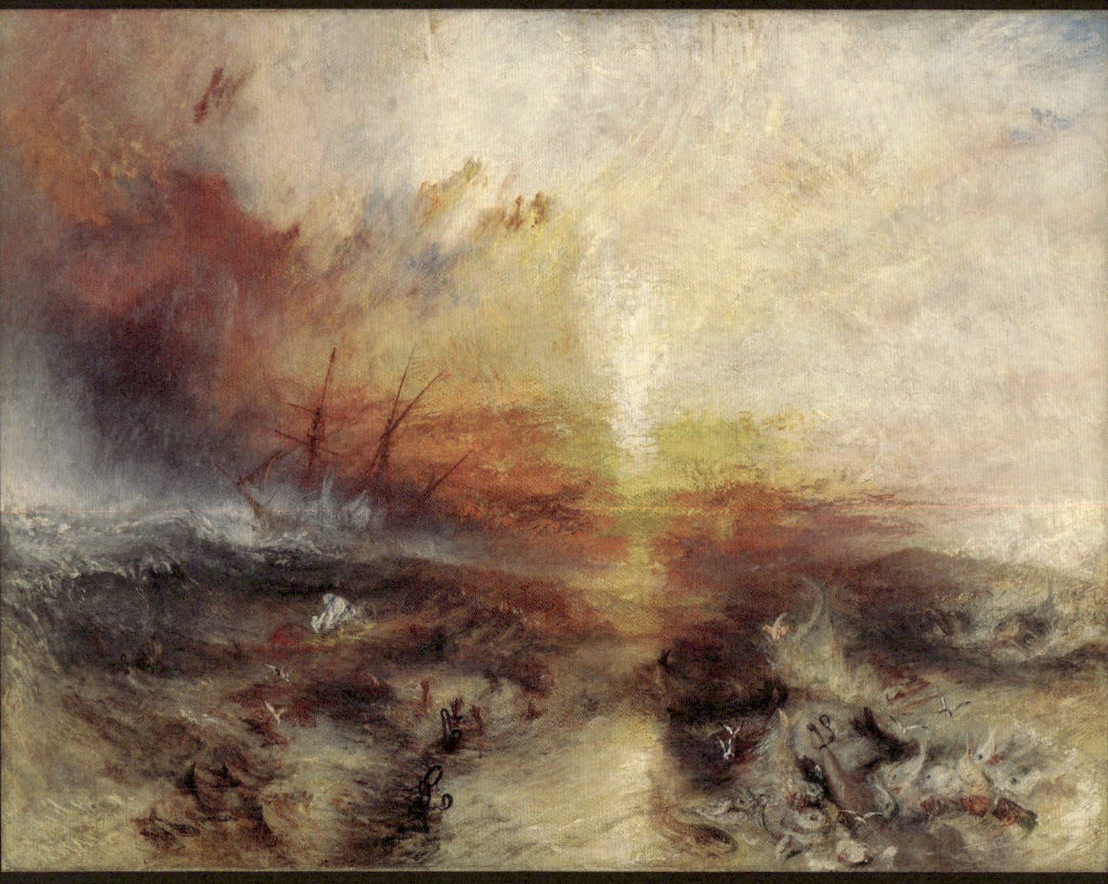

J. M. W. Turner, *Slave Ship*, 1840

It takes a minute to recognize the full horror of what is unfolding on the canvas. At first blush, the smouldering seascape that Joseph Mallord William Turner created in 1840 could be mistaken for just another sublime sunset of the sort for which the celebrated British Romantic was renowned. Anyone affording the work no more than the 17 seconds that researchers estimate most visitors spend looking at a painting in a museum might well walk away from it with merely a vague sense of angst wrung from the blood-orange clouds that unsettle Turner's troubled horizon.[28] For those whose gaze is patient, however, piqued by the tumult of light and mist that agitate the canvas – which the influential Victorian writer and critic John Ruskin believed would assure Turner's 'immortality' – their persistence is at once repaid by the sudden and disquieting realization of what it is that convulses the writhing waves: not flashes of the impending typhoon, encroaching from the top left of the painting and about to engulf the embattled ship, but gruesome glimmers of the still-shackled flesh of drowned and drowning slaves being viciously consumed by fish and gulls and the surging sea. Turner's anguished painting *Slave Ship*, to which he initially attached the more descriptive title *Slavers Throwing Overboard the Dead and Dying – Typhoon Coming On*, is a masterclass in bait-and-switch suspense – savvy choreography that anticipates Banksy's *Mediterranean Sea View*, an affecting triptych devoted to another maritime tragedy.

Turner's painting was created at a moment when the subject of slavery was current in cultural consciousness. Though Britain had outlawed the ownership of people seven years earlier, the Slavery Abolition Act of 1833 had yet fully to come into effect throughout the Empire. To keep the human horror of slavery at the forefront of popular imagination, Turner reconstructs one of the grimmest episodes in its history, recalling the unconscionable actions taken by the captain of the British slave ship *Zong*, who had accidentally steered the ship off course on its way to Jamaica in 1781. Concerned that the slaves he was carrying might die on board from a lack of food and water before reaching the Caribbean, resulting in a loss of inventory that was not covered by the insurance policy he had taken out on the 'cargo', the captain decided cruelly to throw overboard 130 souls so he could later make a claim. If you let your eyes acclimatize to Turner's tempestuous waves, you will begin to make out the desperate flail of wrists and ankles, tethered hopelessly to iron chains.

The comparatively mild title that Banksy, nearly two centuries later, attaches to his triptych *Mediterranean Sea View* (first installed in 2017 in the lobby of his Walled Off Hotel in Bethlehem, which stares straight into the bleak partition separating Israel from the Palestinian territories) belies the true terror of what the artist is depicting. The three-part work was created at a moment when migrants from the Middle East, fleeing countries riven by unrest, were forced to make dangerous crossings across the Mediterranean Sea in the desperate hope of reaching Greece or Italy, resulting in countless deaths. Banksy transforms Turner's iron shackles into tragically useless blood-orange buoys and life jackets, washed up limp and breathless on the rocks and shore – bright and cheery as the futures that so many refugees never reached.

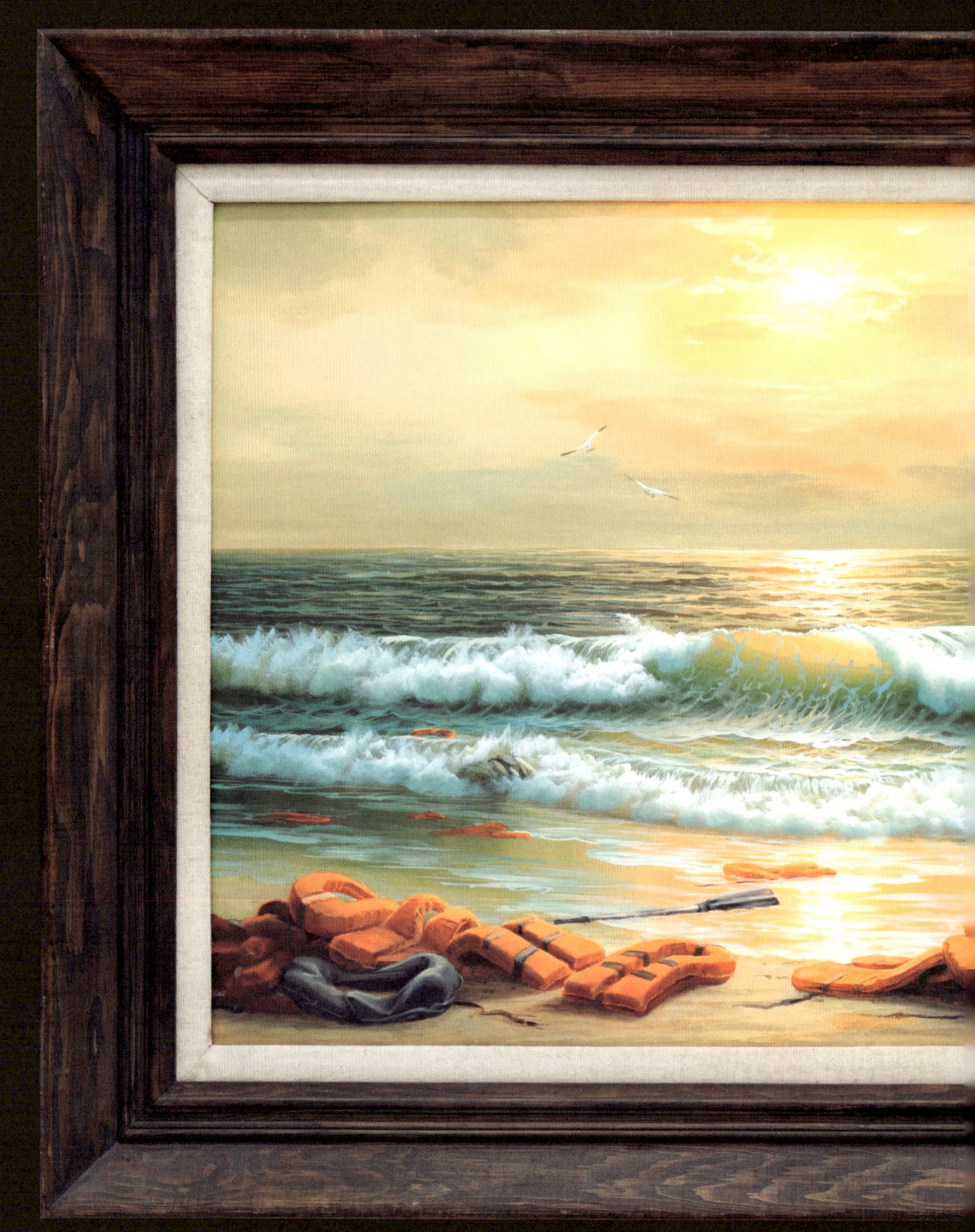

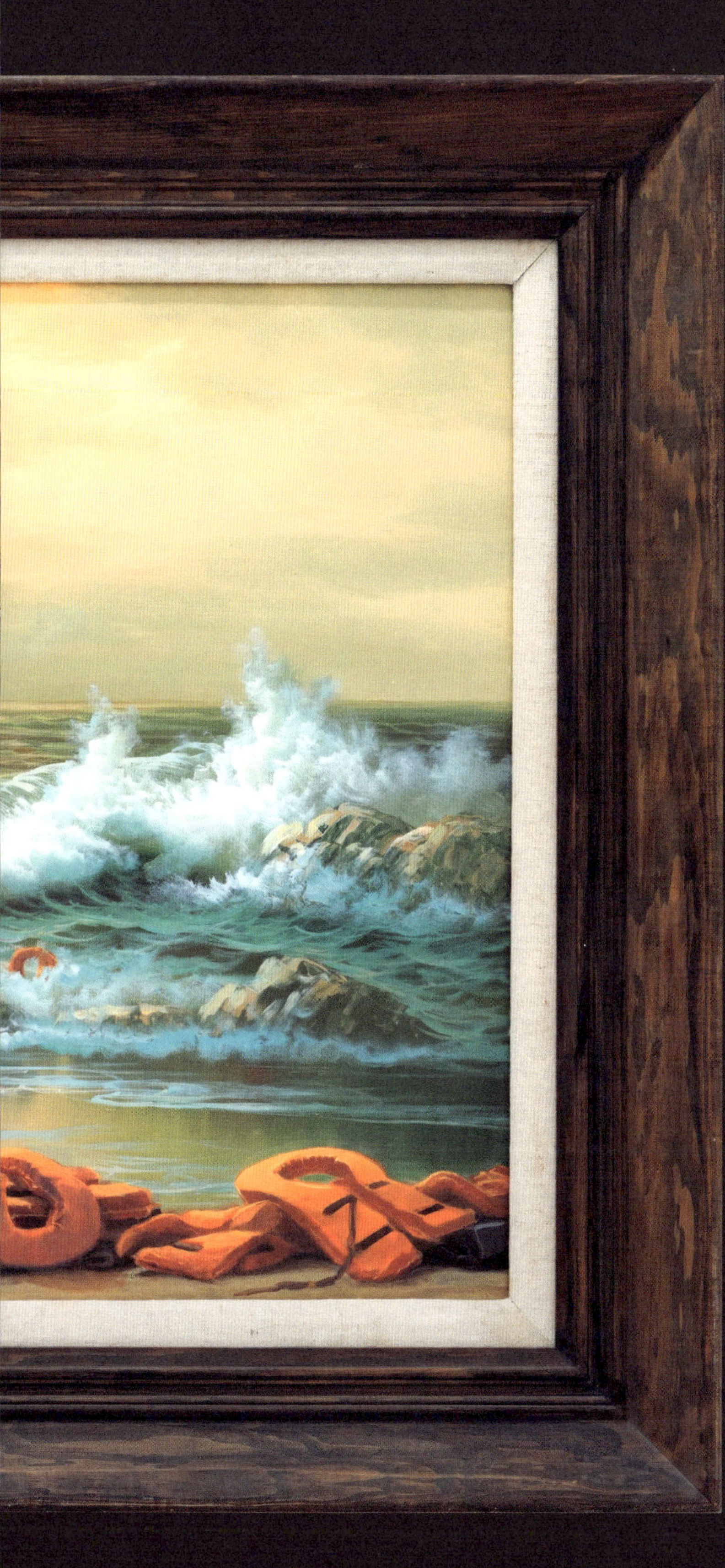

CUT IT OUT

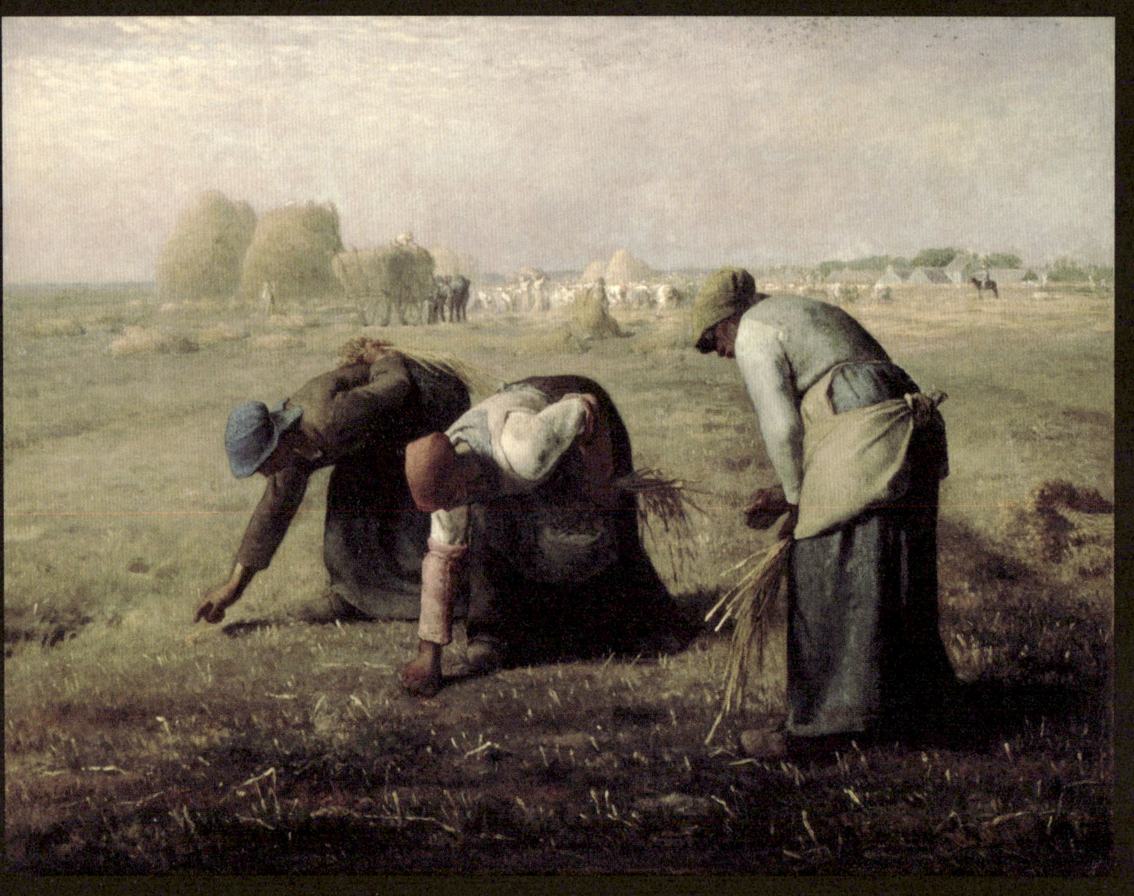

Jean-François Millet, *The Gleaners*, 1857

Don't we owe art a break? After all, even the universe's creator, summoned incessantly since time immemorial to satisfy our every wandering desire, was finally given a breather a century and a half ago, when in 1882 Friedrich Nietzsche declared that God was dead. Yet art has been on duty for at least as long – staring out at us from cave walls, faded ceilings and fatigued canvases without so much as the slightest twitch or tremor, let alone a day off. Imagine the strain of holding a smirk for half a millennia, as Mona Lisa has, or the ache of foisting a flag in the smoke-filled smog of revolution for centuries, like Liberty leading her people. In the case of Jean-François Millet's quietly subversive canvas, *The Gleaners*, which suspends in eternal toil a tireless trio of peasants bent double picking from the ground the teensy bits of grain left behind by harvesters, the agony of their interminable task, let alone the endlessly intractable social struggles for which they serve as symbols, is intolerable to watch. In 2009, Banksy did what no one had ever dared to do before, and cut the groaning gleaners some slack. Literally. In doing so, he dared us to gaze again at a masterpiece that, ironically, we have tended to look straight through as a quaintly antiquated document from a bygone era, rather than a still raw statement – one that has the power to tear our conscience to shreds.

When Millet first exhibited his painting, which evocatively situates the three central labourers, subserviently scrounging for scraps, below the golden haze of a horizon on which the bountifulness of the harvest can be seen swelling in lucrative mountains, the work was widely condemned. Establishment critics and wealthy collectors attending the Salon, the official art exhibition of the Académie des Beaux-Arts in Paris (which, for nearly two centuries, had a reputation for showcasing the art world's crème de la crème), immediately glimpsed in *The Gleaners* a coded call to the poor to take up arms against the prosperous. 'Behind these three Gleaners,' insisted one commentator, making a shocking allusion to the violence witnessed during the French Revolution and the Bloody Reign of Terror, 'on the murky horizon, loom the rioters' pikes and the scaffolds of 1793'.[29] With the Revolution of 1848 (which witnessed the collapse of the monarchy and the start of the Second French Republic) still fresh in the minds of aristocrats, Millet's deceptively quiet canvas was seen as deeply dangerous. Flash forward a century and a half to the contemporary cultural context of the global financial crisis that began a year earlier – once again highlighting the disparity between the wealthy and the poor, the hearty harvesters and the indigent gleaners – and Banksy might well have tried to squeeze from these fatigued physiques a further stint of service by making them scrounge for ultra-processed food, say, or plastics polluting the soil. Instead, with compassion, he seems to be affording the figures, one at a time, perhaps, a respite from their tiresome task of vibrating meaning by freeing them from the frame, and offering them a seat and ciggy. They've earned it. After all, as Banksy knows better than anyone, soulful subversiveness is exhausting business.

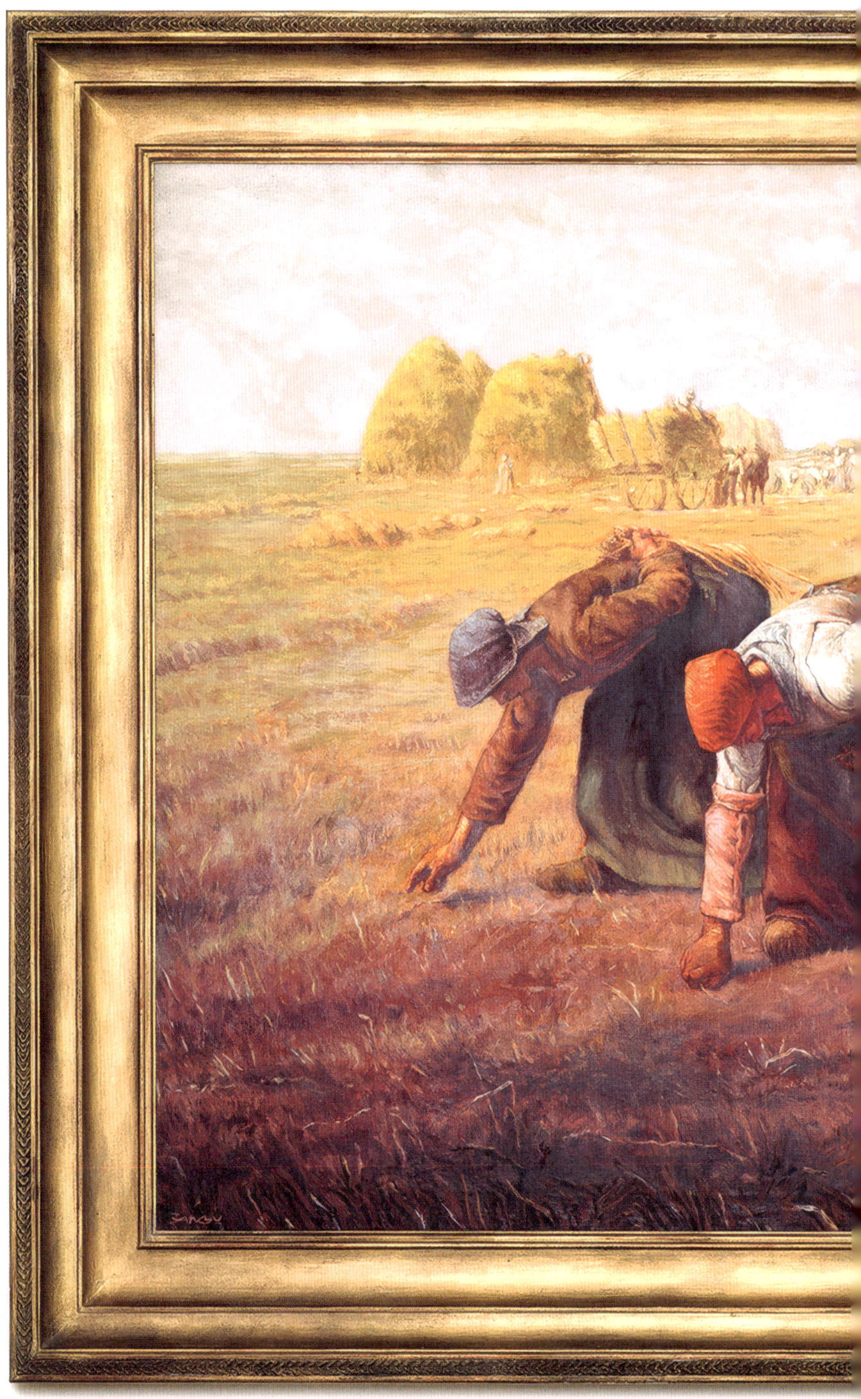

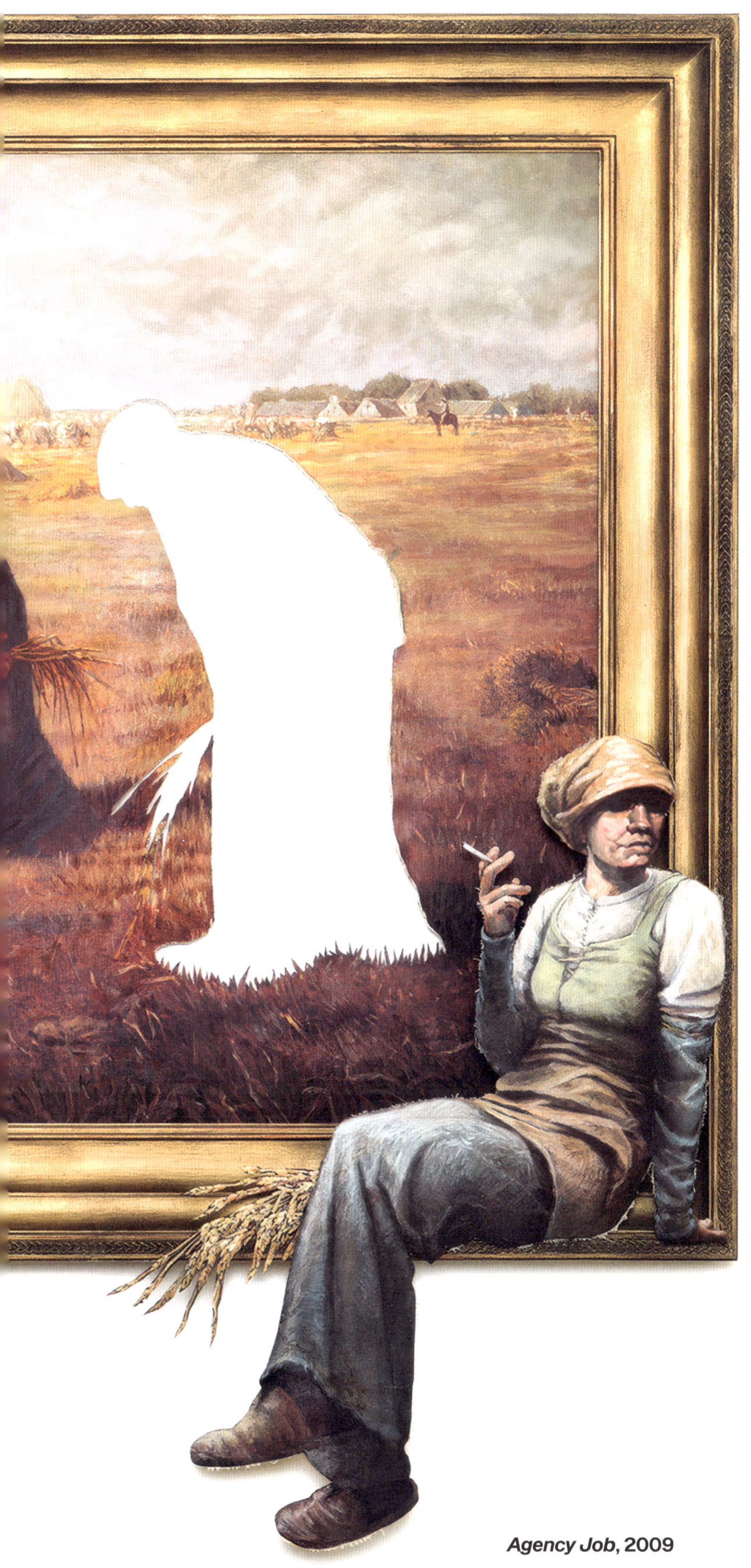

Agency Job, 2009

BEYOND THE VEIL

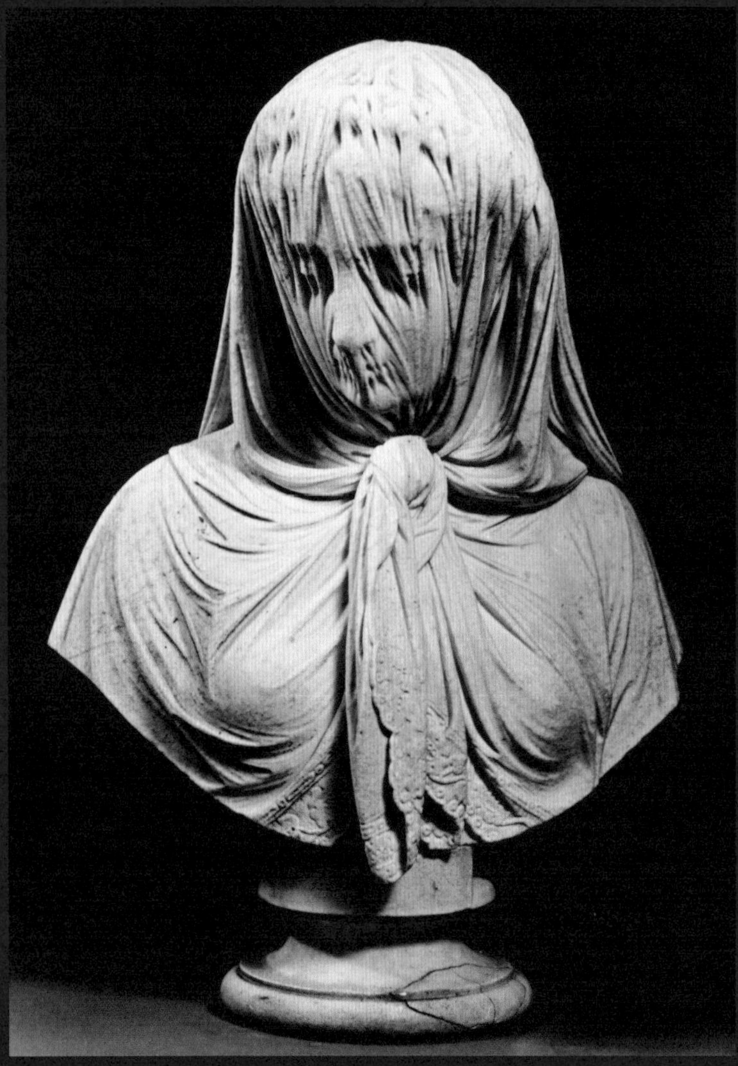

Giovanni Battista Lombardi, *Veiled Woman*, 1869

S ay 'veil' and the softness of that single syllable summons a soulful journey. The word is, after all, derived from the Latin noun *vela*, meaning 'sail', suggesting a stationary voyage, a drifting inward. To pull a veil across one's face, however sheer its weave may be, is to disappear into a near unknown, diaphanously visible yet unreachable. But how do you approximate the gossamer ghostliness of a semi-transparent veil in sculpted stone? The phenomenal finesse necessary to alchemize marble into the ripples of any fine material clinging to skin, never mind the challenges posed by see-through fabric falling across a face, has been a benchmark of a sculptor's skill since antiquity – from the gauzy gowns that enshroud the figures of the Parthenon marbles to the exquisite rumples of Mary's dress in Michelangelo's *Pietà*. Replicating the ethereal effect of creased silk as it gently cascades across a countenance, simultaneously revealing and concealing the subject, is something relatively few sculptors dared to undertake before the Italian Rococo sculptor Antonio Corradini became obsessed with the trope in the 18th century. Done well, the result is a face that seems eternally on the verge of emerging from the stasis of stone only to sail back to its opaque otherwhereness – a restless wraith forever frozen between this world and another, life-in-deathness and death-in-lifeness.

The mournful bust of a veiled woman created by the 19th-century Italian sculptor Giovanni Battista Lombardi in 1869 is one such phantom. Downcast in mourning for some indeterminate loss, the young woman is portrayed as having pulled tight across her sorrowful face a veil whose fragile folds and delicate pleats manage miraculously to preserve a semblance of her youth while offering a prescient glimpse of her complexion's slow shrivel into old age. The bust's ability to hold in equilibrium an innocence that is slipping away and a maturity that may never be reached makes it a fitting source for one of Banksy's most achingly poignant murals. On the exit door of Paris's Bataclan theatre in the summer of 2018, two and a half years after that venue was the site of a terrorist attack in which ninety concert-goers were brutally murdered by Islamic extremists, Banksy stencilled an echo of Lombardi's touching portrait. Portrayed wearing the protective suit of a security service responder, she holds a crocheted handkerchief in one hand and impassive paperwork in another – a ledger, perhaps, on which to keep a tally of those who died when three gunmen stormed the theatre as the American band Eagles of Death Metal played their song 'Kiss the Devil'. Veiled by tears, Banksy's reinvention of Lombardi's bust stood solemn sentry by the door through which many in the crowd of 1,500 tried desperately to escape, haunting the space like a soul summoned from another world.

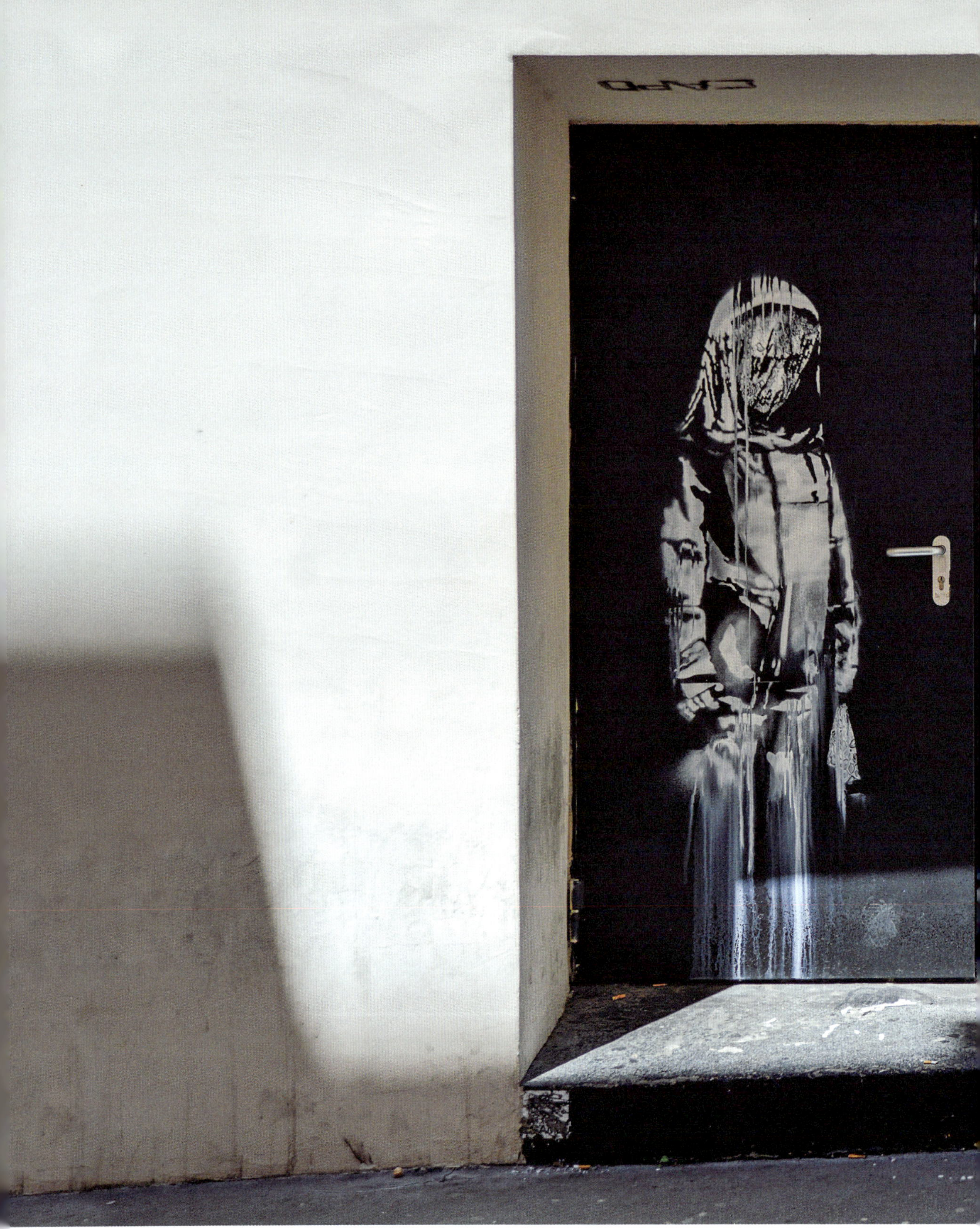

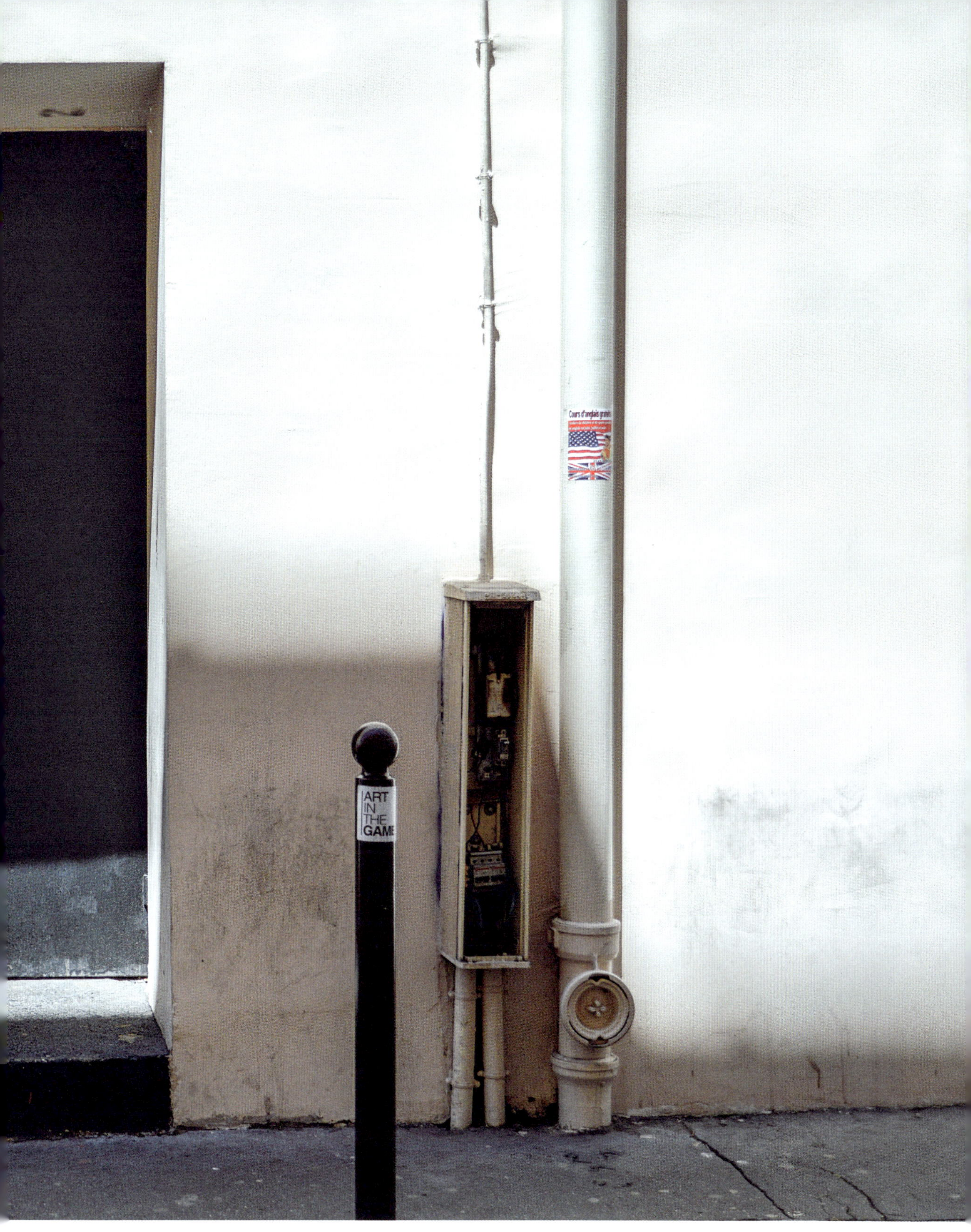

Bataclan theatre, Paris, 2018

ON POINTE

Art needs protection – not just from the natural decay of the perishable materials that comprise it, or from the smashes and slashes of inadvertent damage to which all things are vulnerable, but also, so it seems, from the very hands of the painters and sculptors who create it. For those who find themselves enchanted by the countless portrayals of ballet dancers that the French Impressionist Edgar Degas committed to canvas, paper and wax sculpture in the latter decades of the 19th century, the notion that the supple subjects themselves, captured with such seeming devotion, are in fact forever suspended in a fug of toxic debasement that emanated from the artist who immortalized their physiques may come as a dispiriting shock. In 2005, Banksy unveiled an arresting send-up of one of Degas's most memorable depictions of a young ballerina, the life-size, mixed-media sculpture that he created around 1880, *Little Dancer Aged Fourteen*. In doing so, Banksy invited us to reassess what it is we admire when we stare into the callous haze of the Parisian artist's revered and revolutionary, if morally brutish, handiwork.

The only sculpture that Degas exhibited during his lifetime, the wax effigy of Marie van Goethem, an aspiring dancer at the Paris Opera Ballet, was augmented by the addition of a pleated gauze tutu, a snug silk bodice, fuchsia slippers, and a wig made from horsehair – innovative enhancements that lent a realistic tactility to the work, blurring the lines between art and life. But beneath the added gauze and silk and horsehair, a less salubrious thread had also been woven into the fabric of the piece. It seems that Degas was attracted less to the poetics of the craft than he was to the profound discomfort the dancers suffered while training – an agony that he was happy to help amplify. Referring to the young students, many of whom came from such severe poverty that they found themselves forced into exploitation, as 'little monkey girls', Degas relished in the excruciating strain of the awkward poses he required his models to hold for hours. He loved watching the girls break.[30] Reflecting on his treatment of the ballerinas years later with a fellow painter, Degas admitted that 'women can never forgive me. They hate me, they can feel that I'm disarming them, I show them without their coquetry, in the state of animals cleaning themselves ... they see me as the enemy'.[31]

In Banksy's hands, however, Marie van Goethem is 'disarmed' and powerless no more. Equipped with a military-grade gas mask to protect her from the noxiousness of Degas's inhumanity, she has freed herself from the ungainly pose in which she was imprisoned for a century and is seen mincing merrily off – at long last, the master of her own destiny. As if paying tribute to the other young dancers, referred to in the day as *petit rats*, whom Degas mistreated, Marie is accompanied, at her feet, by a sweet skitter of rodents, Banksy's alter ego, the surest sign that his affections are truly with her.

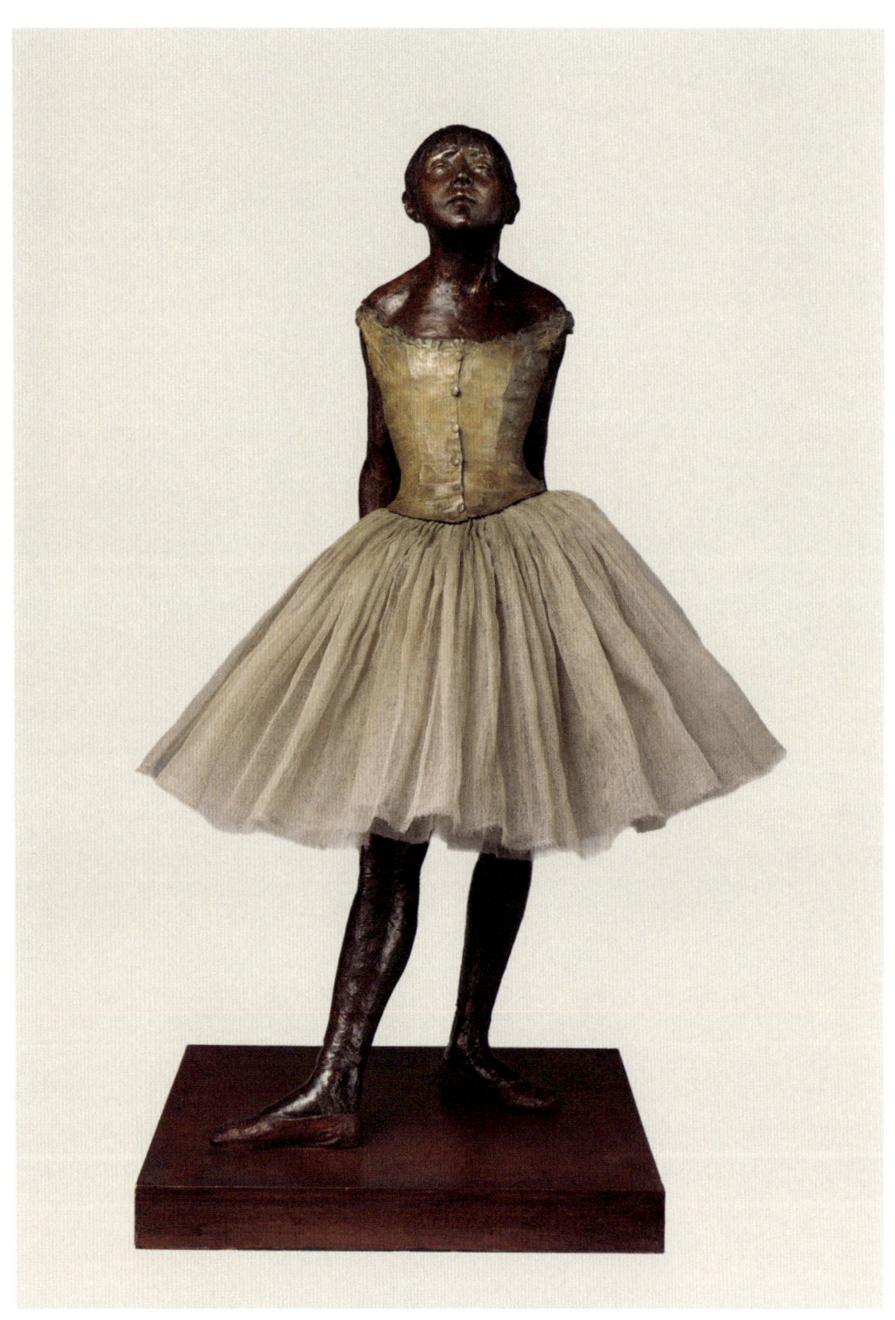

Edgar Degas, *Little Dancer Aged Fourteen*, 1880–81

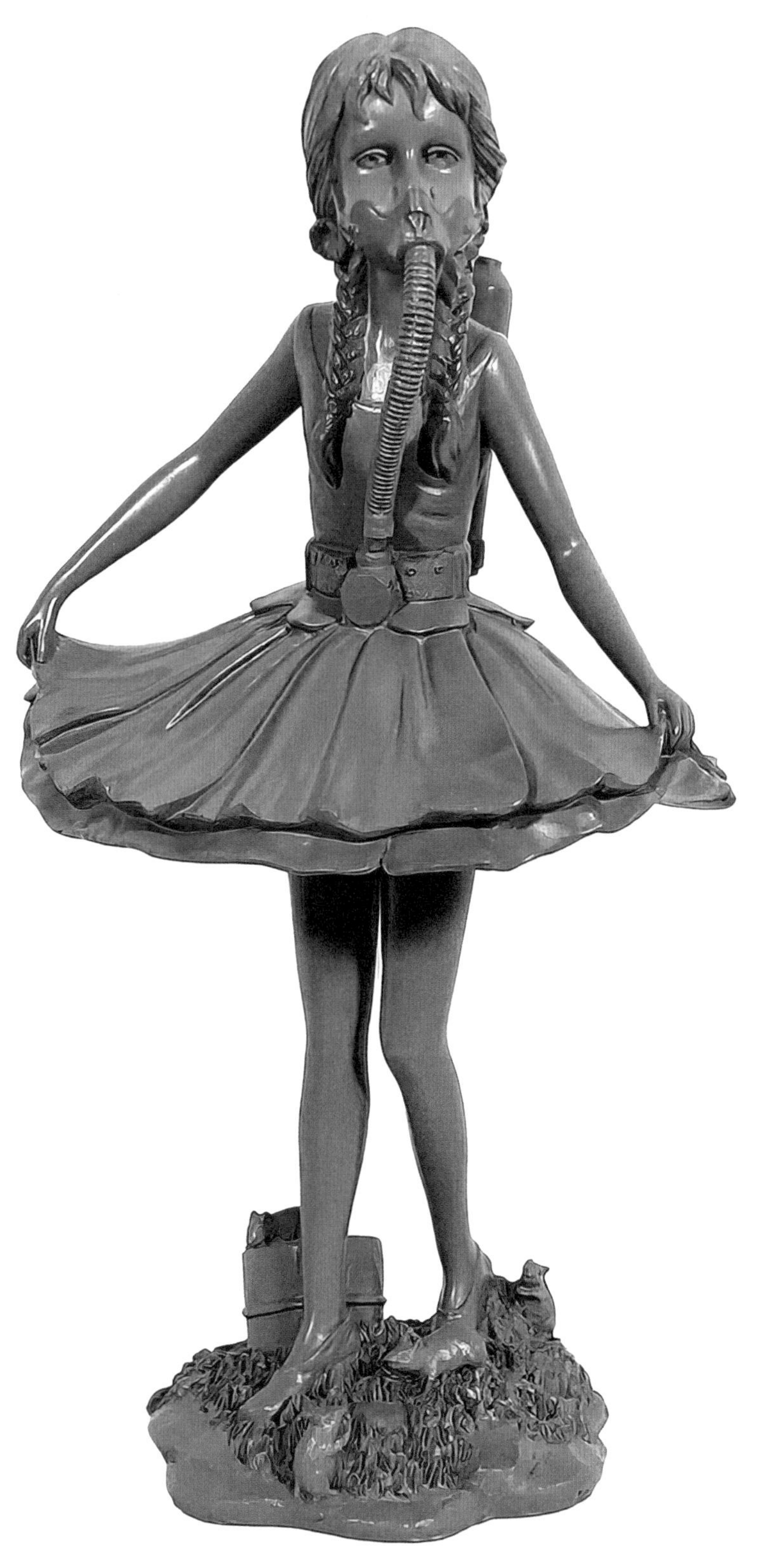

Ballerina with Action Man Parts, 2005

SHORE THING

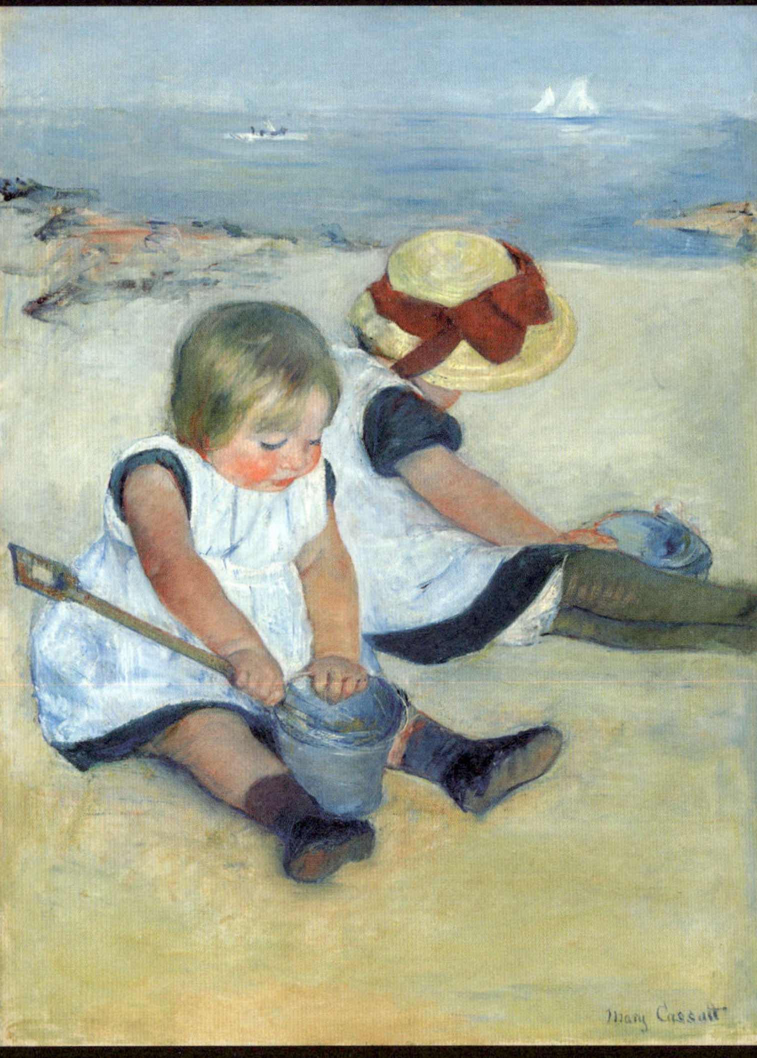

Mary Cassatt, *Children Playing on the Beach*, 1884

The rallying cry coined in Paris during the weeks of intense civil unrest that threatened to topple France's government in May 1968, '*sous les pavés, la plage!*' ('under the pavement, the beach!'), always had a poetic ring to it that transcended the heated politics of the moment. On a literal level, the phrase describes what student protesters, agitating against capitalism and consumerism, were discovering beneath the paving stones that they were prising loose to build barricades against the police – the sandy shores of forgotten beaches that once stretched along the river Seine before the urban sprawl of Paris had buried them under an amnesia of concrete and stone. On a deeper level, the phrase is stirringly romantic, a call to rekindle a repressed consciousness of innocence – that luminous, visionary gleam in which the world seemed bathed when we are children. In that sense, the social and political aspirations of those protesting in May 1968 had an unexpected aesthetic antecedent: the Impressionists had, a century earlier, likewise sought to restore things to their stifled resplendence. Among the more moving examples of that urge to bring back to light the faded refulgence of childhood is Mary Cassatt's glimmering *Children Playing on the Beach*, which the Paris-based American artist painted in 1884.

Likely a tribute to her sister Lydia, whose death in 1882 after a lifetime of illness left Cassatt unable to paint for half a year, *Children Playing on the Beach* portrays two little girls absorbed in the wonder of the sunlit sand on an idyllic summer day. There is a sense of urgency and vigour to Cassatt's brushwork that, despite the fact that she returned to the canvas many times over, creates the impression that the scene is a fleeting flash of memory, freshly excavated from beneath the heavy paving stones of grief. Seemingly as far removed from the concerns of politics as a picture could possibly get, Cassatt's poignant painting nevertheless vibrates with the very vibe that many protestors in May 1968 were desperate to evoke. It was time to lift the sorrowful slabs under which the world was busy burying itself – time to liberate the light and build castles in the sun. '*Under the pavement, the beach!*'

In August 2021, as part of a spree of works that Banksy christened 'The Great British Spraycation', a playfully hybrid piece – part mural, part installation – that seemed lit up from inside with the mingled spirit of the Paris protest slogan and Mary Cassatt's powerful elegy to her sister appeared in the East Suffolk coastal town of Lowestoft. Banksy stencilled the image of a little boy kneeling, his face sensibly shaded by a floppy summer beach hat, on a drab wall on London Road North, a short stroll from the beach. The small child, who holds in his hands an outsized crowbar, stares outside the mural to the large and very real sand castle that rises before him on the pavement – a work of wonder he seems magically to have freed from beneath a pair of paving stones that he has just prised loose. Was Banksy making a political point, or was he just being playful? Yes, it's definitely one of those. Or neither. Or both.

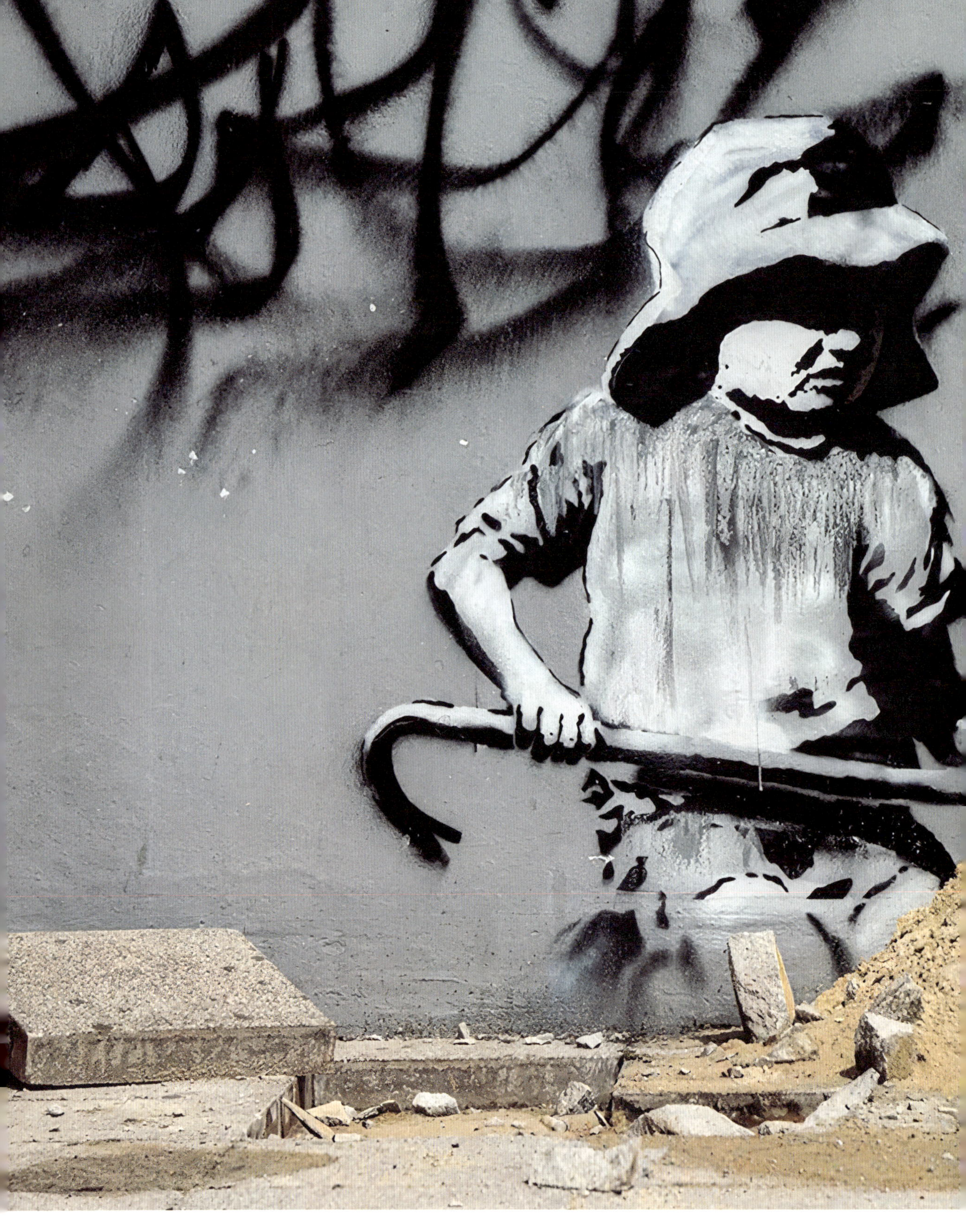

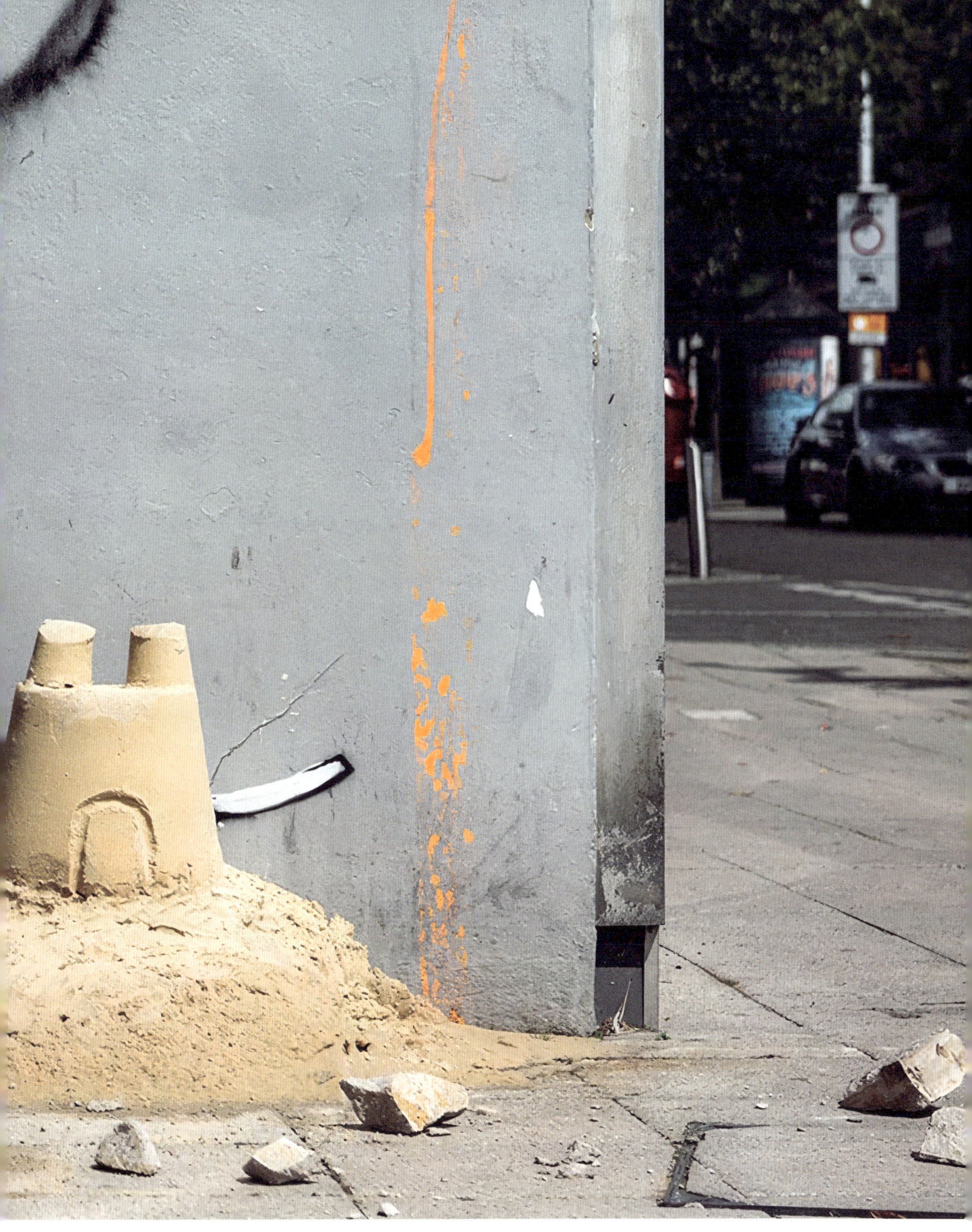

Lowestoft, 2021

OIL PRESSURE

In October 2005, crude oil was clogging the world's brain. Images of the
human and environmental tolls taken by Hurricane Katrina, a devastating
Category 5 storm that had ravaged the coast of Louisiana two months earlier,
claiming nearly 2,000 lives, displacing approximately 1 million people, and
spilling more than 7 million gallons of oil into the Gulf of Mexico, were still
saturating international news. The Iraq War, perceived by many as more a
strategic operation for control of the region's oil reserves than a righteous fight
against terrorism, was still in its early years. In America, a heated battle over
legislation either to permit or to prohibit drilling for oil in Alaska's threatened
Arctic National Wildlife Refuge saw energy nationalists, determined to exploit
the country's native reserves, and enraged environmentalists, desperate to
curb America's reliance on climate-endangering resources, pitted against one
another. Oil was everywhere.

It was against this highly agitated cultural backdrop that Banksy unveiled a
wry riff on one of Vincent van Gogh's most revered works, *Sunflowers* (1888–89).
Wittily rechristened *Sunflowers from Petrol Station*, Banksy's acerbic reimagining
of Van Gogh's famous vase of thrumming perennials was included in his
sensational exhibition 'Crude Oils: A Gallery of Re-mixed Masterpieces,
Vandalism and Vermin', which saw several send-ups of seminal works from
art history sharing space with a scrum of two hundred rats that were left to
scamper about the gallery. Far from diminishing the meaning of the famously
effulgent affirmations of life (which Van Gogh said expressed 'gratitude'),[32]
Banksy sculpts from the suspended explosion of blooms a poignant portrait
of looming desolation that fracks into a reserve of swelling anxiety.

Van Gogh's original canvas, one of seven devoted to the subject of sunflowers that the Dutch Post-Impressionist would undertake between 1888
and 1889, was begun in keen anticipation of the arrival of his friend and fellow artist, Paul Gauguin, with whom he was planning to share a rented house
in Arles, in the south of France. Unfortunately, an altercation with Gauguin in
the days before Christmas, 1888, in which Van Gogh turned a knife on his
friend before using a razor to slice off a portion of his own left ear, has since
complicated the lustre of the works Van Gogh created at this troubled time.
As if seizing on the complexity of the canvas's connotations, as a talisman of
hope curdled into trauma and despair, Banksy strips the bouquet's now-stooping
stems (which he's slimmed from fifteen to four), and scatters about the table
on which the vase sits a ragged carpet of shrivelled florets, like so many severed lobes. By drolly dislocating Van Gogh's intensely intimate canvas to the
seemingly out-of-the-way context of 'petrol stations' and 'crude oil', Banksy
challenges us to consider to what extent meaning in art, like fossil fuels in
earth, is a finite resource that we can only exploit for so long. Eighteen years
before *Sunflowers from Petrol Station*, Van Gogh's work sold at auction for nearly
$40 million (£22.5 million), the highest price ever paid for a painting at the
time, marking a turning point in the hyper-valuation of works of art. But
how long can we greedily extract profit from these precious cultural deposits?
At some point, the vessel is empty. And so are we.

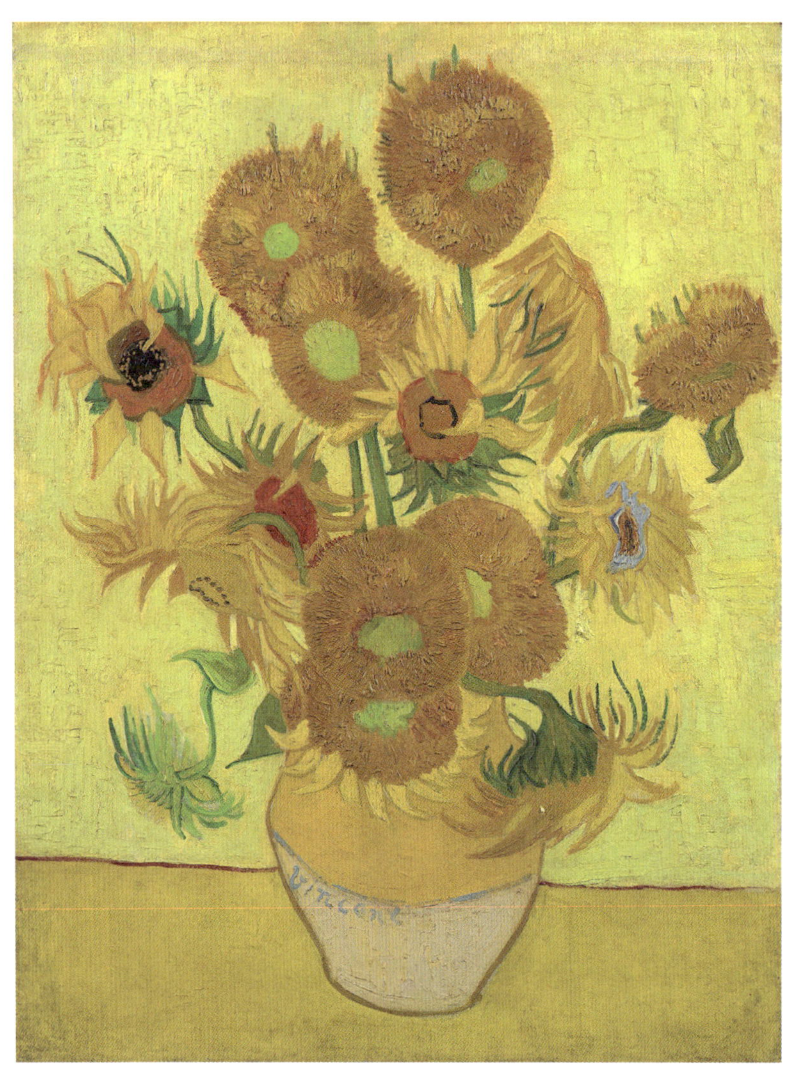

Vincent van Gogh, *Sunflowers*, 1888–89

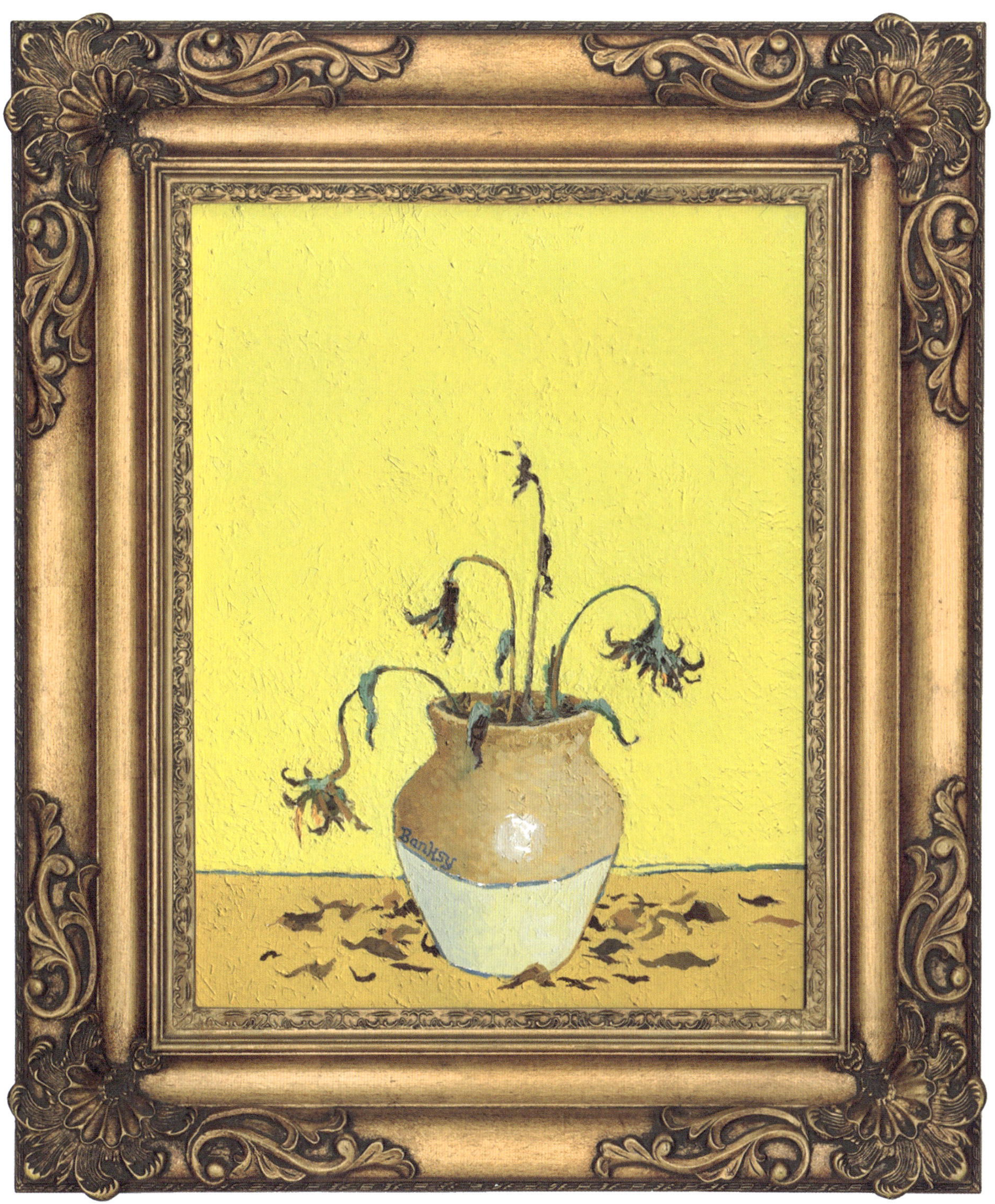

Sunflowers from Petrol Station, 2005

BURNING BRIDGES

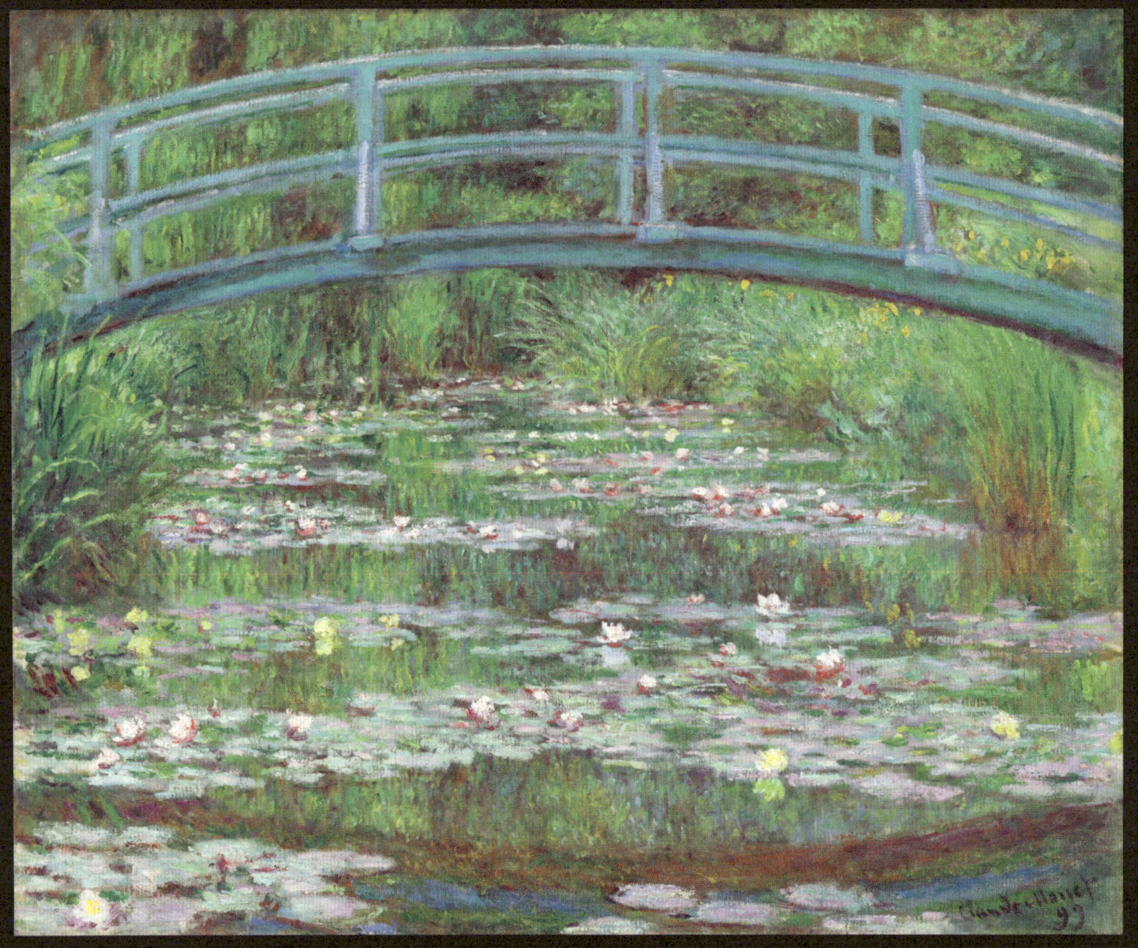

Claude Monet, *Japanese Footbridge*, 1899

In early May 2004, under a headline that reads 'Waterlilies don't come cheap', *Time Magazine* reported to its readers the recent sale at auction of a painting by Claude Monet that depicts a pond in the French Impressionist's garden in Giverny, north of Paris. Though the $17 million that Monet's lyrically luminous *Le Bassin aux Nymphéas* (1917–19) fetched paled in comparison to the $104 million that Pablo Picasso's painting *Boy with a Pipe* bagged in the same sale (the highest price ever paid for a painting at the time), it was Monet's canvas that grabbed *Time*'s headline. Perhaps there was something about the perceived tension between the enormous price tag for Monet's work and the pulsing purity of its sun-dappled subject that *Time*'s editors believed was especially surprising. A year after the Sotheby's sale in New York, Banksy inserted himself into the conversation by intervening, as only he could, in a clever conflation of three separate instalments of the water-lily series that preoccupied Monet's imagination for the last thirty years of his life: *Le Bassin aux Nymphéas* (1899, Philadelphia Museum of Art); *Water Lilies and Japanese Bridge* (1899, Princeton University Art Museum); and *The Water-Lily Pond* (1899, The National Gallery, London). In doing so, Banksy succeeded in scraping away memorably at Monet's seemingly impenetrable mystique and bringing to the surface of his revered work a clutter that was always there, but had slipped out of sight.

Monet's famous footbridge and the enchanting pond of intermingling petals, pads and reflected sky over which it gently leaps frames one of the most charming settings in all of art. To many, the series evokes an idyllic realm of unsulliable beauty far removed from the bustle and rancour of an ever-modernizing world that is increasingly fraught with the clamour of commerce. This is Paradise Regained. Or is it? Far from portraying an unspoilt tract of nature left to rewild itself into unadulterated innocence, Monet's canvas pulses with hostility. For one thing, those dazzling blossoms that unfurl themselves into eternal splendour do so in direct defiance of local law. Interlopers in the native environment of northern France, these plants were specially imported by Monet from Egypt and South America. Worried the invasive aquatics might poison the area's water, the local council insisted Monet remove them. He refused. It wasn't his only run-in with authorities. At the same time that the artist contented himself with capturing the tranquillity and stillness of the poetic pedestrian byway he portrays in his paintings, Monet was busy amass-ing a collection of expensive automobiles that he enjoyed roaring through the streets of Giverny and nearby towns, his compliant chauffeur at the wheel. It is said that notices published by the village's mayor demanding drivers slow down were squarely designed for his eyes alone. Not long after painting his famous fleet of Japanese footbridges (he made seventeen in all), Monet was stopped for speeding in the village of Franeuse. Seen in the unexpected light of the artist's obstreperous attitude to authority, Banksy's *Show Me the Monet* – with its defiantly dumped shopping trolleys (perfect for wheeling imported plants to the self-checkout till) and deviously discarded garish traffic cones (the sort used to slow the speed of incorrigible drivers) – takes on added interest.

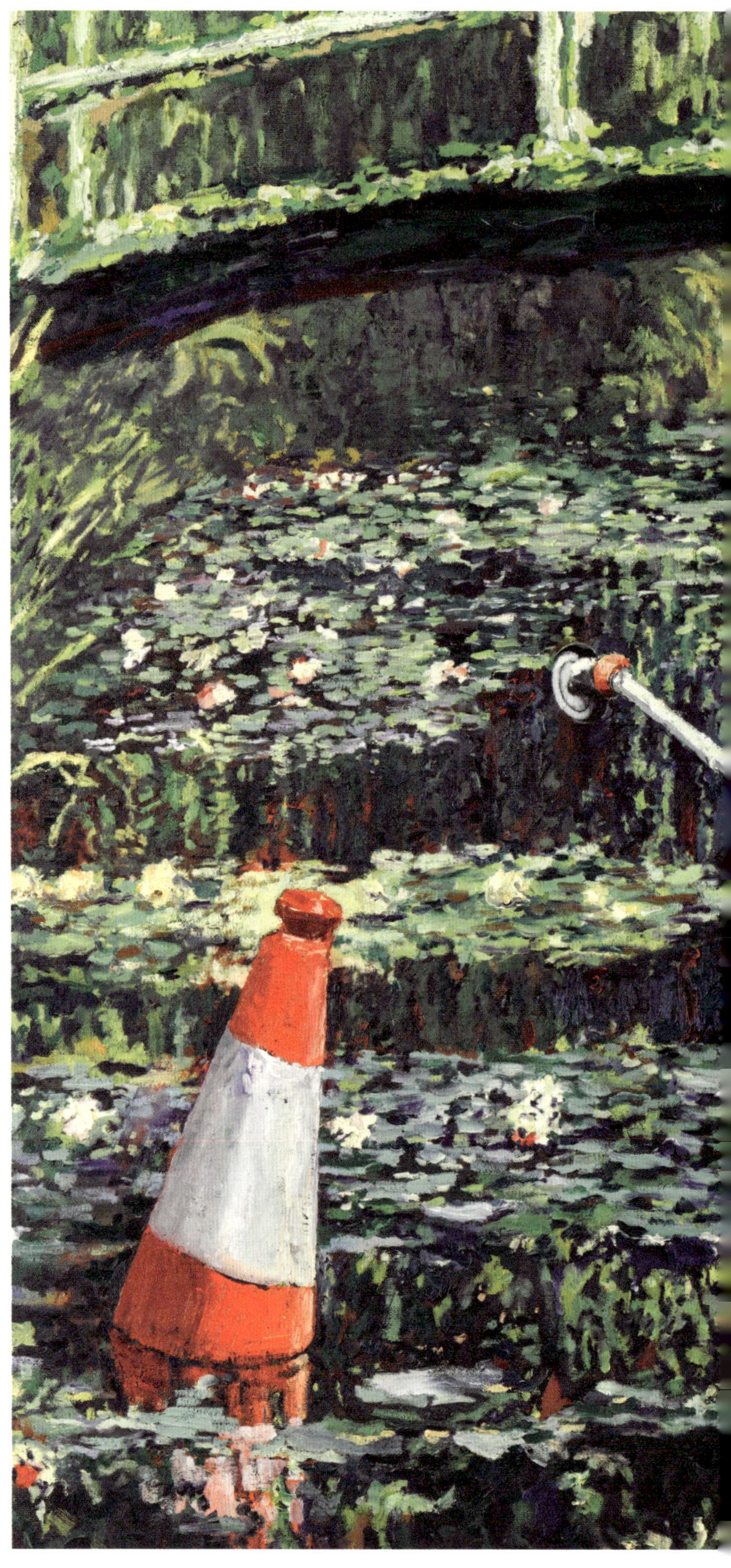

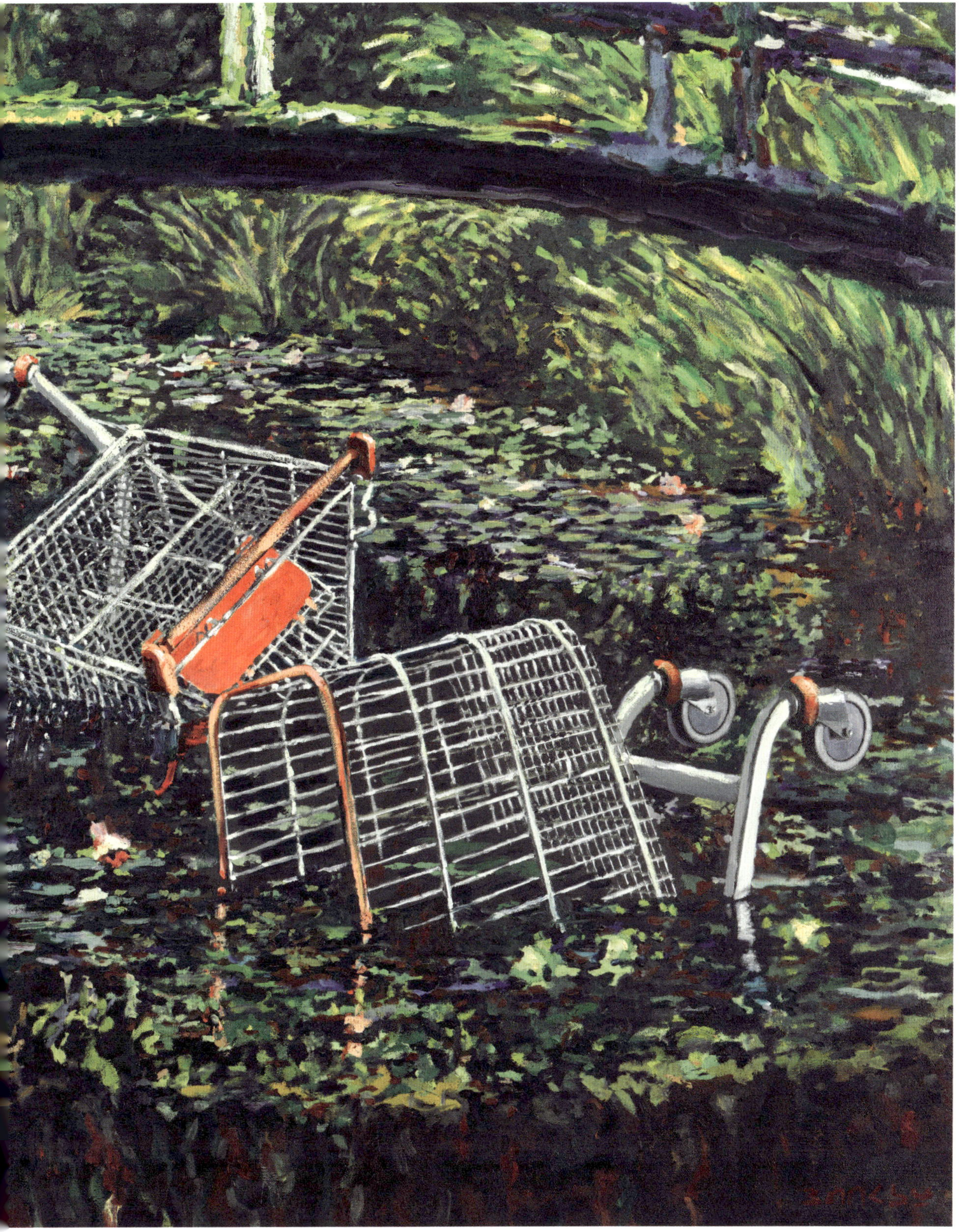

Show Me the Monet, 2005

DON'T EVEN DRINK ABOUT IT

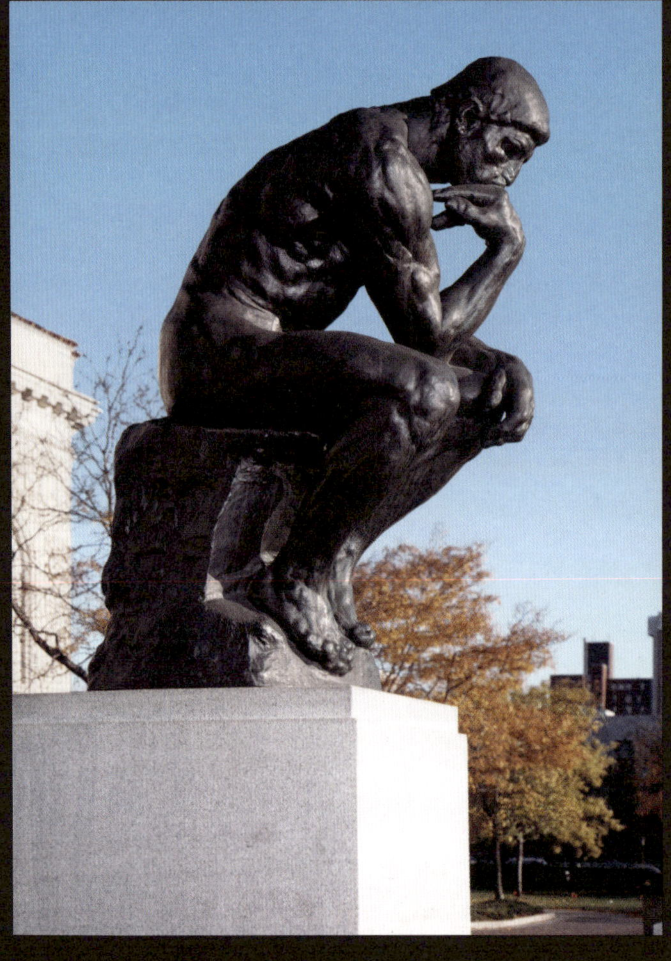

Auguste Rodin, *The Thinker*, 1904

In March 2004, Banksy stealthily installed on a bustling Shaftesbury Avenue in London's West End a full-scale send-up of French sculptor Auguste Rodin's famous statue, *The Thinker*. Though bold in scale (and complete with elevating plinth on which the sculpture could cerebrally squat), Banksy's intervention was rather restrained. Apart from scuffing up the pioneering bronze's polished complexion, Banksy merely fitted the nude figure, hunched in thought with chin resting uncomfortably on the knuckles of his right hand, with a dashingly cocked dunce cap fashioned from an overturned traffic pylon and rechristened him *The Drinker*. But far from debasing one of the most iconic works in art history, Banksy succeeded in reapplying to the original sculpture a complexity of resonance whose lustre had dulled in the century since it was first unveiled in Paris in 1904.

Think of *The Thinker* and we tend to conjure an unambiguous archetype of pure contemplation – a figure whose absorption in the energies of mind transcends the dense and murky materiality of its engrossingly cumbersome physique: the ill-fitting proportions of his oversized hands and the awkward ergonomics of his right elbow straining to reach the left knee. In truth, Rodin's eternal avatar of fierce fathoming was, from the first, a coil of competing cultural and intellectual connotations. Initially conceived not as a large stand-alone effigy at all, but merely a small component in a crowded scene depicting the Gates of Hell from the 14th-century Italian poet Alighieri Dante's *Divine Comedy*, *The Thinker* was originally envisioned by Rodin as a poet – perhaps Dante himself, ironically reimagined as a strapping athlete whose muscles could make Michelangelo's brawny nudes feel body-shamed. It is thought that Rodin modelled his portrayal of the figure on the body of a man he encountered in Paris's red-light district – a boxer, wrestler and muscle-man by the name of Jean Baud. Even the deep patina that gives Rodin's work its broodingly soulful sheen cannot be separated from baser elements that complicate the sculpture's meaning as a straightforwardly intellectual invention. To hasten the emergence of the alluring layer of tarnish that, over time, attaches naturally to the surface of bronze, Rodin was known to direct his studio staff to urinate on his newly created sculptures. From the outset, *The Thinker* teetered between bawdy and soul.

In the century or so since Rodin himself reimagined his squatting sculpture – prised it loose from the burning bustle of the Gates of Hell, enlarged it exponentially, and changed its name from *Le Poète* to *Le Penseur* – the figure has slipped the chrysalis of its making and crystallized in cultural consciousness as symbol of pure thought. By fitting the sculpture with a traffic pylon (with which Banksy has crowned other unsuspecting statues, including one of the Duke of Wellington outside the Museum of Modern Art in Glasgow), Banksy taps into the same spirit of complex forging in which the work was initially created. While the tapered topper does of course call to mind the conicity of 'dunce caps', its meaning in cultural history is multivalent and can also allude to the similarly-shaped hat worn by Hephaestus, the Greek god of artisans and sculptors, or the ancient Phrygian cap that came to be a symbol of liberty during the American and French Revolutions. And that's the point.

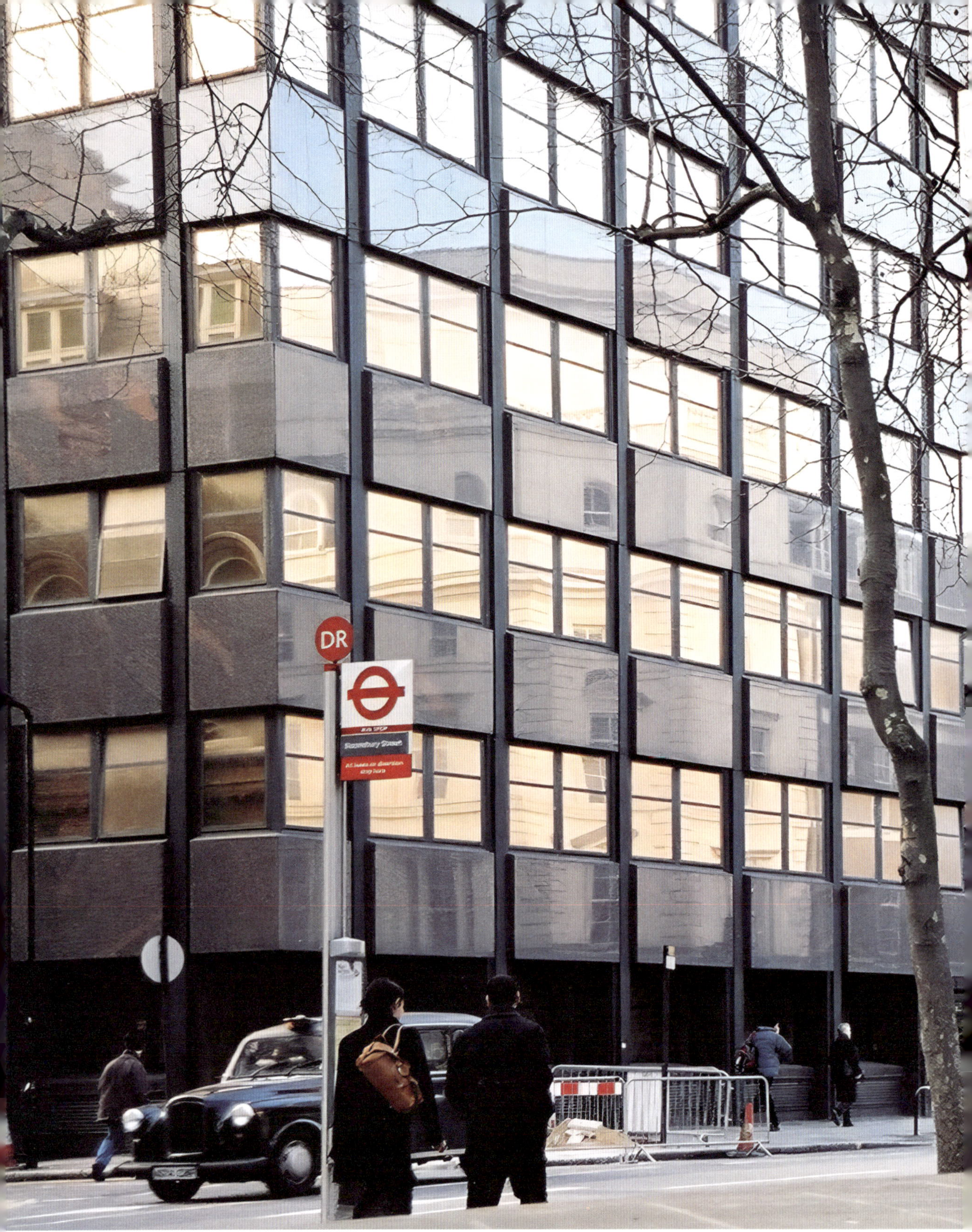

DR

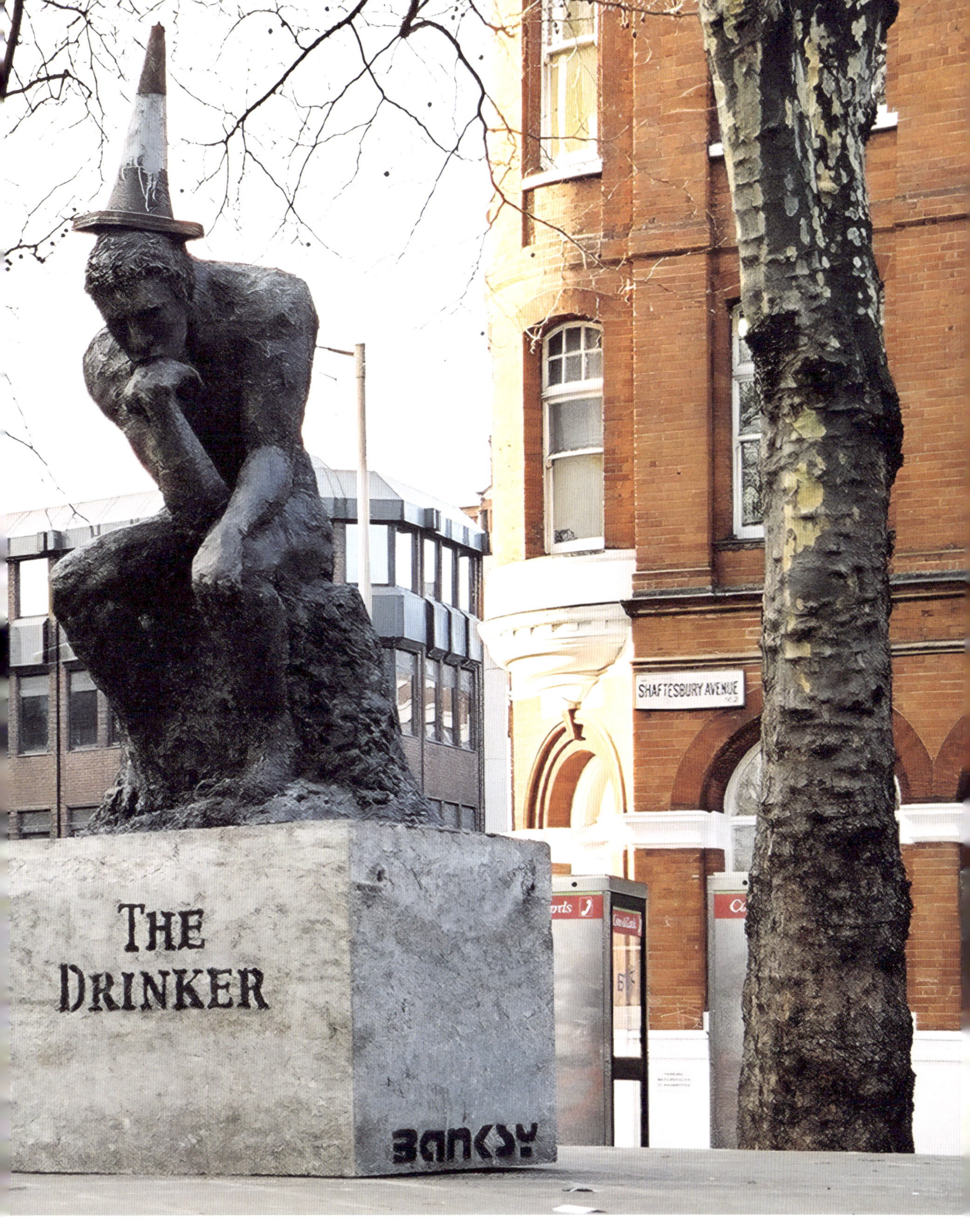

The Drinker, 2004

SPIN CONTROL

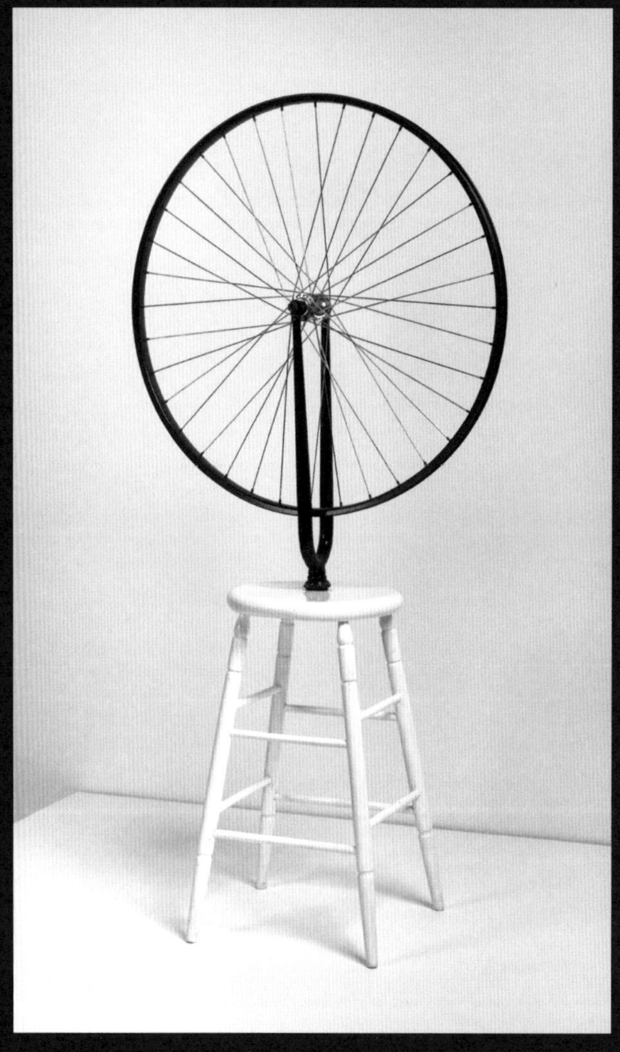

Marcel Duchamp, *Bicycle Wheel*, 1913

On 11 October 2020, the world reached a morbid milestone. On that day, over 1 million new cases of Covid-19 were recorded internationally for the short span of the three preceding days, indicating that the virus had begun to spread more rapidly than at any moment since the global pandemic had been declared six months earlier. The sudden surge in Covid infections triggered fears that fresh lockdowns might be deemed necessary, leading to the closure of businesses and schools and forcing people once again to stay put and stay apart. Two days later, against the background of widespread angst, an incongruously cheerful work of art, or so it seemed, appeared beside a beauty salon in Nottingham, England, lifting local spirits.

Stencilled with black and white spray paint onto a red brick wall, the work appeared to consist, at first glance, of little more than a slightly larger than life-size image of a young girl joyfully hula hooping on her own, blissfully oblivious to the whirling anxieties of the world around her. But those who looked more closely at Banksy's work (which he officially acknowledged four days later by posting it on his Instagram account) quickly realized that the spinning hoop that held the girl entranced in its tilting orbit was not a toy at all, but the back tyre of a battered bicycle we see chained to a lamppost beside the wall. The girl's resourceful repurposing of the broken bicycle's redundant treads as a vehicle not for travel but self-sustained stationary enjoyment serves as an emblem of the artist's own impromptu ingenuities in the making of his work and cleverly echoes the contours of the very first instance of so-called readymade art from a century earlier.

In 1913, the French avant-garde artist Marcel Duchamp found himself dislocating the utilitarian function of a bicycle's front wheel by flipping it (still attached to its fork and head tube) upside down and inserting it surreally into the top of a high kitchen stool, to watch the spin of its spokes and tyre, disconnected from their intended purpose. Duchamp soon christened his provocative reassignments of ordinary objects as works of art – a project that famously included, two years later, a porcelain urinal flipped on its side and signed with the *nom de plume* R. Mutt – 'Readymades', a coinage that suggests a kind of irrefutable completeness. Readymades are seemingly self-sufficient in both their making and meaning.

Placed side by side with Duchamp's repurposed bicycle wheel, a pioneering work that is often credited as a seminal moment in the emergence of conceptual art, Banksy's hula-hooping girl becomes a poignant symbol of joyful self-actualization in a run-down world of severed ties. By salvaging a scrap from a broken bike and recycling it as a prop for self-reliant joy, the girl becomes an alluring aspiration – an icon. That Banksy chose to share his work with a neighbourhood still haunted by the closure in 2002 of its last Raleigh bicycle factory, which made bikes for 114 years, ensured its profundity would remain spinning in local consciousness long after it was removed.

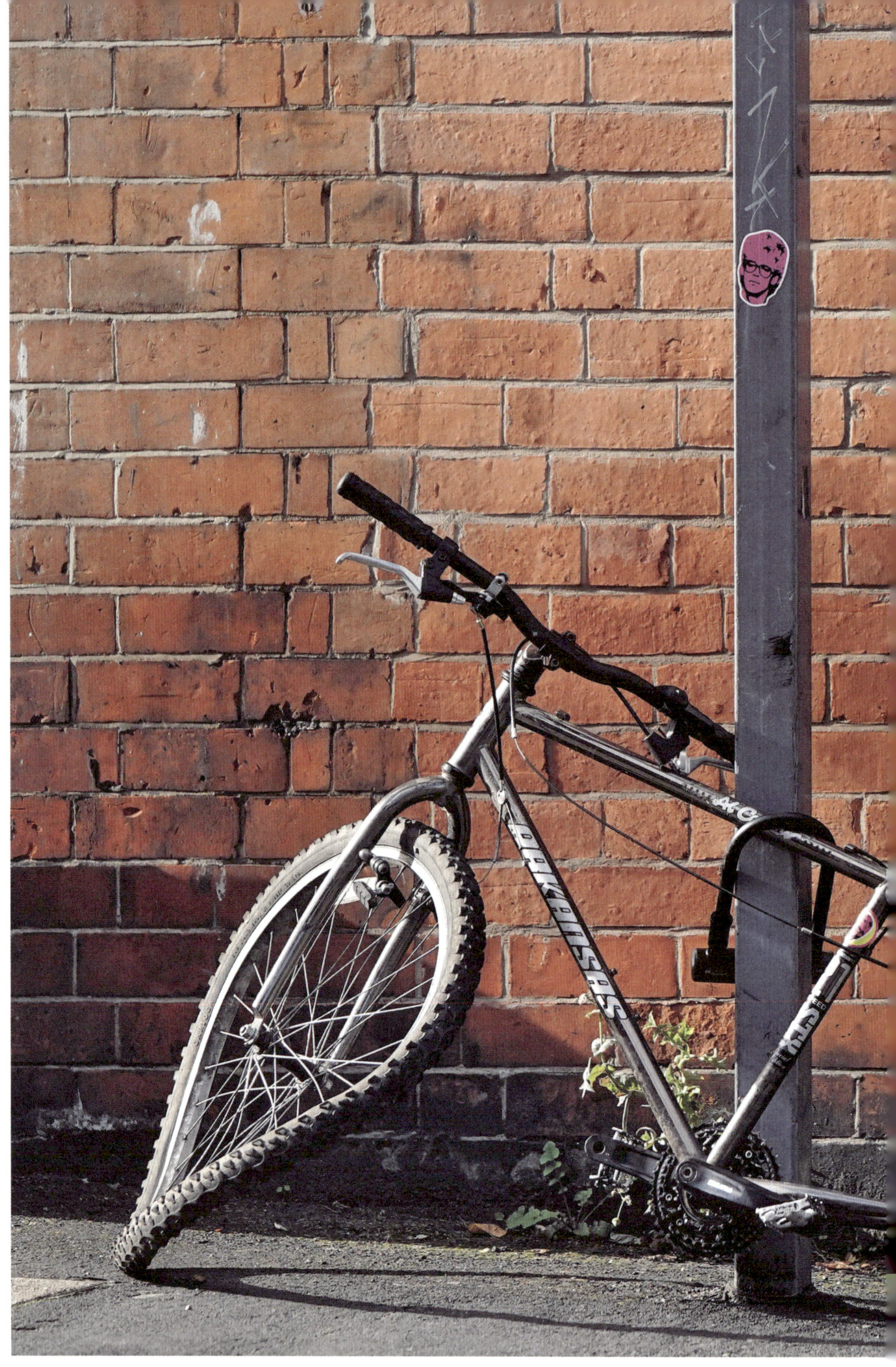

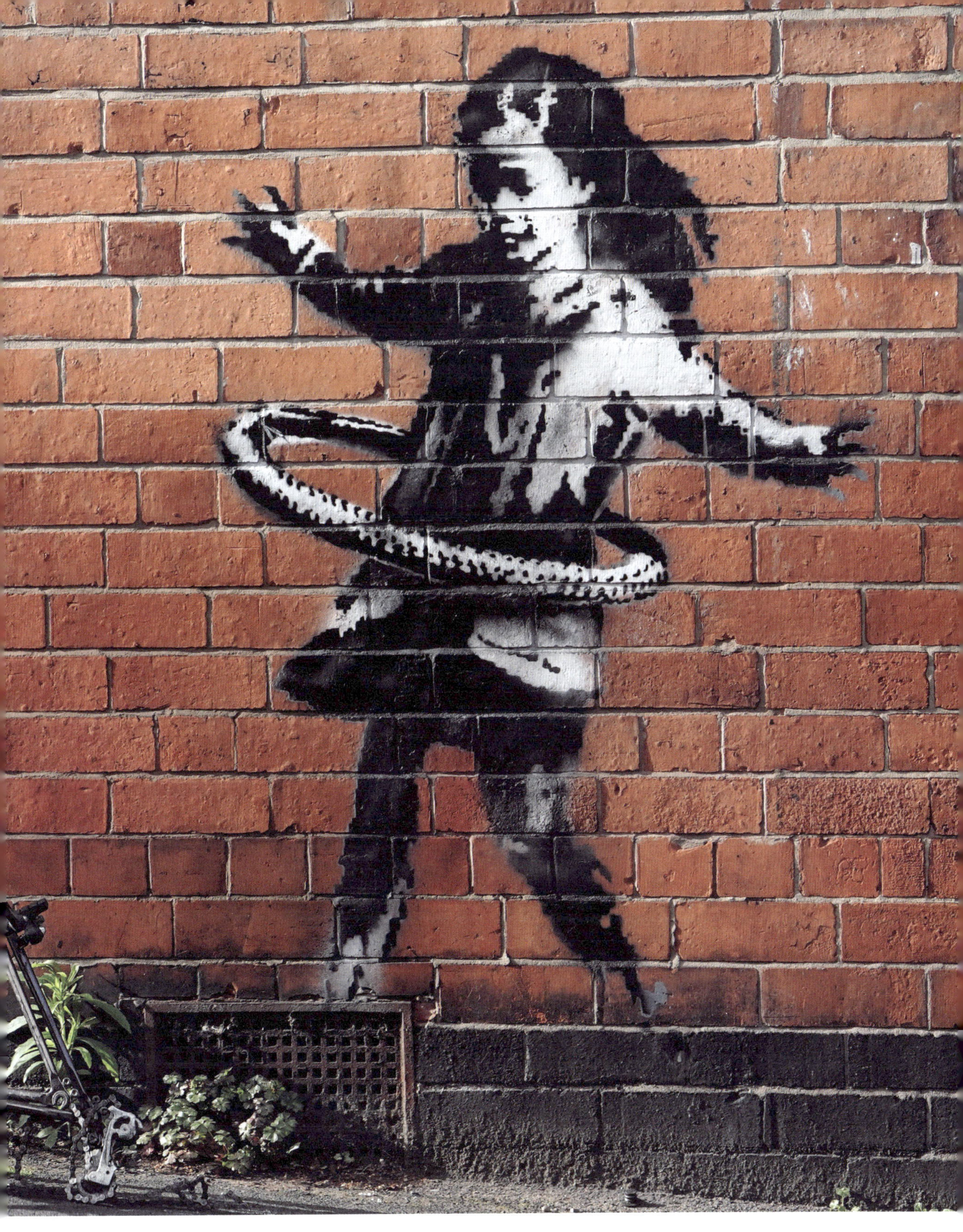

Nottingham, 2020

MONKEY BARS

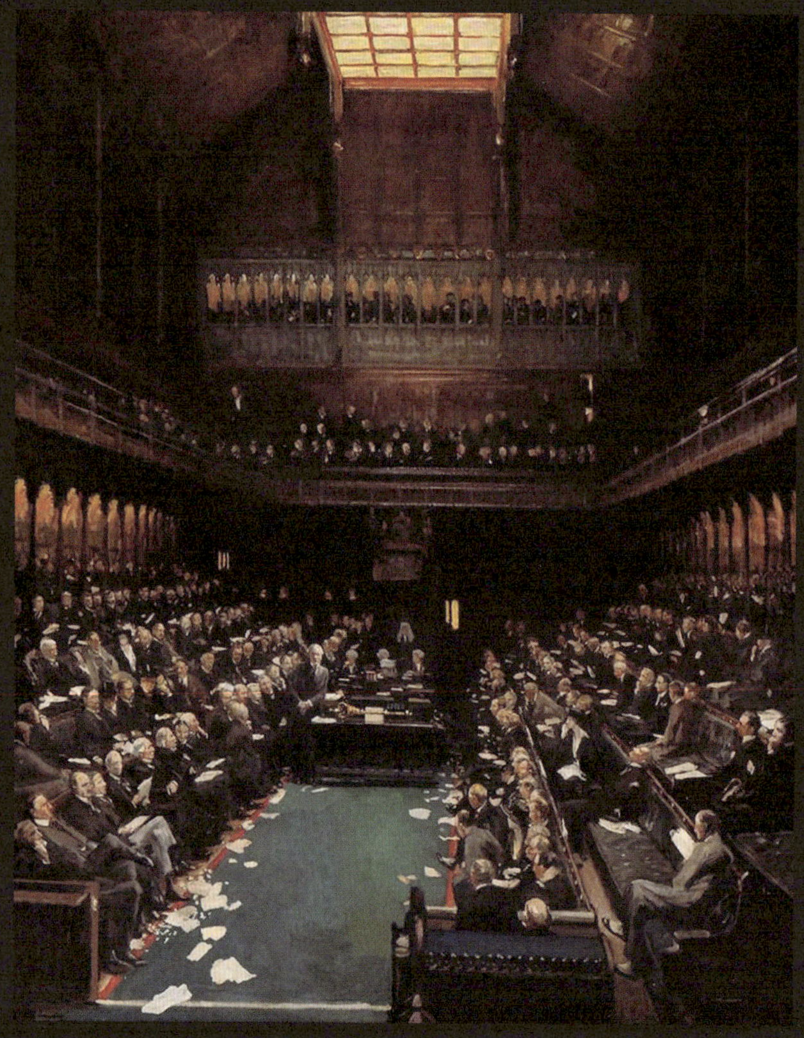

John Lavery, *The Right Honourable J. Ramsay Macdonald Addressing the House of Commons, 1923*

The tradition of mocking the ethical integrity of the United Kingdom's deliberative chamber, the House of Commons, is long and venerable. The institution's purported reliance on the honesty of its elected members, the future US President Thomas Jefferson observed in 1782, 'would be rational ... if honesty were to be bought with money.'[33] The humourist P. G. Wodehouse, whose lampooning of those who wield wealth and power is legendary, was even less flattering in his assessment: 'Have you ever been in the House of Commons and taken a good look at the inmates? As weird a gaggle of freaks and sub-humans as was ever collected in one spot.'[34] Even those who have endeavoured to paint a less pejorative portrait of the body's workings, such as Irish artist John Lavery, were unable to conceal the shocking shambles of decorum displayed by those who serve in the chamber. Lavery's *The Right Honourable J. Ramsay Macdonald Addressing the House of Commons* (1923) chronicles the discourteous dishevelment of MPs, seen nattering and napping while ripped and rumpled papers, strewn across the carpet, line their pen. In 2009, for an exhibition at the Bristol Museum, Banksy joined in the jeering of parliament's perennial dysfunction when he unveiled the largest canvas he has ever undertaken, a canvas echoing the solemnity of the House of Commons captured by artists such as Lavery, replacing the body's bodies with an oafish army of chimpanzees whose demeanour, ironically, is marginally less unruly than what many witness inside the actual chamber.

When first shown in 2009, in the final full year of the Labour government's twelve-year term in office, Banksy's impressively plush and elaborate chamberscape of guffawing chimps bore the title *Question Time*, in reference to the session of parliament devoted to questioning ministers. A decade later, Banksy re-unveiled the work under a new title that made it clear that the piece had grown into its stretched linen skin as a fresh reflection on Britain's decision to leave the European Union three years earlier. Now christened with clever double entendre *Devolved Parliament*, the painting also contained a few further adjustments for those with patience to notice. The chimp nearest the work's observer, for example, can now be seen holding a banana whose curved posture has been flipped from swerving up to dangling down. More than merely implying a banana-republicness to the body, Banksy may have intended the fruit's frowny, thumbs-down droop as a subtle reference to one of the many myths that circulated around the time the UK voted for Brexit, namely that continued EU membership would mean that Britain could only buy bananas whose shape conformed to strict EU regulation. The slippery claim, widely debunked, was aped by prominent politicians.

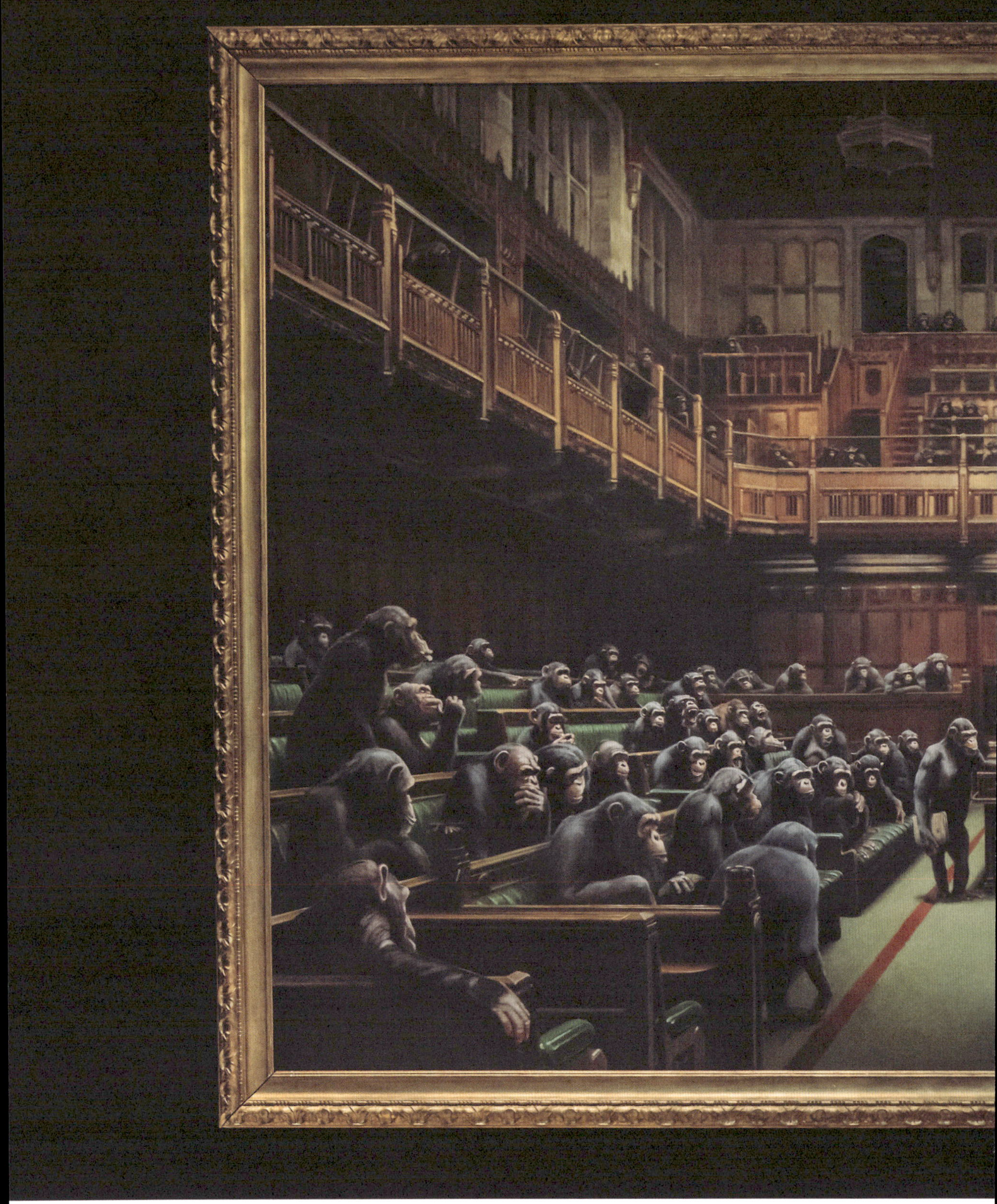

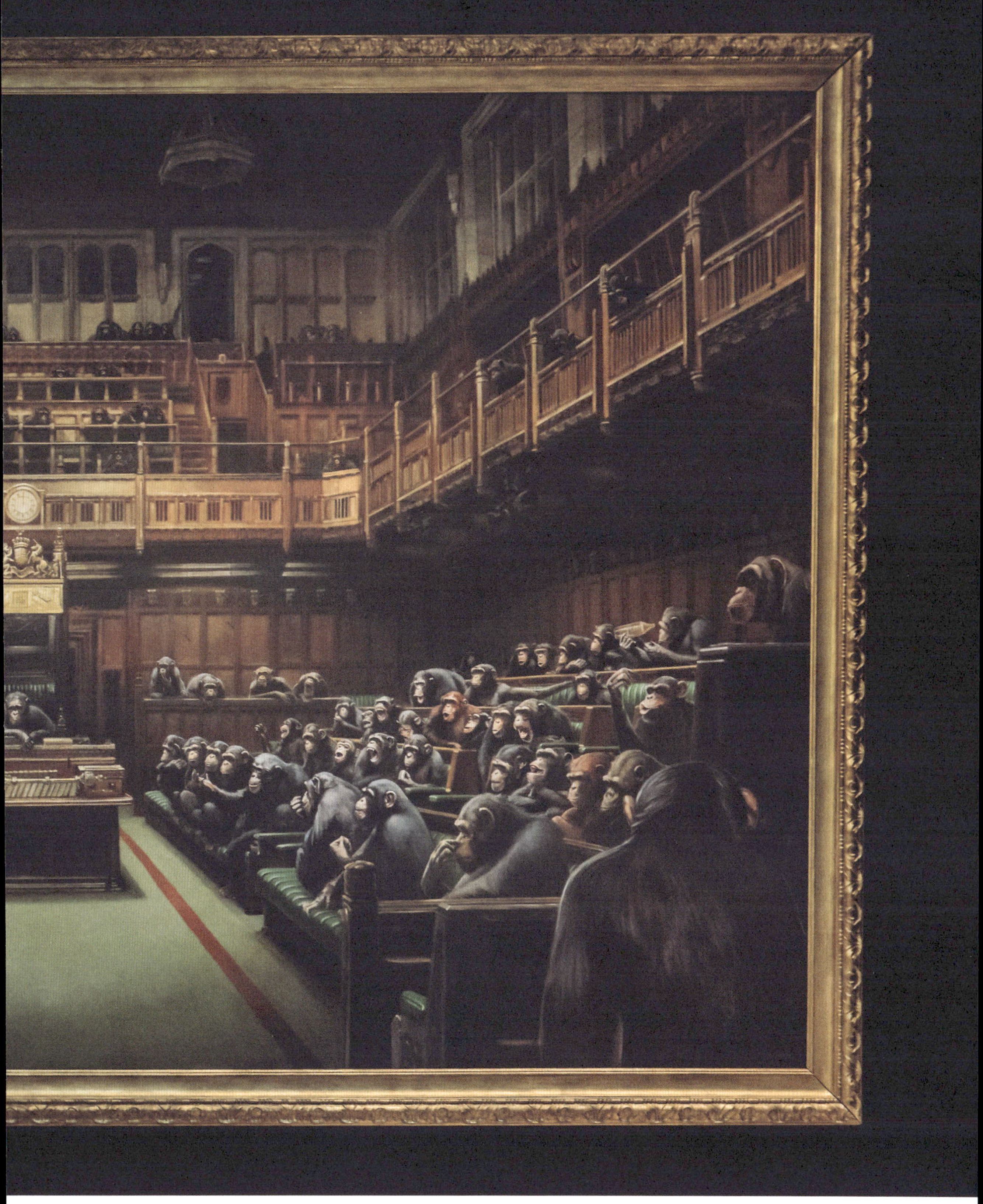

Devolved Parliament, 2009

FOLLOW THE HEART

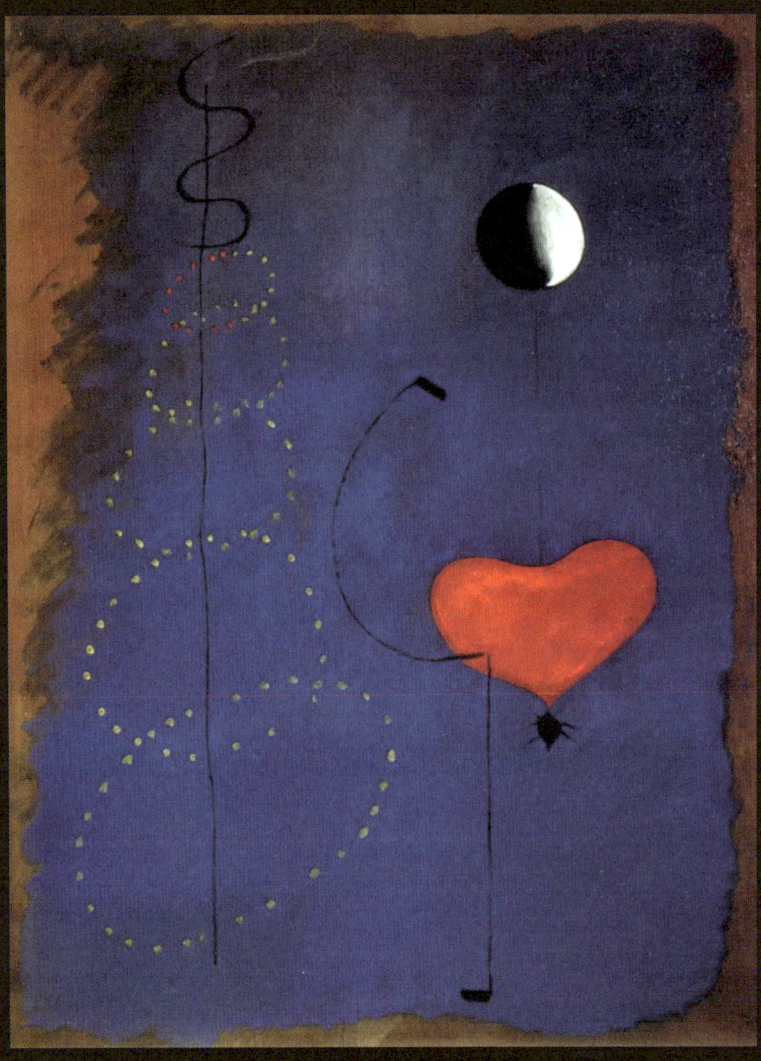

Joan Miró, *Dancer II*, 1925

Where other artists politely allude to works and movements that came before them, Banksy pulls his hood down, flips on the shredder of his imagination, and feeds its insatiable blades one revered masterpiece after another. What comes out the other side, stripped to an irreducible rawness, is an image that vibrates with intensified urgency and poignancy – not a puerile parody of the antecedent that underlies its inception, but a compression of the icon into something rough and unrefined, unpolished and pure.

Girl with Balloon is one of those. Among the best-known images in all of contemporary art, the famous print began life in 2002 as a stencilled shadow on a concrete stairwell wall on Waterloo Bridge in London's South Bank. It would soon be etched in the age's brain. How you choose to interpret the deceptively simple story that the image tells (is the girl letting her heart go in a soulful expansion of self, or is her innocence being torn away from her by the callous gusts of the unfeeling world?) says more about you than it.

My own mind can't help riffling back through the pages of cultural history to the ambiguous squiggles and splotchy symbolism of a painting that Banksy may or may not have intended to wad up and put a match to as kindling for *Girl with Balloon*: Joan Miró's inscrutable scribble *Dancer II*, which the celebrated Catalan Surrealist created in 1925. In Miró's painting, a levitating red heart near the centre of the canvas is the anchor for a floating black-and-white balloon that hovers above it. In truth, both shapes in Miró's mythology represent over-stylized parts of a dancer's body. The sphere is her head; the heart her hips. The two long lines that squirt beneath the heart are the ballerina's legs. She is holding one foot up, while spinning on the other. She may be brittly abstract, but at least she's intact. Happy and whole.

Nearly eighty years later, as the world braced itself for another war in the Middle East, Banksy was less elusive and roundabout in *Girl with Balloon*. He was also more brutal. Any way you slice it, Banksy's girl is being torn apart, her heart ripped from her. In October 2018, a version of Banksy's poetic image went up for auction at Sotheby's in London. Immediately after bidding was concluded and a stunning price of over £1 million stamped on the sale, the girl began to slip through the bottom edge of the weighty wooden frame that surrounded her, which had been fitted with a hidden shredder. Auction-goers looked on in horror. The world gasped. Had Banksy really engineered his own work's self-destruction? Or was he merely illustrating what happens when we attempt to monetize what isn't really ours – what happens when we put our soul under the hammer?

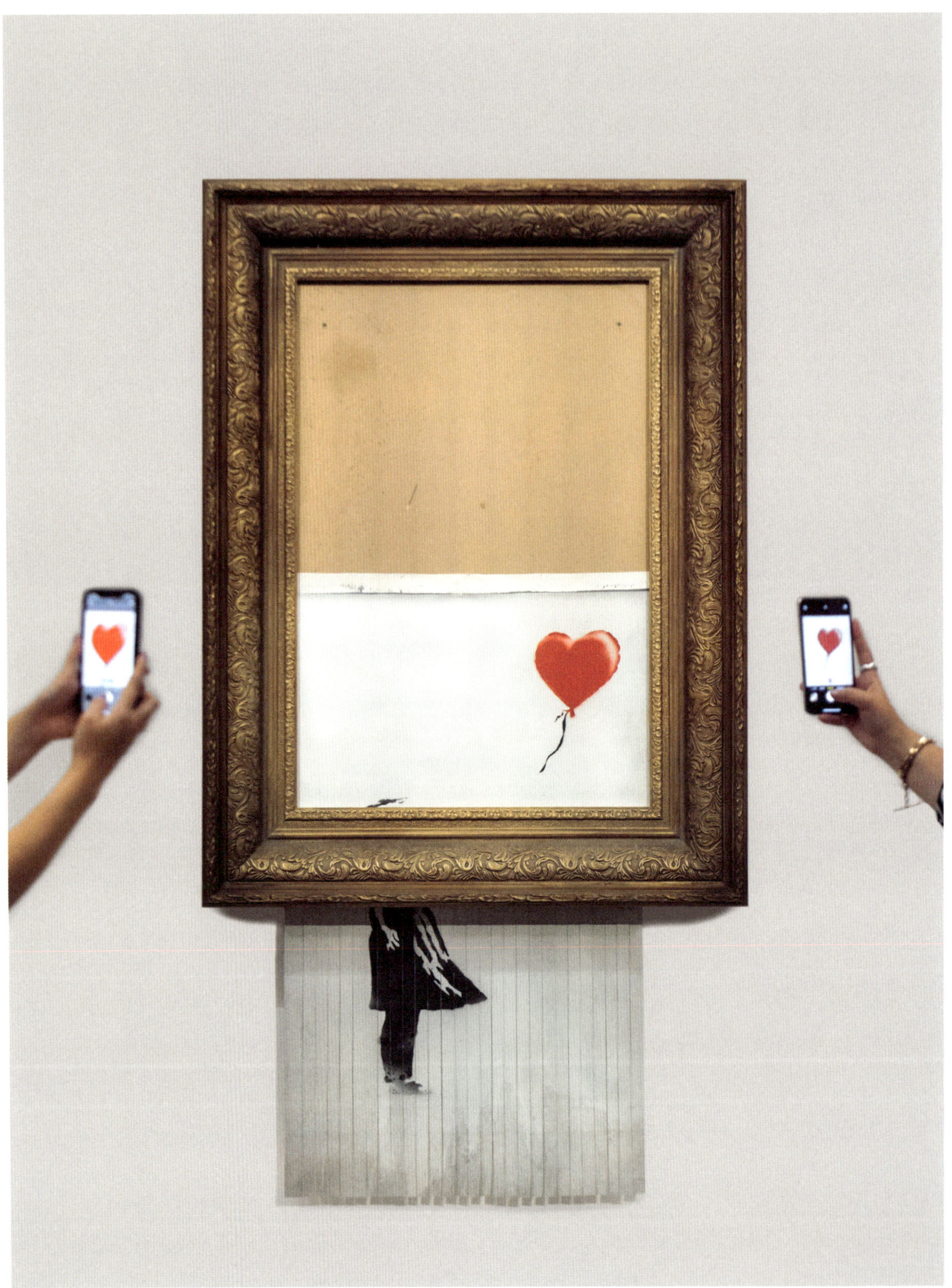

Love is in the Bin, 2018

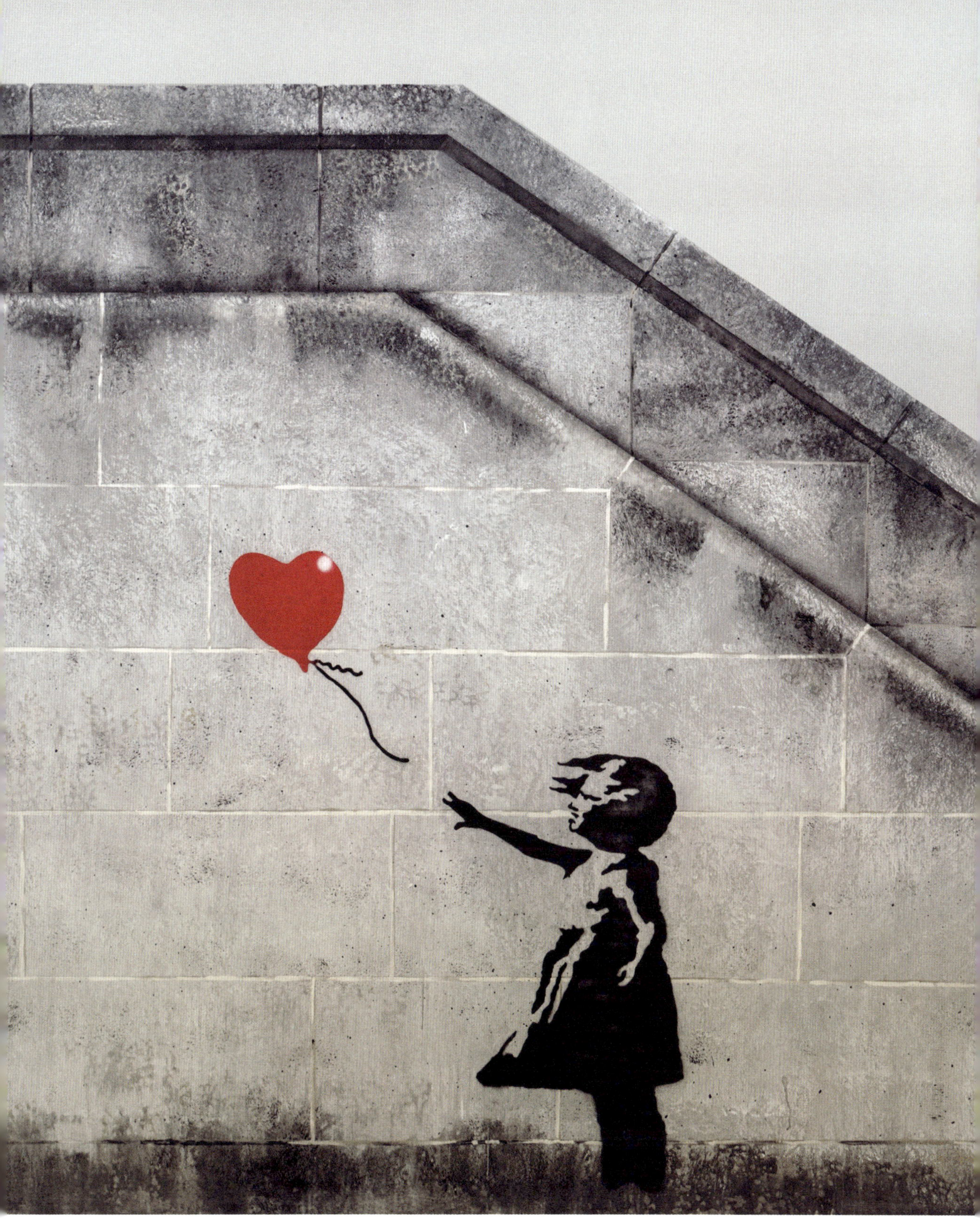

Waterloo Bridge, South Bank, London, 2002

DEEP DIVE

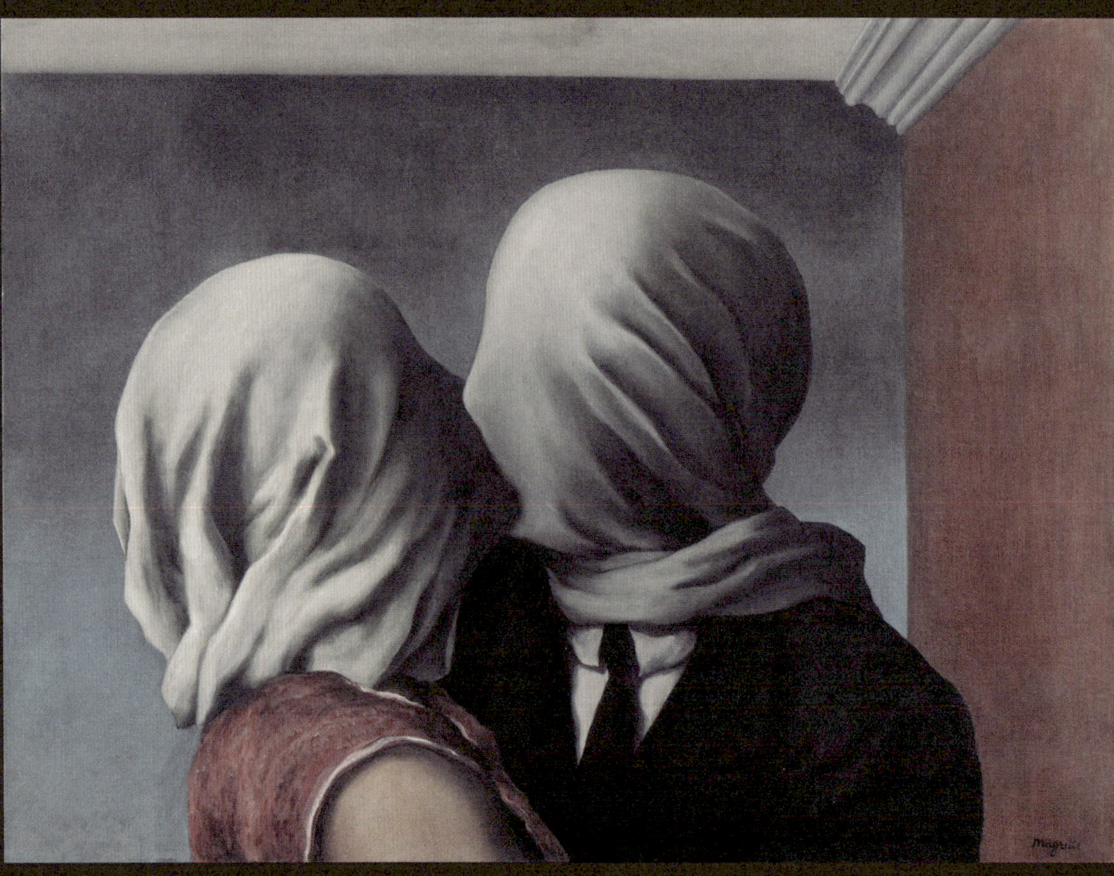

René Magritte, *The Lovers*, 1928

When the Belgian Surrealist artist René Magritte was thirteen years old, he witnessed the recovery of his mother's drowned body from the river Sambre, near the city of Châtelet. It had been over two weeks since she had managed to escape from a bedroom in the family home, where she was locked each evening to protect herself following repeated suicide attempts. Though Magritte would never discuss the incident, according to family myth the nightdress that his mother had been wearing when she entered the water was still clinging to her bloated and marbled flesh and had pulled itself tight across her face. The traumatic, spirit-sealed image of a shrouded countenance haunted Magritte. It became a recurring motif in his paintings, which seem, themselves, to dredge the stagnant stream of his subconscious where the memory of his mother ceaselessly churned. Take, for example, his disquieting canvas *The Lovers*, which features a couple passionately kissing in spite of the fact that their heads are veiled by tight-fitting sheets. The striking work appears to epitomize the impenetrability of existence and has been interpreted as a comment on the irresolvable estrangement of people from one another, no matter how intimately involved.

In 2003, Banksy echoed the disconcerting contours of Magritte's work when he was commissioned to design the cover for the British rock band Blur's seventh studio album, *Think Tank*. Retaining the theme of alienation at the heart of Magritte's painting, Banksy has replaced the suffocating fabric that hems Magritte's subjects off from each other and from our gaze with comically bulkier diving helmets that carry with them an expanded art historical symbolism. In 1936, Magritte's fellow Surrealist, Salvador Dalí, introduced the diving helmet as an indispensable element in the movement's lexicon when he paid a visit to a diving shop in England and asked to be fitted for one. Dalí had come to the UK for the opening of the sensational International Surrealist Exhibition in 1936, which introduced to Britain many of the movement's leading figures, including Giorgio de Chirico, Max Ernst, René Magritte and Dalí himself. Keen to know just how far down the artist was intending to dive, the shop owner was taken aback when Dalí explained that he was planning to plumb to the depths of the human mind. Whatever wisdom may have reverberated from that remark was quickly rescinded by the ludicrous sight of the Spanish Surrealist nearly asphyxiating himself while wearing his new diving helmet as he delivered a lecture on paranoia during the exhibition. Freighted with conflicting connotations of profundity and absurdity, the helmets in Banksy's work load the lovers' embrace with an alluring ambiguity. At once affecting and preposterous, Banksy's reinvention of Magritte's claustrophobic clinch delves deep into the cultural subconscious to salvage an image that is at once extremely familiar and impossible to unmask.

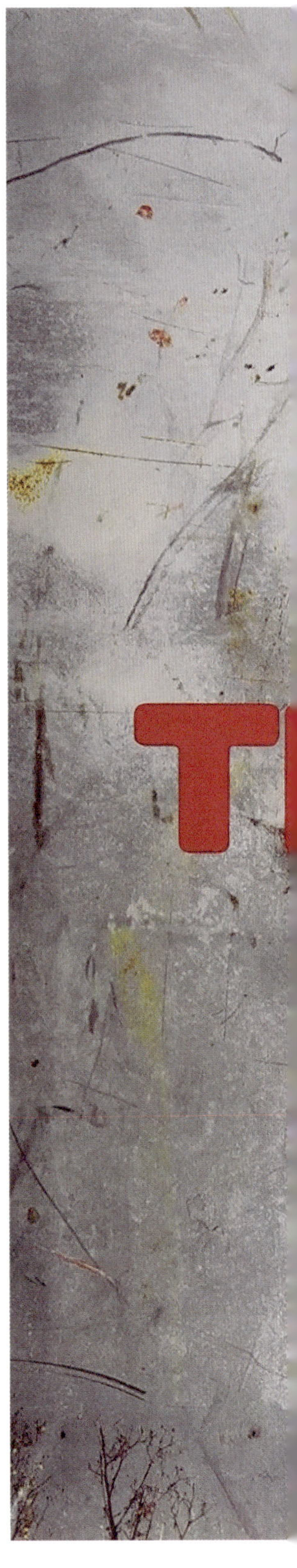

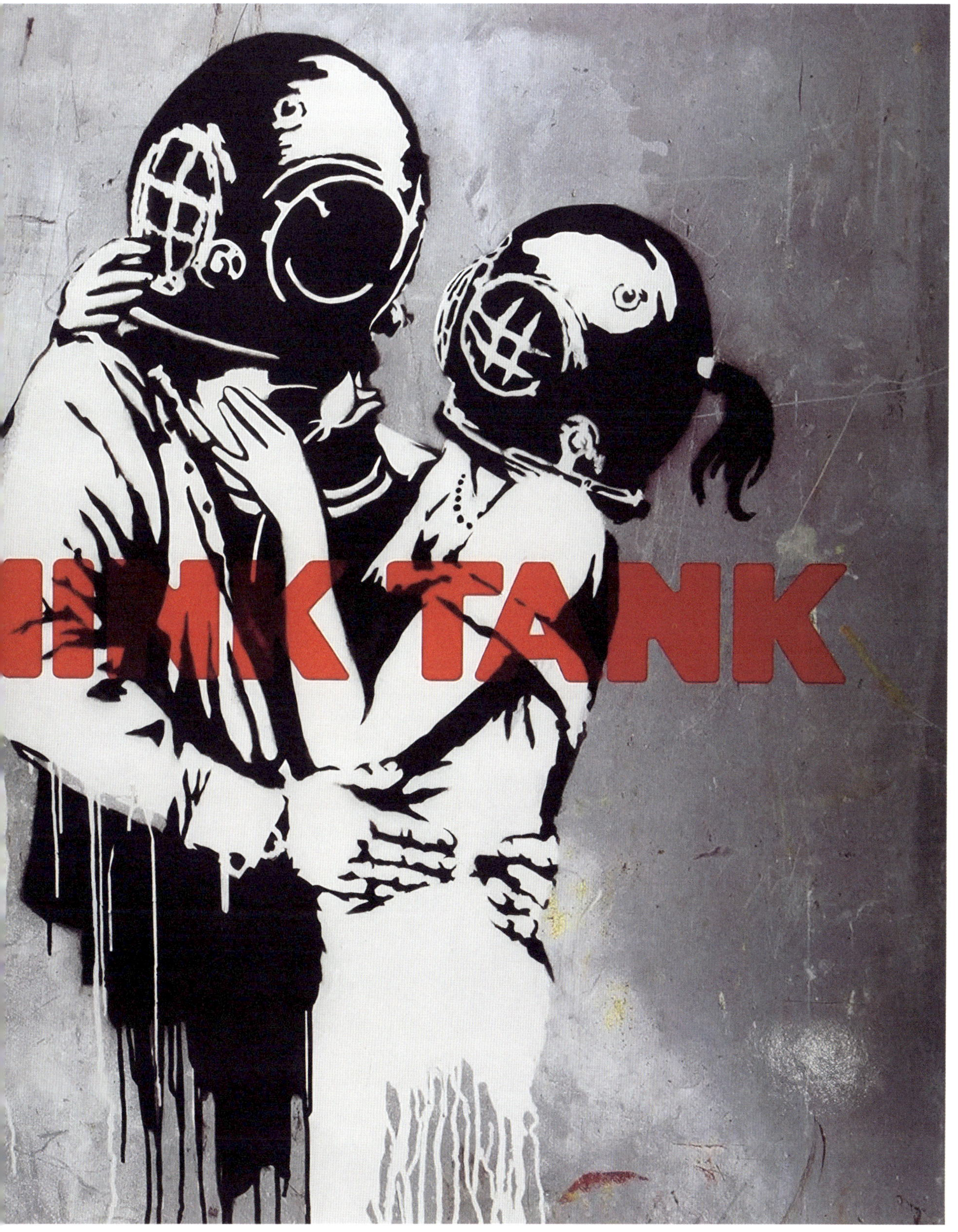

Think Tank, 2003

PIPE
DREAMS

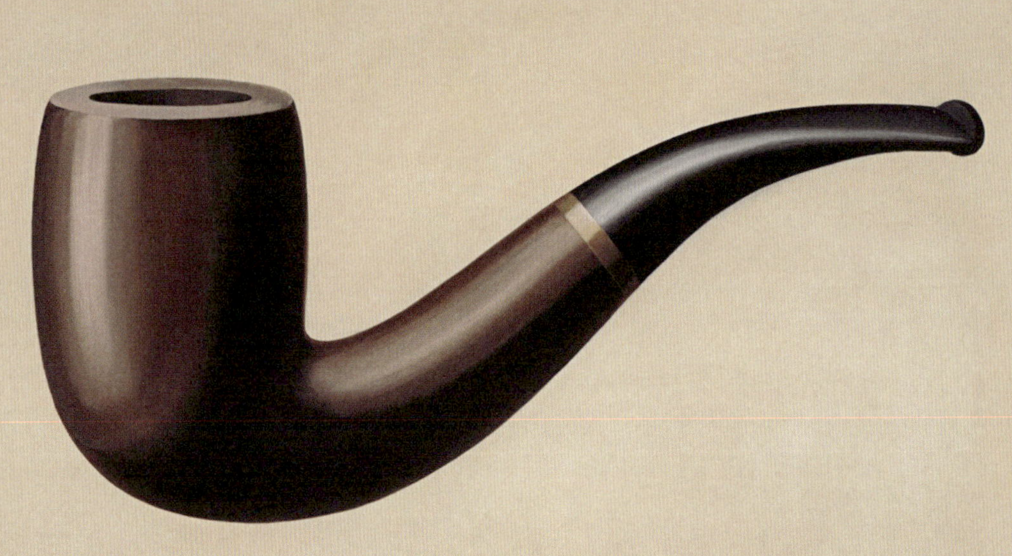

René Magritte, *The Treachery of Images*, 1929

Is anything ever what we say it is? According to René Magritte's provocative painting *The Treachery of Images*, which places an emphatic depiction of an enormous tobacco pipe, suspended in space, above the curious counterclaim, scrawled in impeccable cursive, '*Ceci n'est pas une pipe*' ('This is not a pipe'), the answer is no. Nothing is ever what we depict it as being, nor can it be. A thing's existence and our description of that thing's existence (whether in words or in images) are not only distinct from each other, they are at odds. Magritte's philosophically floating form – which hovers gracefully in the same neutral void and with the same mystic sheen as George Stubbs's timeless portrait of an Arabian stallion, *Whistlejacket* – may well resemble a pipe, in the same way that Stubbs's canvas resembles a horse, but it is not one. It's a painting. Nor is there any essential relationship between the idea of this portrayed object and the arbitrarily assigned word 'pipe'. 'Pipe' comes from the Latin *pipare* (meaning 'to chirp' or 'to peep') and has come to attach itself to a device for smoking tobacco only by the slow and sloppy slippage of language over time. Unlike nearly every other artist who ever created an image or the likeness of something or someone before him, Magritte doesn't want you to mistake for a second that what he has depicted is what he appears to have depicted, visually or verbally. Rather, he wants you to float with him in the neutral void where being and representation are delightfully disjoined. He wants to earn your trust by convincing you that his painting, in truth, is a lie. Magritte is determined to take things whose status and stability you take for granted – pipes and paintings, things and the names of things – and smash them to smithereens. He wants to shake up your mind.

So does Banksy. It is therefore not surprising that in 2011, Banksy should decide to take Magritte's famous painting – which has ironically become one of those very things whose status and stability in cultural history we take for granted – and turn the work on its head. By constructing a rough and ready replica of Magritte's work and wittily replacing his un-pipey tobacco pipe with what is, in fact, a very real water pipe alongside the seemingly straightforward assertion 'This is a pipe', Banksy has created a work that could easily be seen as heckling the pretentiousness of the famous original – one that refuses to play pompous postmodern games and tells it like it is. But nothing is ever what it seems in Banksy. *This Is A Pipe* was created at a moment when alarm at the scarcity of clean drinking water around the world was accelerating – a cause and concern Banksy addresses in earlier works, including *Everything but the Kitchen Sphinx*. Banksy's incorporation of an actual, but rusting, dysfunctional tap, one incapable of performing the very function for which it is intended, calls into question the legitimacy of its claim to being what it says it is. In that sense, it resuscitates rather than refutes the riddle of Magritte's head-scratcher by demanding we consider how a pipe that pipes nothing can be a pipe at all. Just because something says it's real doesn't mean it really is.

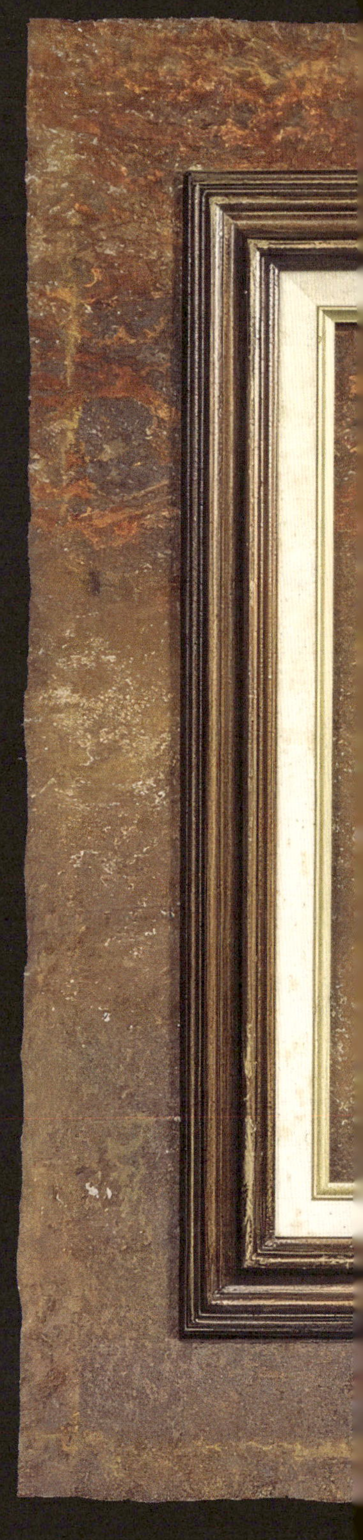

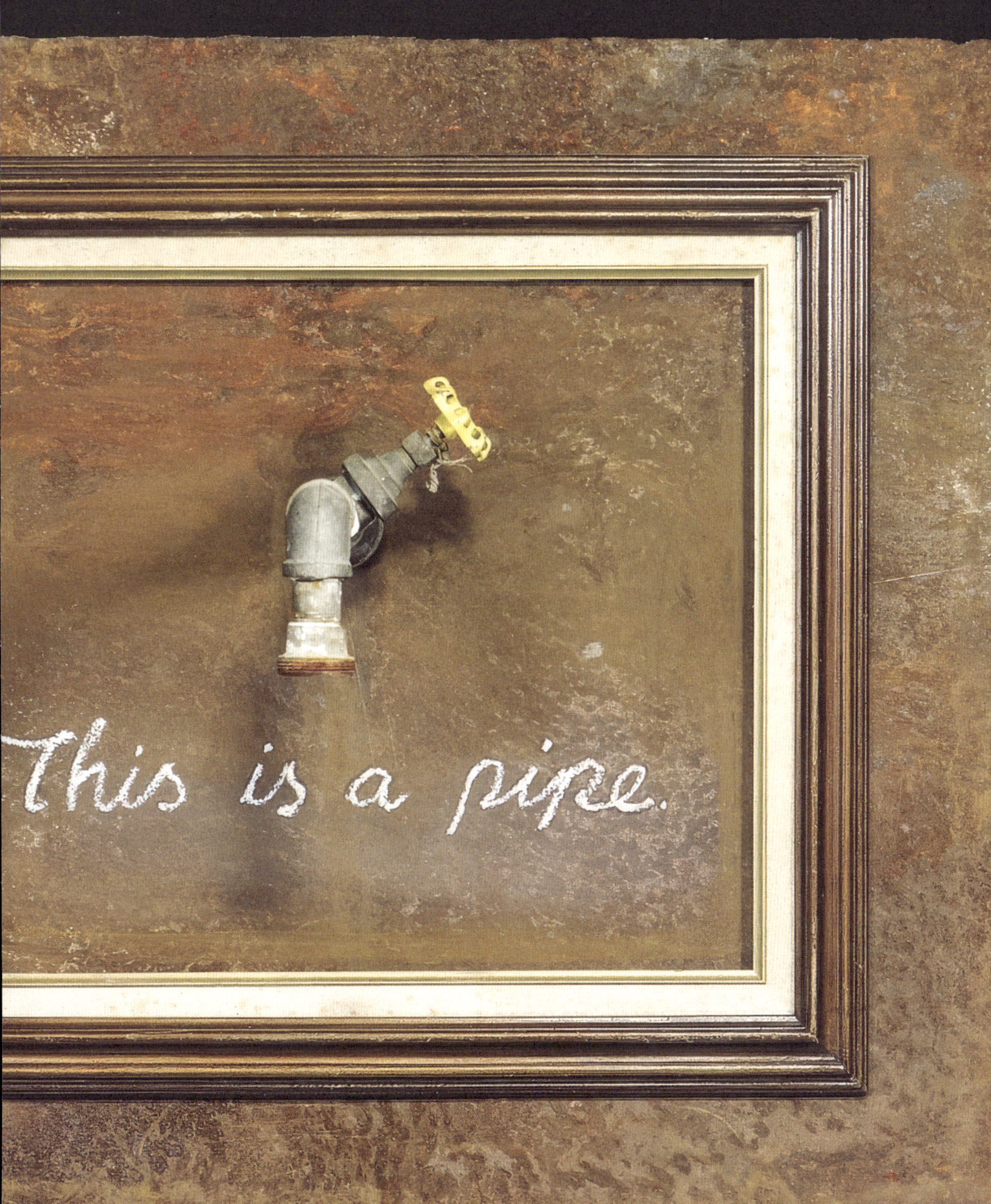
This is a pipe.

SICK NOTE

In November 1996, twenty-two-year-old Canadian student Jubal Brown filled
his belly full of blueberry yoghurt, blue cake icing, and blue Jell-O and set off
for the Museum of Modern Art in New York. It was there that he leaned in
close to the spare geometry of Dutch artist Piet Mondrian's abstract painting
Composition with Red and Blue and spewed cerulean all over the canvas. Initially,
Brown satisfied the dismayed museum officials that the incident, which left a
discordant spatter on the priceless work that restorers managed successfully
to remove, was not a deliberate assault on Mondrian's proto-Minimalist grid,
but merely the result of an upset stomach. Something he ate, perhaps. He later
confessed, however, that his act was in fact entirely premeditated – a defiant
statement against what he called 'oppressively trite and painfully banal'[35] works
of art. Nor was it his first outburst. Earlier that year, Brown had erupted red
on a painting by French Impressionist Raoul Dufy in what was the first instalment, he later explained, of an envisioned trilogy of primary-colour gags he
called 'Responding to Art'. Rather menacingly, 'yellow' has remained stuck
in the pipeline.

Fast forward seventeen years and the memory of Brown's bilious acts,
with which he moronically sought to merge the visceral and the visual, washed
back across cultural consciousness when Banksy released in 2013 a pseudo-
self-portrait, stencilled in shadowy black on a whitewashed urban wall, bent
double holding a spray-paint can and vomiting flowers – real flowers, which
were fortuitously squeezing through the fissure between two abutting build-
ings. The image, which skilfully fuses found realities and illicit expression,
accompanied the announcement of a month-long residency that Banksy was
about to embark upon, during which he dared himself to create a new work
of art every day on the streets of New York in October 2013. The campaign,
'Better Out Than In', caused a stir. Crowds gathered to see each instalment
before it was removed by municipal authorities or destroyed by rivals. The
mayor put the city on high alert to catch him in the act. Everyone's eyes
were peeled. New York was forensically scrutinizing the aesthetics of itself,
every neglected wall and aerosolized enunciation, like never before. Just as
Mondrian's austere grids nudged us to reimagine the geometric essence of
urban matrices, which he mapped not from above, as they first might seem,
but from deep inside, Banksy invited us to see afresh the lines and spaces of
the rigid cityscapes we look at every day but fail to see. Unlike Brown's artless
act of asinine vandalism, which threatened serious damage to priceless works
and left a repulsive mess for others to clean, Banksy's 'Better Out Than In'
– a riff on Cézanne's observation to his friend, the novelist Émile Zola, that
'all pictures painted inside, in the studio, will never be as good as those done
outside'[36] – was thoughtful, executed with extraordinary stealth, and risked
no injury to anyone or anything. Yet it was Banksy's joyful tableaux of wit
and wonder that garnered unbridled abuse by art critics. New York art-world
insider Jerry Saltz superciliously dismissed the images as the work of a 'bird-
brain' and a 'turd' and wrote that Banksy should 'fuck off'.[37] On Jubal Brown
and his suspended threat of a potentially destructive yellow explosion inside
a museum, critics were largely silent. Kind of makes you sick.

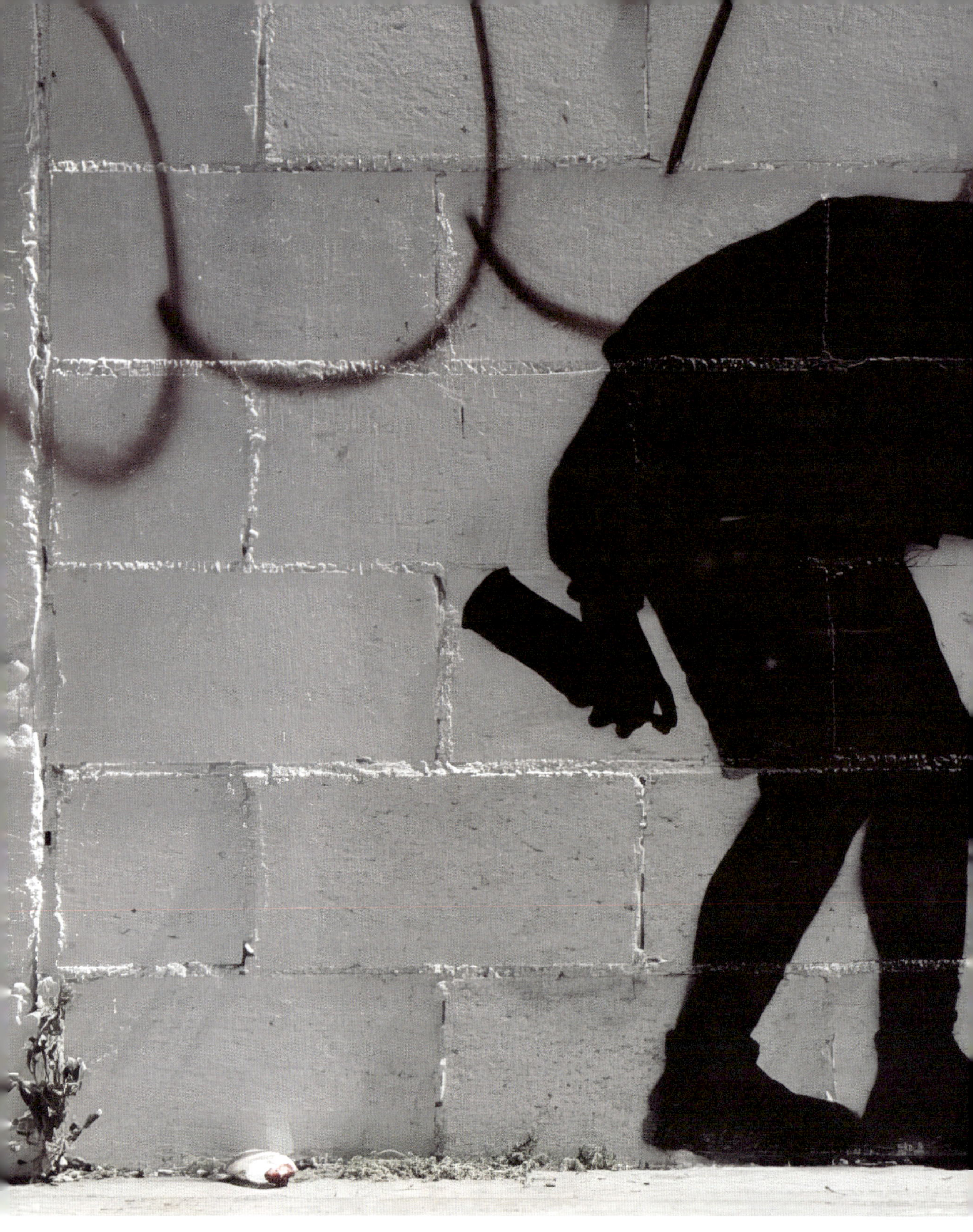

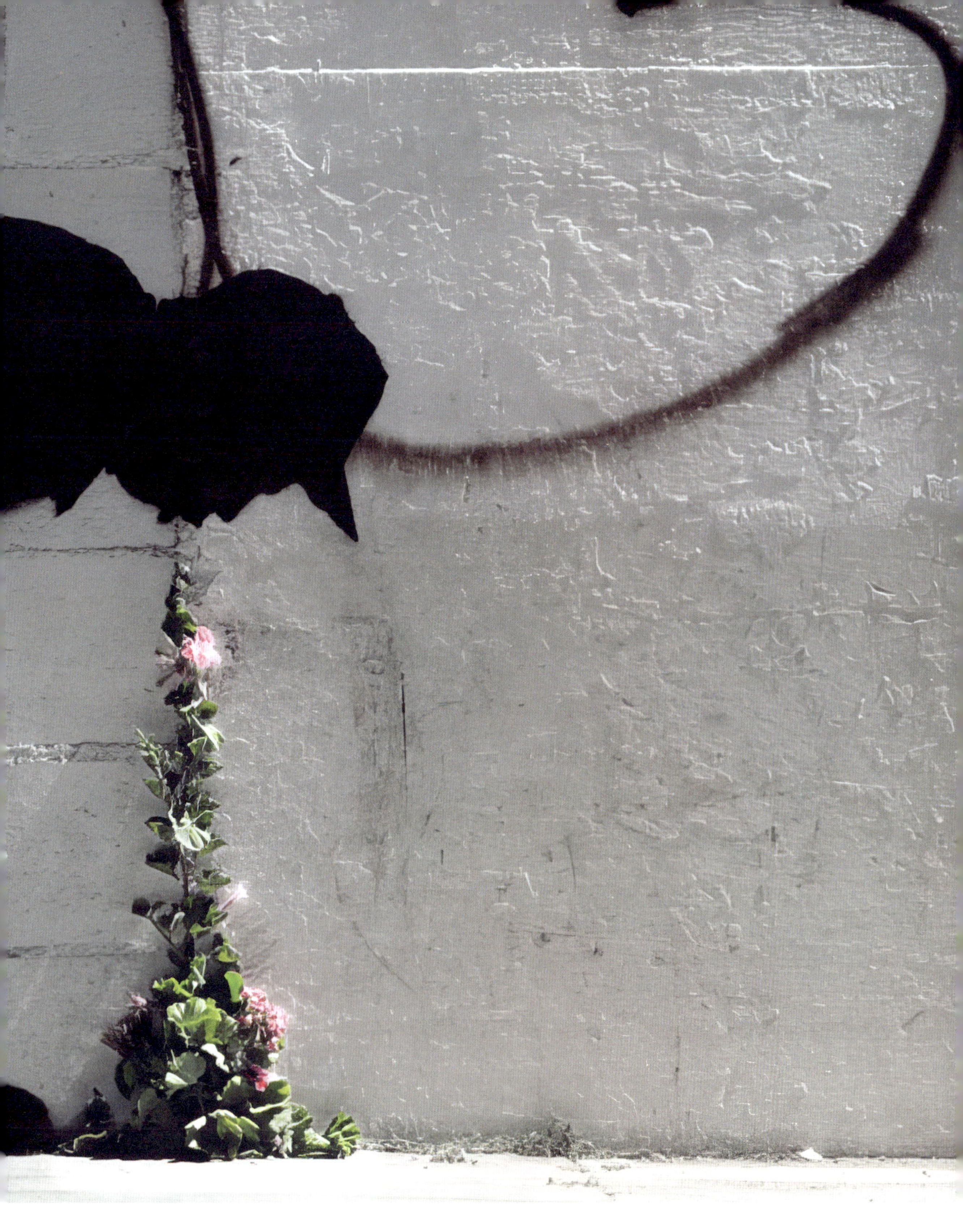

New York City, 2013

STRIPPED AWAY

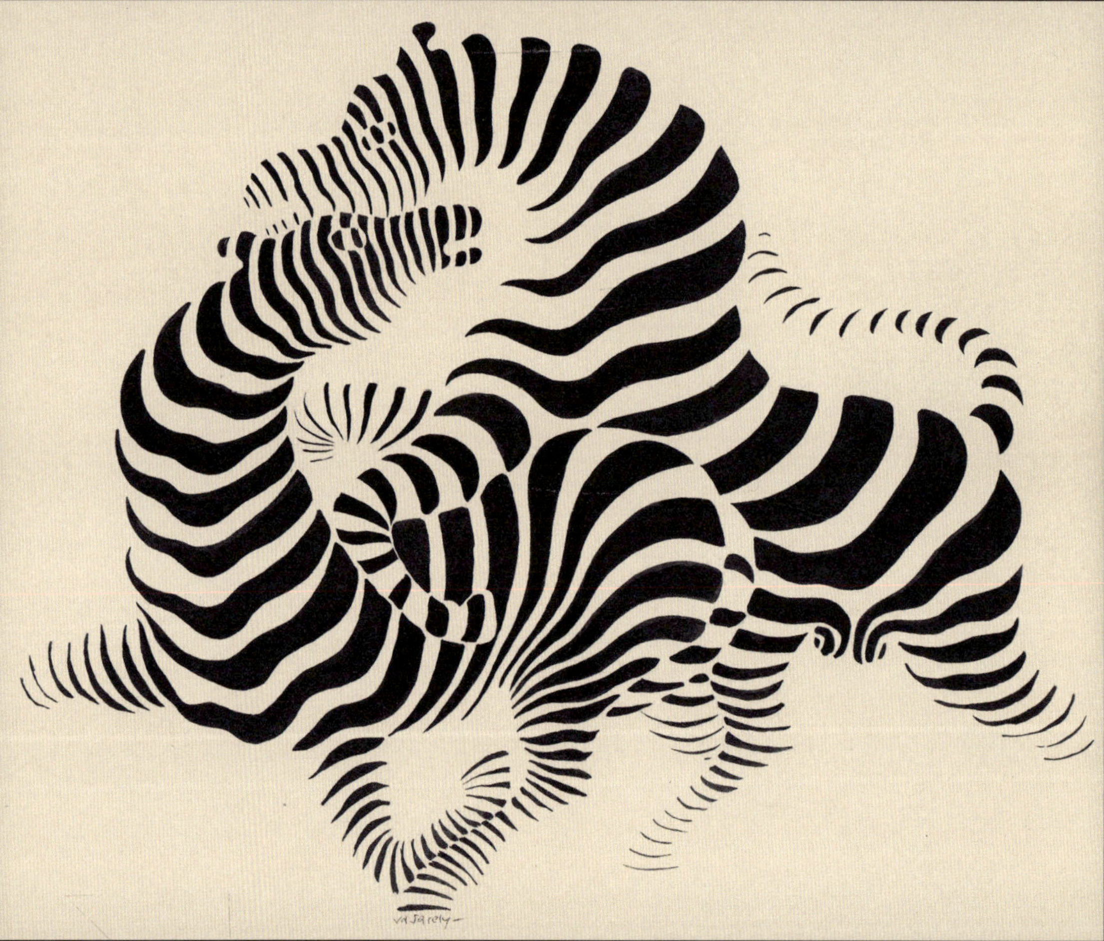

Victor Vasarely, *Zèbres-A*, 1938

Great art keeps us guessing. It resists easy and easily exhaustible caption. Can you think of any enduring masterpiece whose perennial allure isn't amplified by mysteries of its making or meaning? From the frozen flurry of prehistoric handprints on cave walls to the sphinx-like stare of the inscrutable hayseeds in Grant Wood's *American Gothic* (1930), crypticness is essential to art's imperishability. Yet the mastery of mystery itself has proved teasingly elusive. It is impossible to contrive. The Impressionists tried, with uneven success, to do so by engineering the enigmas of light. The Surrealists sought to fossick mystery by dredging the murky subconscious. In the 1960s, so-called Optical Artists resolved to riddle our retinas with intricately woven illusions of rippling lines. By befuddling our eye, they seemed to suggest, perhaps the soul could be seduced into awe. A seminal work in the inception of Op Art is the Hungarian-born Victor Vasarely's portrait of an entangled pair of frolicking zebras that the artist created in 1937, two decades before the movement he is credited with fathering truly took off. Seven decades later, a baffling mural by Banksy, which echoes the conundrums of Vasarely's unravelable canvas, likewise strips the question of what art is down to an irreducible essence – a thing of provocative pleasure that deliciously defies definitive explication.

Despite the liquid lyricism of its bold markings, which seem deliberately designed to inspire legends, the zebra is not, in fact, strongly associated with any definitive cultural connotation. Unlike its close cousin the horse, associated with myriad classical and folk myths, the zebra has largely escaped the reigns of fable and lore. The indelible scrawl that half hides the zebra's hide is, ironically, a blank page. So much so that when the young Vasarely, a gifted graphical artist and trained typographer, selected it for the entwinement of black and white stripes that pretzel our pupils, he did so knowing that the mesmerizing music of his engrossing graphic would not be undermined by minds fixated on decrypting symbolism. The wonder of dichromatic muscles strobing between darkness and light, and the untranslatable cantations of the creatures' pulsing striations, allow the work to inhabit a perceptual plane where seeing prances unbridled by thought. It's a mystery. So too is Banksy's own ambiguous ode to the enigmatic zebra, which appeared on the wall of a house in the Malian city of Timbuktu in 2008. In it, a washerwoman is seen carefully hanging on a clothesline the stripes she's surreally stripped from a zebra's back and scrubbed clean. So accustomed are we to reading Banksy's work as sharp social statements, however teasingly ambivalent their messages may be, we cannot help attempting to distil a socio-political sentiment from the beguiling mural. Our mind twists with the potential readings it auditions and rejects. Is the washerwoman a cog in a machine of social cleansing? Is individuality a superficial mirage? Are we all the same deep down? Perhaps Banksy is simply saying that meaning itself, like the flickering lines in Vasarely's work, is ultimately an alluring illusion – that life is delightfully absurd.

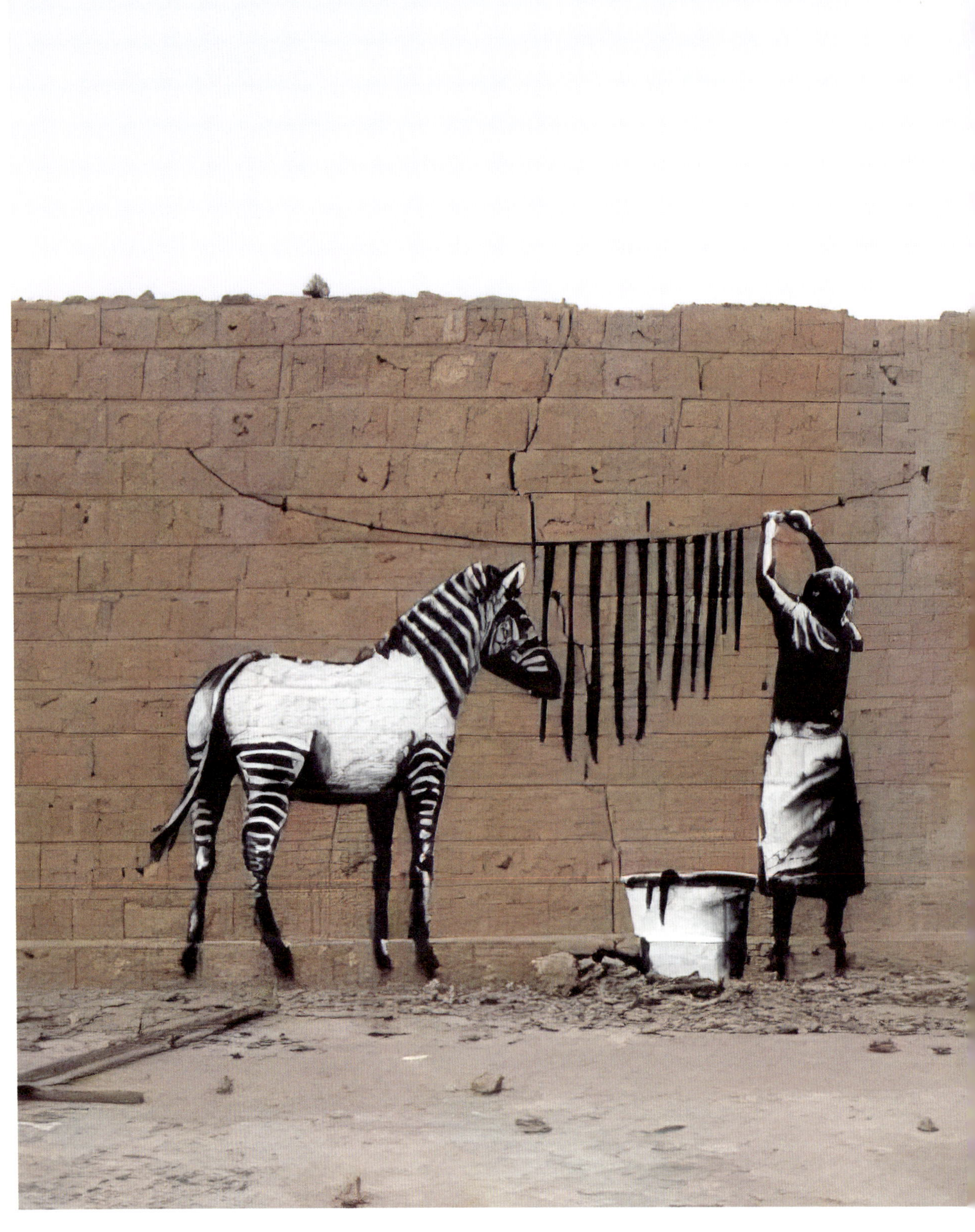

Timbuktu, 2008

IN STITCHES

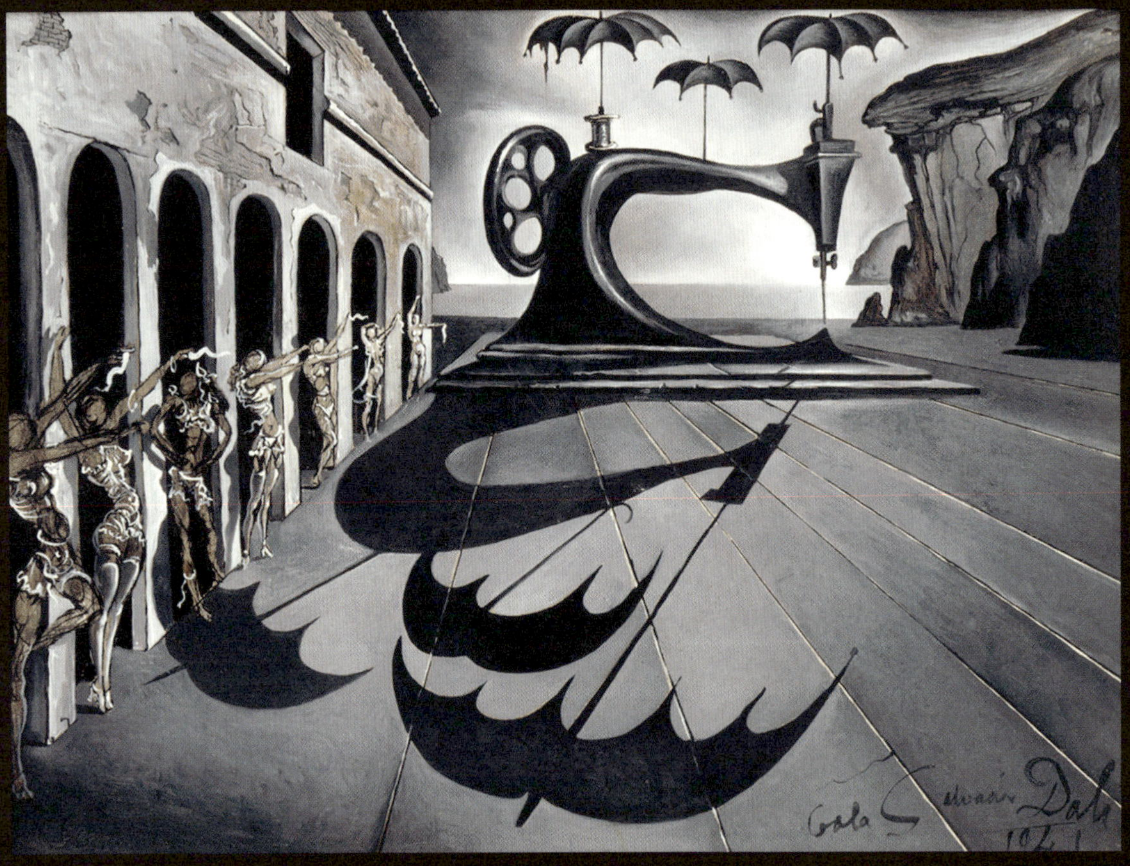

Salvador Dalí, *Sewing Machine with Umbrellas in a Surrealist Landscape*, 1941

'One has to watch out for engineers', the French writer and filmmaker Marcel Pagnol warned in his 1949 essay 'Critique des critiques' (or 'Criticism of Critics'). 'They begin with the sewing machine and end up with the atomic bomb.'[38] Ironically, decades before there even was an atomic bomb, the sewing machine itself was already launched in cultural consciousness as a powerful projectile waiting to strike. Inspired by an arresting phrase by the Uruguayan-born French poet Isidore Ducasse (the self-styled Comte de Lautréamont) – 'handsome ... as the fortuitous encounter upon a dissecting table of a sewing machine and an umbrella!'[39] – the Surrealists glimpsed in the sewing machine an explosive symbol of foreboding and unease. In 1920, American-born avant-garde artist Man Ray invoked Ducasse in the making of an ominous quasi-readymade sculpture, *L'Enigme d'Isidore Ducasse* (*The Enigma of Isidore Ducasse*), which is comprised simply of a sewing machine tightly wrapped in a dark woollen blanket, cinched with string like a hastily bundled corpse. A photograph of the portentous work, which featured on the very first page of the inaugural issue of the Surrealist magazine *La Révolution surréaliste*, was embraced by fellow artists as an anthemic emblem of subconscious fears – of something piercing and pulsing just beneath the heavy curtain of consciousness. The sewing machine, while doubtless designed initially as a liberating gadget, had quickly become an instrument of exploitation to which women and children could be tethered in sweatshops.

A generation after Man Ray's work, in 1941, Salvador Dalí returned to the same forbidding elements that unsettle and invigorate Ducasse's description for his painting *Sewing Machine with Umbrellas in a Surrealist Landscape*. In Dalí's inscrutable vision, umbrellas are seen perching on the humped back of a dinosaur-sized sewing machine, like huge primeval bats waiting to swoop, in a dreamlike plaza. While the long and sinister shadow cast by Dalí's nightmarish machine may not have eclipsed better-known works by the artist, such as *The Persistence of Memory*, it does inflect our reading of one of Banksy's signature works, which appeared one morning in May 2012, stencilled to the side of a Poundland shop in north London. The image portrays a barefoot boy, around seven years of age, hunched over a sewing machine on his knees, stitching Jubilee tat – cheap Union Jack bunting – a real-life stretch of which Banksy has cleverly affixed to the mural, as if it were flowing magically from the pulsating needle of the depicted machine. The mural was widely interpreted as a comment on revelations made in recent years that the bargain chain was trading goods supplied by sweatshops in India, where a seven-year-old had been discovered working more than 100 hours a week. Banksy's bold rehabilitation of a seemingly moribund cultural symbol wove fresh intensity into powerful works whose relevancy had begun to slip and ripped at the stitches of social conscience.

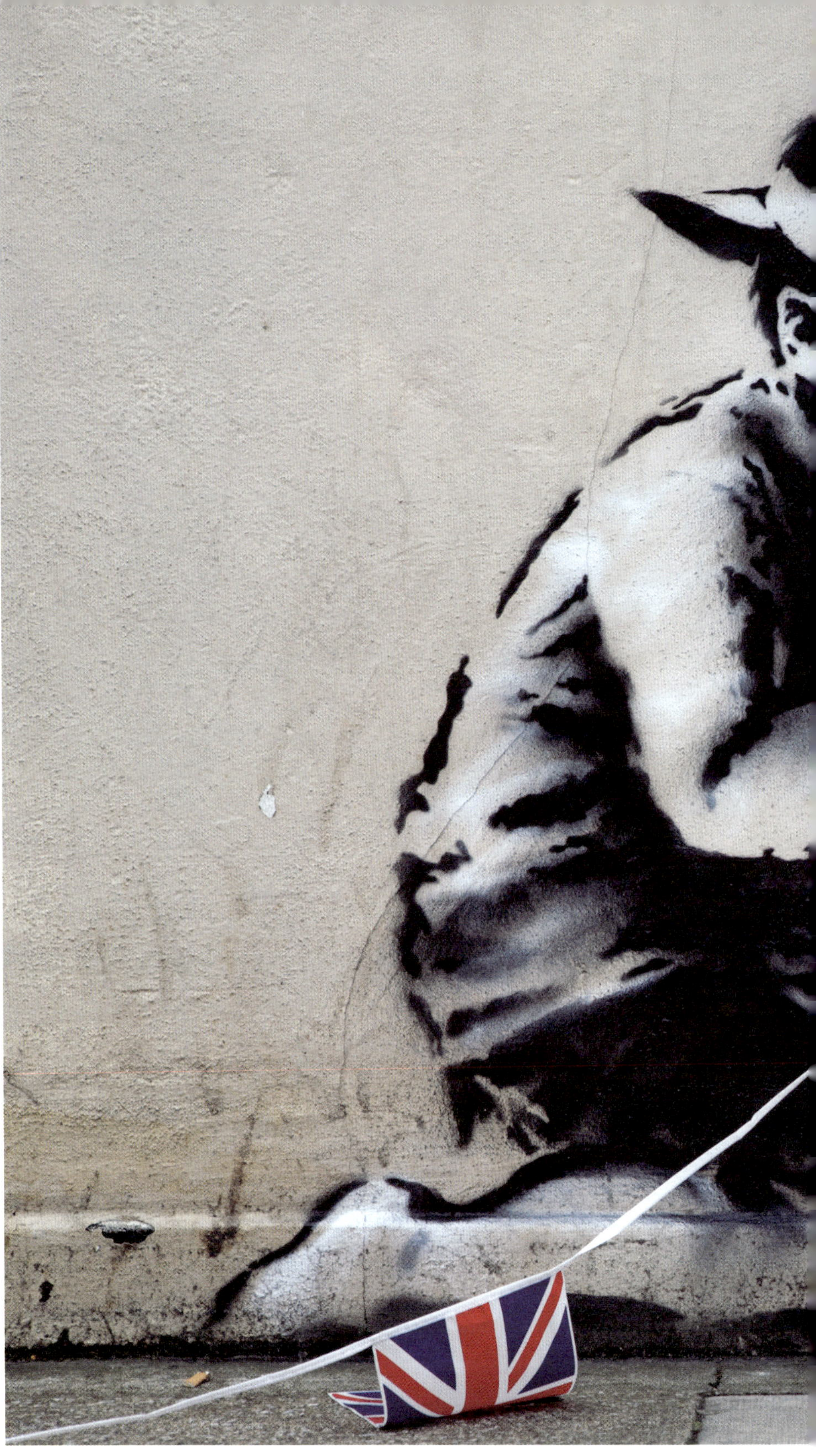

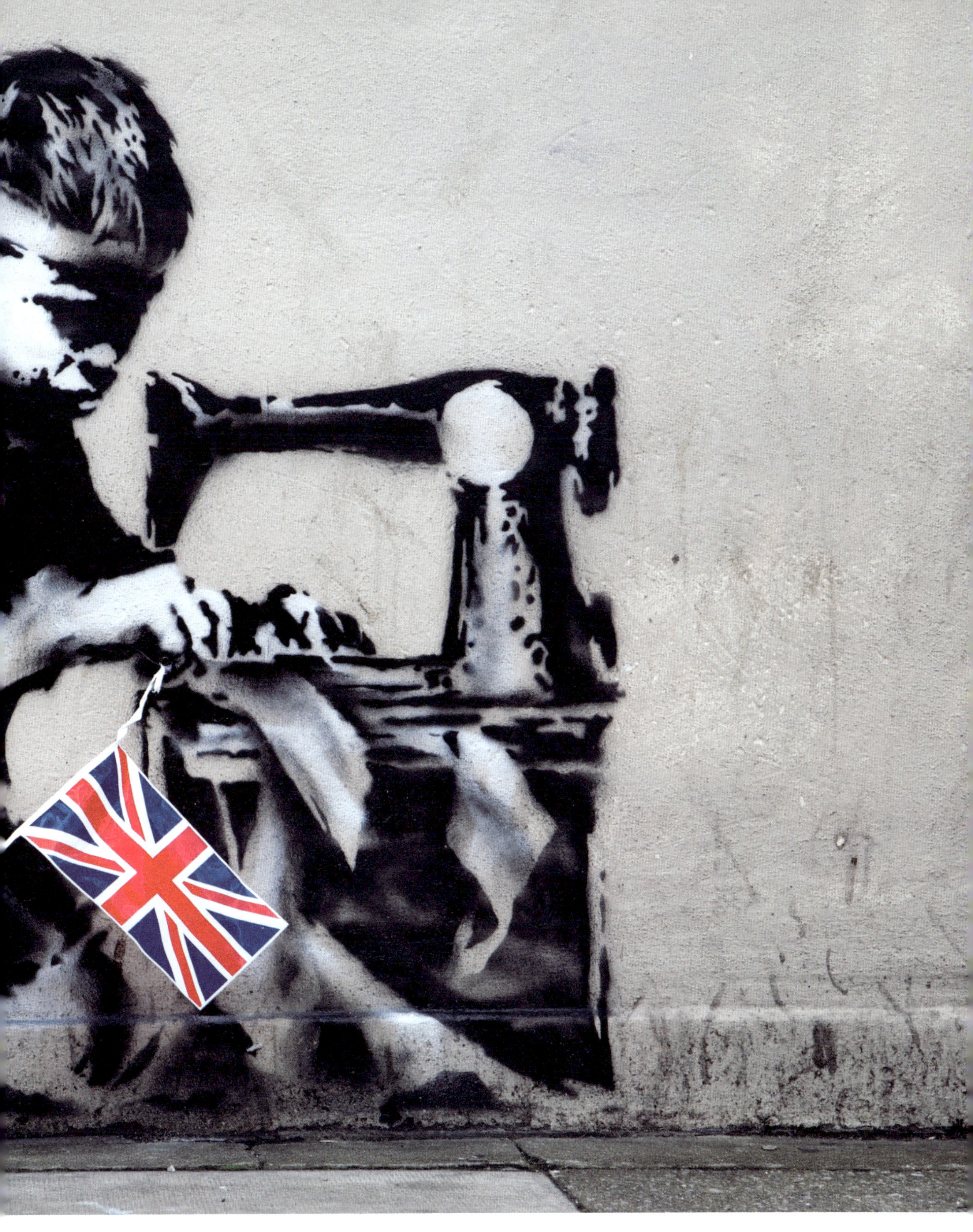

Wood Green, London, 2012

WINDOW DRESSING

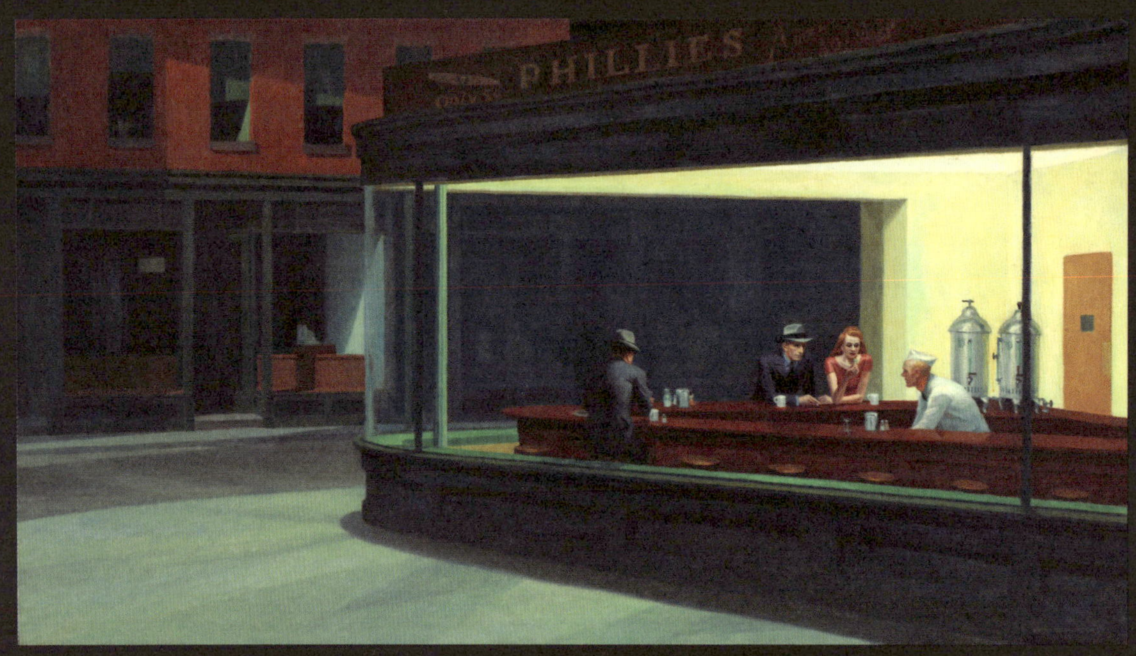

A shirtless yob wearing Union Jack boxer shorts grips a can of beer as he stands on a street corner, hurling abuse at the startled patrons sitting inside a late-night diner. A pair of plastic lawn chairs that he has just used to smash the restaurant's windows lie strewn across the lamp-lit pavement. What makes the scene so arresting isn't the laddish display of anti-social behaviour as such, but its surreal dislocation in time and place from an English city centre on any given night in the past quarter century to the mythic desolation of mid-century America as famously memorialized by Edward Hopper in his iconic ode to urban loneliness, *Nighthawks* (1942). Where Hopper's famous painting nostalgically preserves a fleeting ambience behind a protective pane, Banksy's augmented reality cracks open that hermetic seal and illustrates just how dramatically a society's soul can coarsen.

Hopper's original painting was created at the height of the Second World War. The cold, crisp geometrics of the empty city street and soulless fluorescence of the chilly artificial light, accented by acidic greens, gloam portentously from inside the diner and amplify the sense of loneliness that throbs existentially from the four figures who only incidentally occupy the same sealed space but who are, in truth, profoundly cut off from each other – each isolated in the impenetrable capsules of their own anxieties. Ironically, Banksy's anachronistic interjection of a seemingly foreign figure provides the foursome, who turn their gaze his way, with a common focus for their otherwise wandering attention. He's the ghost of alienation future, who shocks them out of their tightly clenched selves. Look closer at Hopper's painting, and there is no entryway into or exit from this pristine isolation. We can see a pair of doors at the back of the diner, but they offer no escape, only access to deeper corridors of despair. The architecture doesn't add up. But the angry hooligan in Banksy's reinvention, who seems to be an exaggerated projection of the imprisoned foursome's fermenting spirit, as urban anguish simmers over time into the rage of social marginalization, pierces their suffocating confinement. The chaotic cracks he's left on the pane that spreads sparklingly wide in Hopper's canvas, where the plastic chair has popped the painting's bubble, introduce into the work an almost liberating disorder – a breath of fresh air.

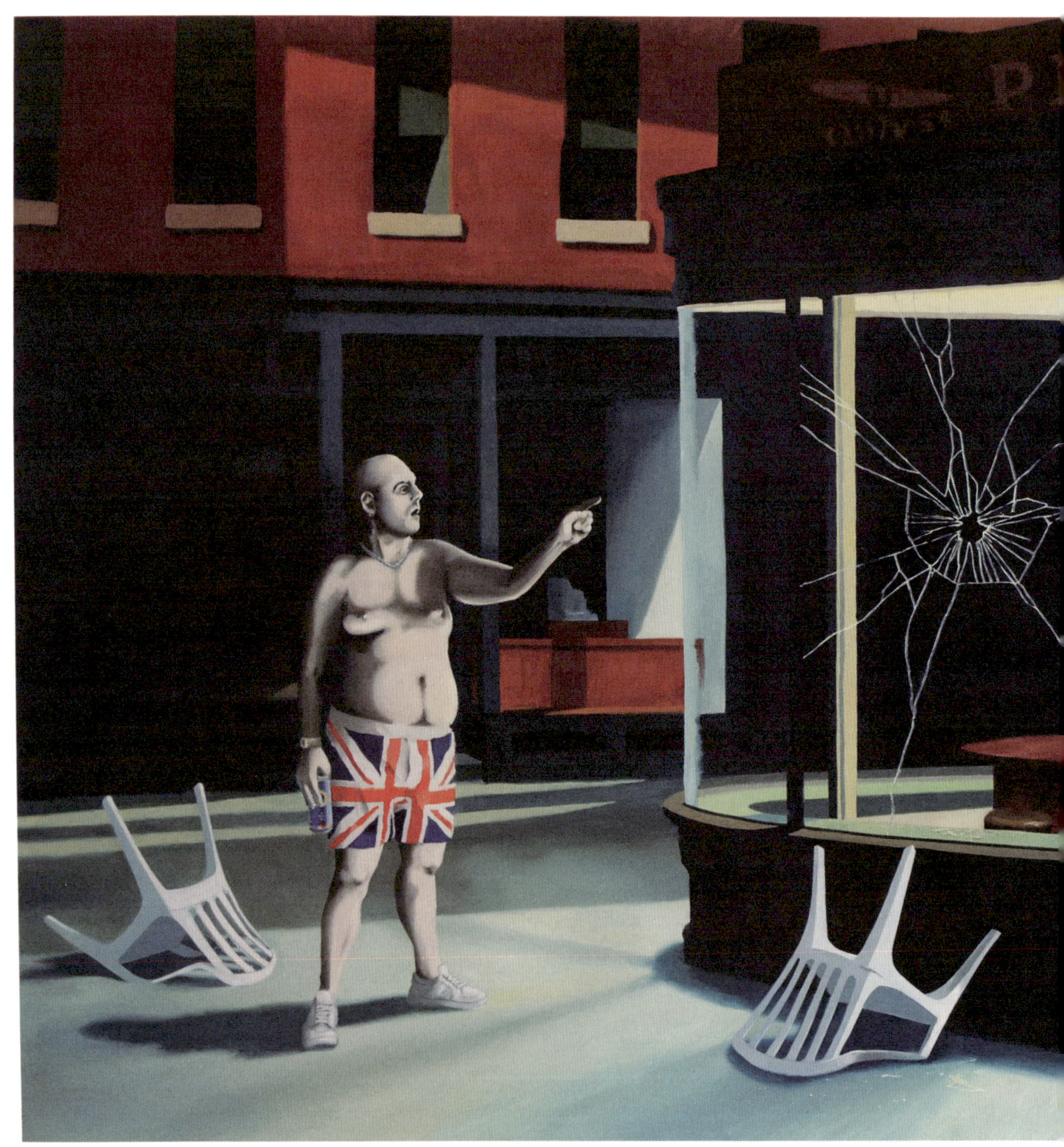

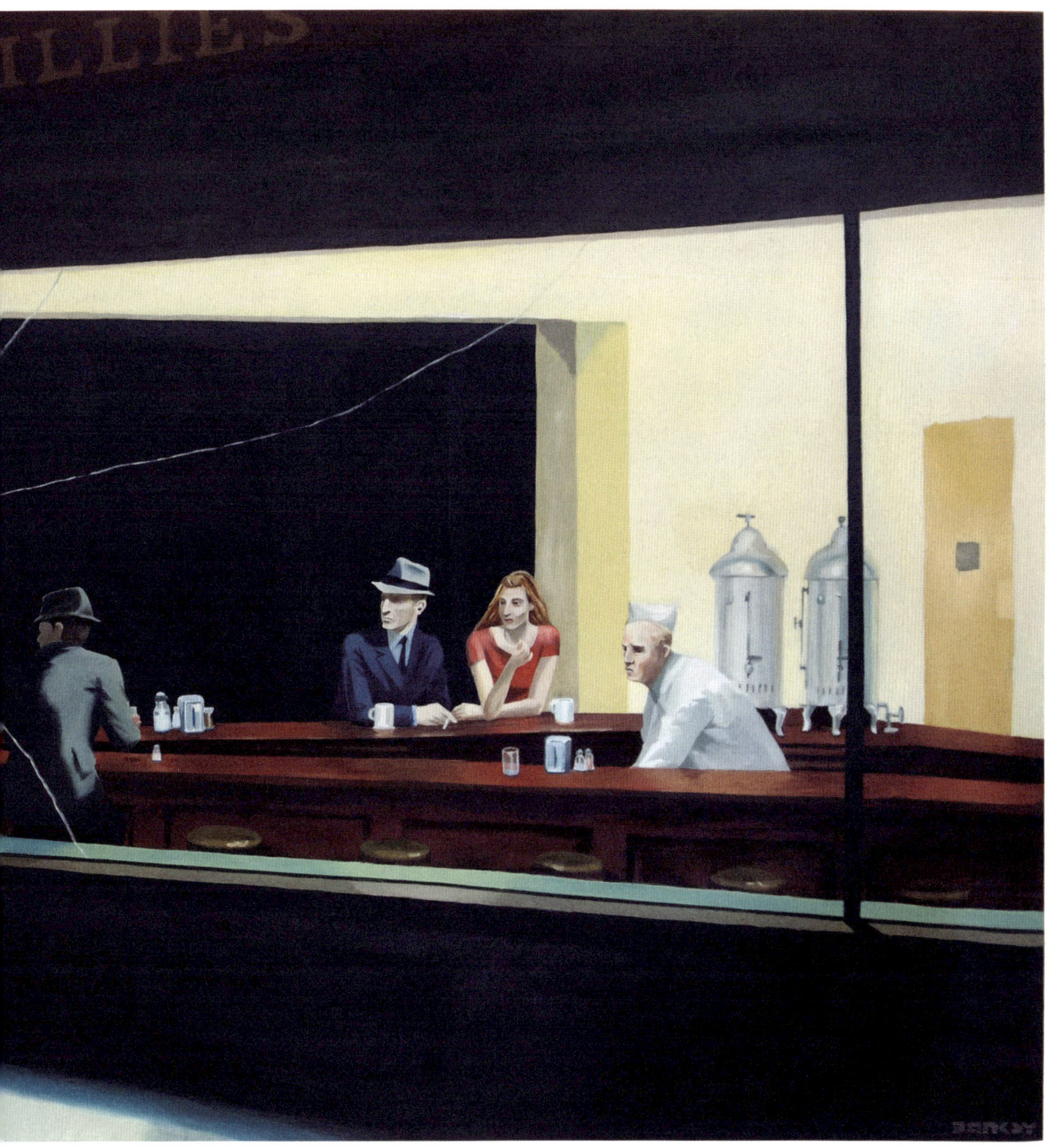

Are You Still Using That Chair?, 2005

POLE POSITION

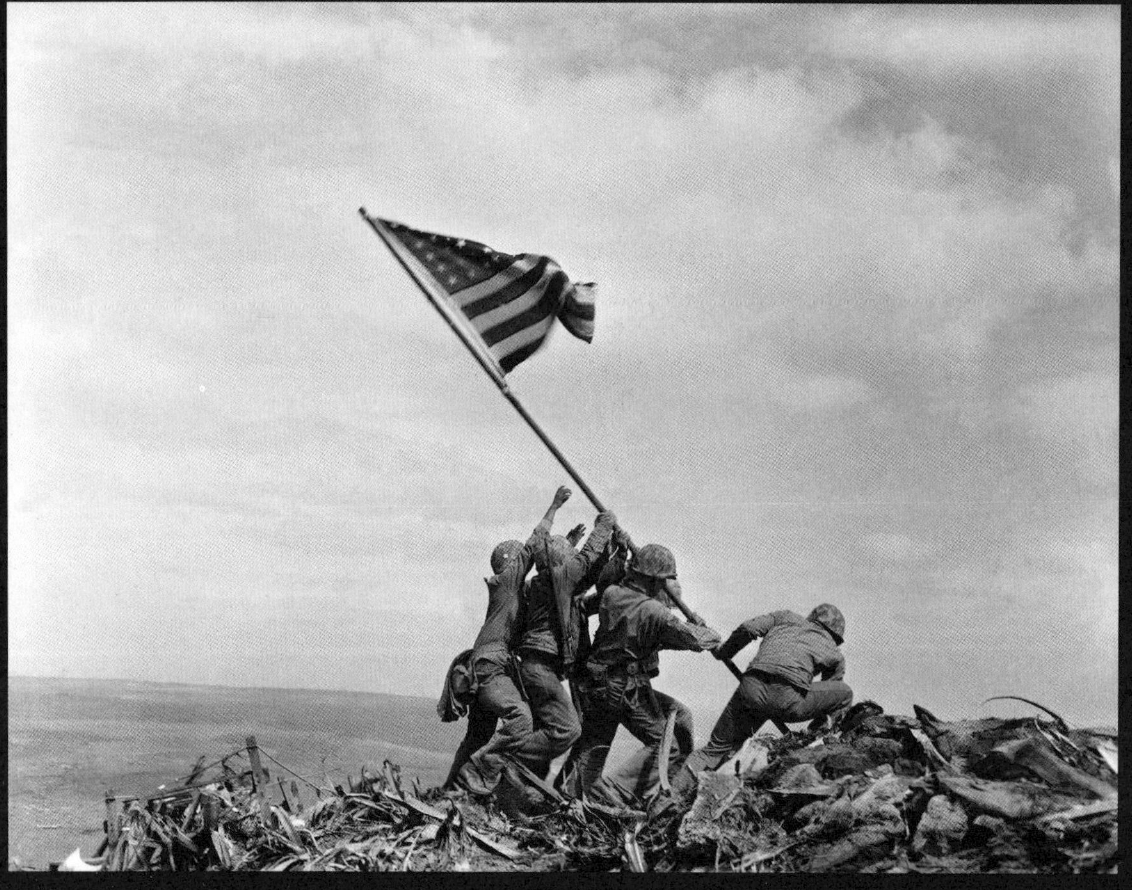

Joe Rosenthal, *Raising of the Flag at Iwo Jima*, 1945

Every picture hides a story. Take, for example, the famous photograph of US Marines lifting a hefty flagpole against the gusts of war above Mount Suribachi on the Micronesian island of Iwo Jima during a decisive battle for control of the strategic Pacific Ocean outpost in the final throes of the Second World War. The rousing image, captured serendipitously in February 1945 by American photojournalist Joe Rosenthal, garnered the cameraman a Pulitzer Prize and inspired a large sculpture of the event by the American artist Felix Weihs de Weldon, which stands near Arlington National Cemetery in Virginia. While the intense tableau of six soldiers working as one to stake the Stars and Stripes in the scruffy ground served as a symbol of courage and determination that nudged a nation towards geopolitical and economic domination in the second half of the 20th century, the image is also fraught with personal tragedy. A poignant satire by Banksy of Rosenthal's endlessly reprinted photo seems implicitly to appreciate that the memorialized moment is troubled by truths that no flag, however deep or wide, can ever fully occlude.

By the time Rosenthal reached the summit of Mount Suribachi, which overlooks the volcanic island that Japan had been using as an early warning station for approaches by enemy bombers, a small American flag had already been mounted. It was only by chance that Rosenthal was on hand when a decision was taken to replace the first flag with a much larger one, in the hope of lifting the American troops' morale as they fought to win control of the island base. Only three of the six men whom Rosenthal captured raising the second flagpole survived the month-long battle, which would see nearly 22,000 Japanese and 7,000 US soldiers killed, and tens of thousands severely wounded. Among the trio to make it off the island was twenty-two-year-old Corporal Ira Hayes (the soldier on the far left of the photo) – an Arizona-born Pima Indian who struggled terribly with depression, survivor's guilt and alcoholism in the years following the battle. Though crucial to the chaotic choreography of an iconic image that superficially embodied American grit and resolve, Hayes was unable to fit into the society whose spirit he'd help lift. Hayes was arrested over fifty times for public intoxication in the decade following the publication of Rosenthal's photo, before dying of exposure after a drunken fight in his native Pinal County in 1955.

In Banksy's reimagining of the famous scene (which he released in 2006 as a limited-edition series of signed and unsigned prints in 'formica gold' and 'formica silver'), the scrum of US soldiers has been replaced by a scrappy band of restless youths who clamber atop an abandoned, burned-out car. With the wheels of the vehicle long-since chopped and shopped, the rusting husk offers no promise of conveyance out of their privation. The charred chassis is merely an urban eminence from which the group can survey the desolate landscape. Rather than helping hoist a hollow emblem of hope, one of the kids endeavours to snap off the car's flimsy antenna, and with it, symbolically, any channel of communication with the world that has abandoned it. Seen in the solemn light of Ira Hayes's sad story, Banksy's riff on the famous image from Iwo Jima isn't an insolent subversion of its message but rather a fearless fulfilment of it.

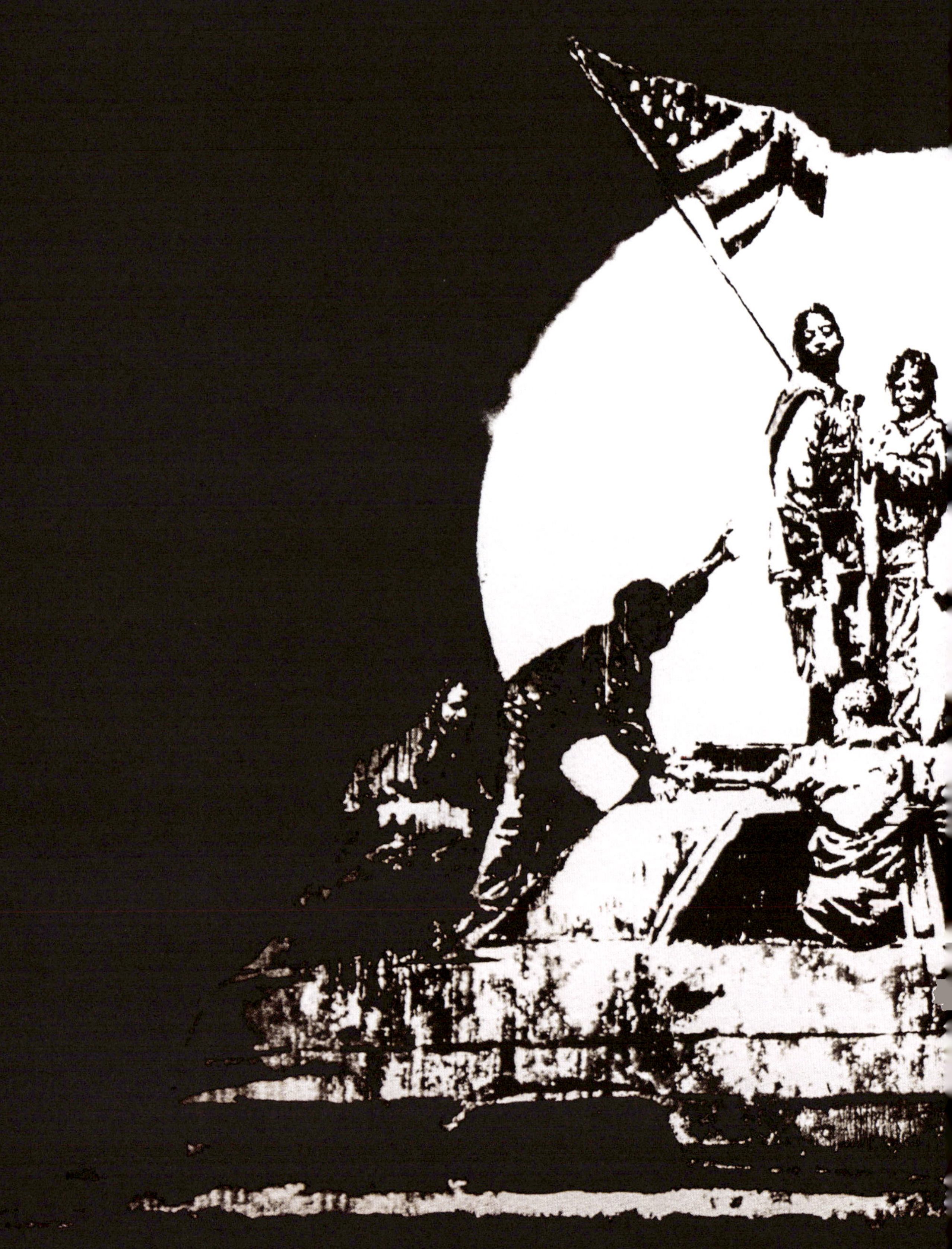

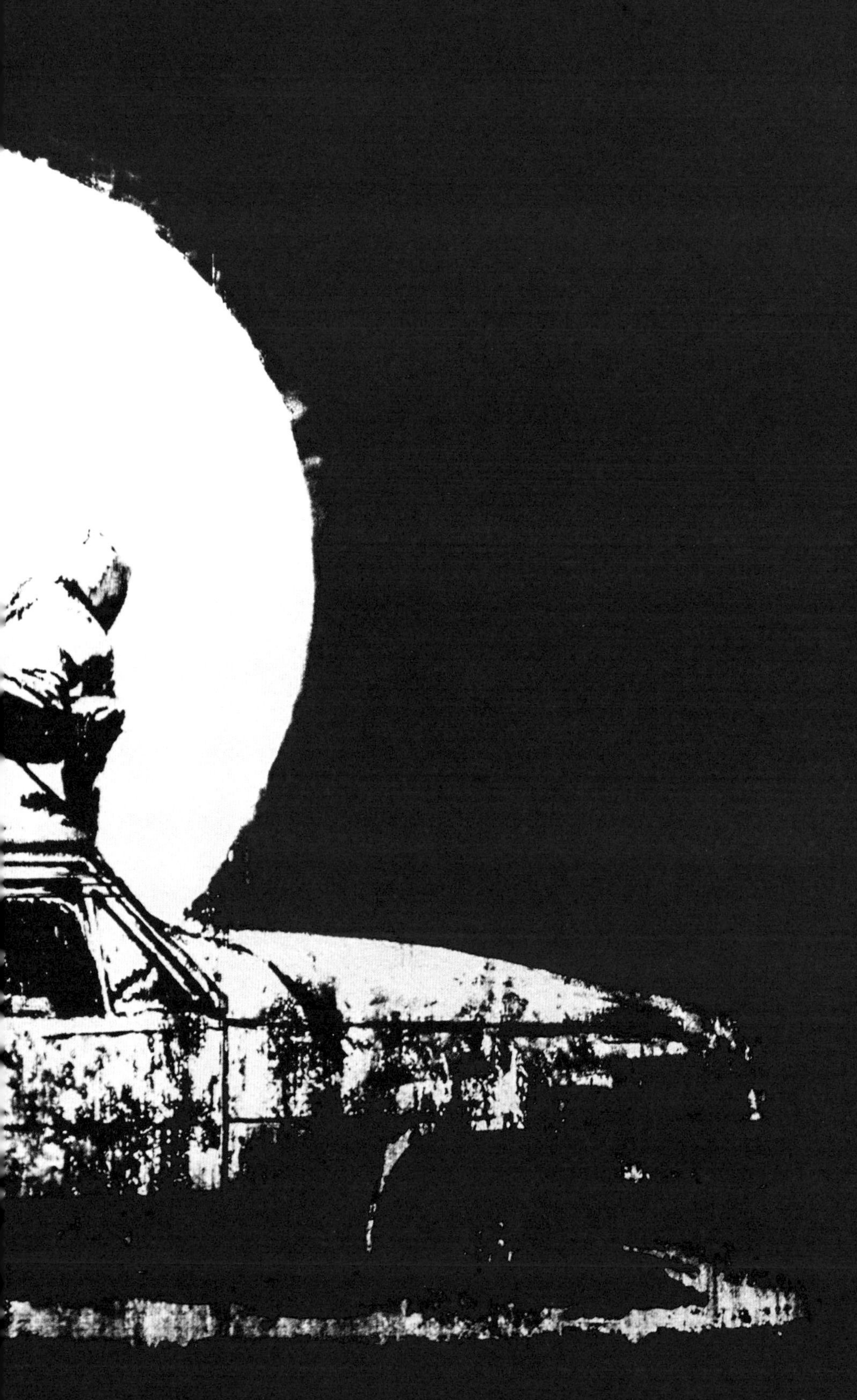

Flag, 2006

HOT TIN SPOOF

Among the principal points of the Pop Art movement, which came to prominence in the late 1950s and early 1960s, was to pierce prevailing presumptions (and pretentiousness) about what art is and could be. Take, for example, Andy Warhol's now legendary *Campbell's Soup Can* series, which the thirty-four-year-old commercial illustrator and printmaker began developing in the summer of 1962. The painterly devotion traditionally shown to religious subjects, lyrical landscapes, scenes of historical consequence, or the faces of significant figures was audaciously redirected to the cold charisma of a super-market staple. Fast-forward four decades and Banksy out-pops Pop by pushing that outmoded movement's elapsed edginess to the very edge. Banksy's *Tesco Value Soup Can* (2004) is not so much a recycling of Warhol's once-controversial conceit as it is an aggressive price-war play for market share and shelf-space in cultural consciousness. By peeling away the labels of Warhol's over-inflated icon and reformulating the spit-and-vinegar spirit that once filled it, Banksy reveals an unexpired potential in the original.

When Warhol first unveiled his hand-painted portraits of mass-produced pantry tins at the Ferus Gallery in Los Angeles in July 1962, his first solo show, the reaction was largely one of bemusement by casual visitors and critics alike. The art world had, of course, seen the same striking crimsons, whites and golds deployed before by such venerable masters as Duccio, say, in his pious *Maestà* altarpiece. But never had such an ennobling attentiveness been lavished on such a seemingly trivial object, one that risked devaluing the cultural precursors it echoed. We now know that Warhol, who was brought up in the Ruthenian Catholic tradition and attended the St John Chrysostom Byzantine Catholic Church in Pittsburgh, Pennsylvania, likely loaded the deceptively disposable cans of tomato soup with an intensely intimate symbolism. Having emigrated to America from a village in Austria-Hungary (today Slovakia), Warhol's parents struggled. His father was a coal-miner and the one reliable lunch that could be afforded each and every day throughout the future artist's childhood was a bowl of Campbell's soup. The comfort and reassurance it brought him became a wellspring into which the artist continued to tap deep into adulthood. For Warhol, the Campbell's soup can was not a disposable receptacle to kick down the road with kitschy abandon, but a spiritual font to which he regularly returned. When Warhol assembled a collage of some thirty-two simulacra of the treasured tins in 1962, his intention was not to generate a rude gesture to the solemnity of art history, but to fashion a deeply personal rood screen of the soul.

Whatever the lofty intentions behind them may have been, Warhol's soup cans would prove incapable of keeping themselves unsmirched by the grubby grip of the art world. When the exhibition closed in 1962, Warhol was delighted when one of the owners of the Ferus Gallery, Irving Blum, offered him $1,000 for all thirty-two of the paintings. A generation later, in 1996, the Museum of Modern Art paid Blum $15 million for the group – marking the steepest ever price jump in the history of canned goods. By rebranding Warhol's tin as a stripped-down, no-frills budget basic, Banksy seeks to rewire the ticking clock strapped to a contemporary art market that seems dangerously to have only one setting: boom.

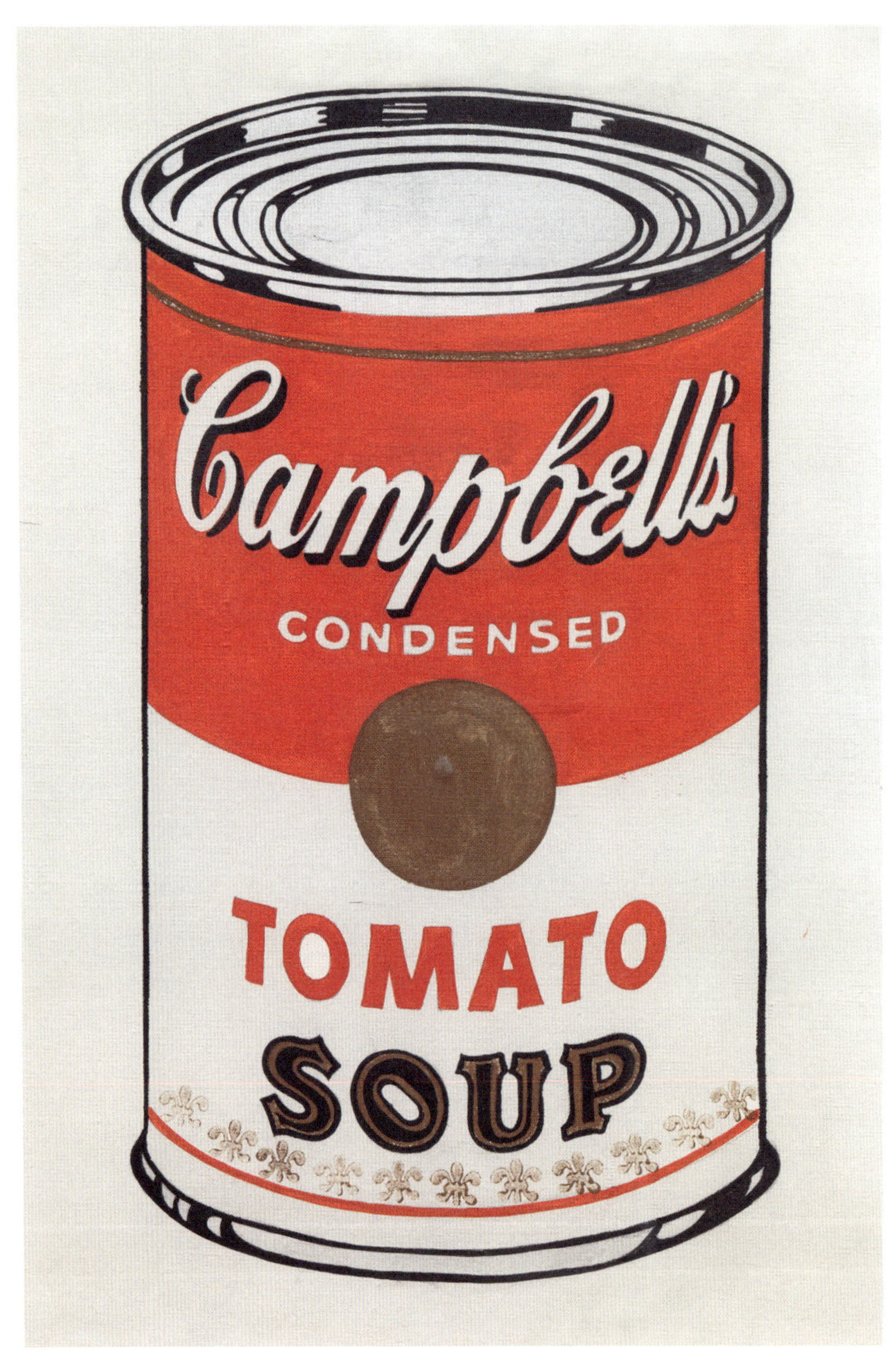

Andy Warhol, *Small Torn Campbell's Soup Can (Pepper Pot)*, 1962

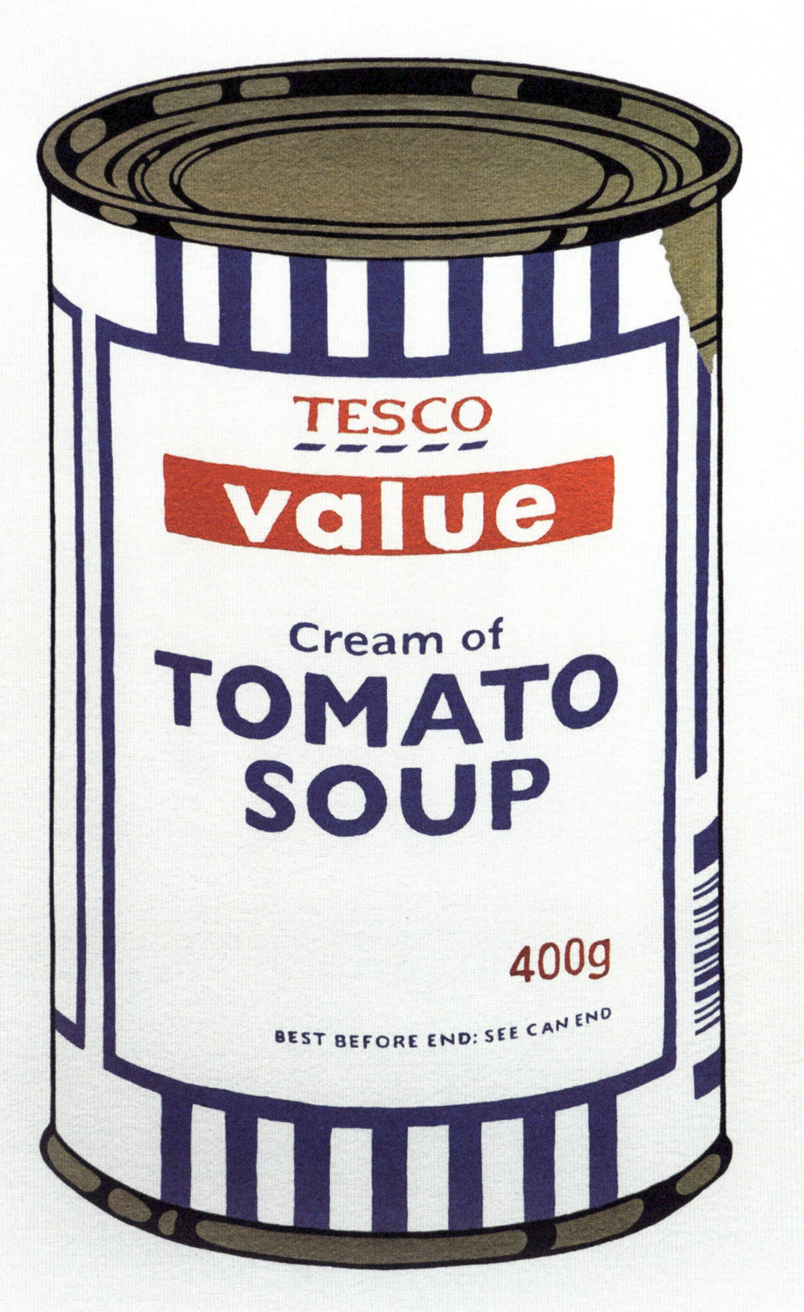

Tesco Value Soup Can, 2004

SOME LIKE IT FRAUGHT

When it comes to great portraits, the eyes have it. In some, they follow you around the room, *Mona Lisa*-style, tracking every move you make. In others, the eyes seem eerily to pierce right through us, as if we weren't there at all – a penetrating propensity that Frida Kahlo's self-portraits have down pat. In the case of Andy Warhol's iconic screen-print portraits of Marilyn Monroe, which the Pop artist began producing in 1962, shortly after the Hollywood starlet's untimely death, there is a disquieting disconnection between Monroe's gaze at us and ours at her. Try as we might, we cannot quite get our stares to sync. The result is a teasing detachment of intimacy that keeps us both, sitter and seer, artwork and observer, desperately searching for each other. That curious uncoupling of pupils, an underappreciated aspect of the portrait's power, is skilfully seized upon by Banksy in his simultaneously vibrant and vexing 2005 portrait of British supermodel Kate Moss.

On first seeing Banksy's portrait of Moss, whose waifish style and natural appeal propelled her into cultural consciousness in the 1990s, one's eyes are forced to do a double take. She's there and she isn't. She is her and someone else at the same time. The close cropping of Moss's face into a claustrophobic, postage-stamp square and the bee-stung glisten of her scarlet lips make her a dead ringer for Warhol's original. And yet, the closer you look at Banksy's small, oversaturated screen prints of the 'anti-supermodel', which he produced in a limited series of seven clashing electric colour combos (blue/grey, red/lime, pink/yellow, green/turquoise, purple/orange, apricot/gold and monochrome black-and-white with red lips), the more difficult it is to pin down which aspects of the likeness have been borrowed from Monroe and which are distinctly Moss's. There's little doubting that the wavy bob of bleached hair has been lifted wholesale from Warhol's original. But what about that beauty mark? Moss doesn't have one. Monroe does, but it's on the other side of her face. And the lips? They're plump enough to be Moss's, but the expression they're pulling is neither one we associate with her nor with Monroe. If anything, it's pure Elvis.

The more you reflect on Banksy's absorbing double-exposure of past and future selves, of the living and the dead, what ultimately emerges as most unsettling is the uncanny coincidence of the celebrity subjects' unmeetable stares. As it happens, Moss suffers from the same ophthalmological condition that Monroe did: strabismus, a misalignment of vision that makes it difficult, if not impossible, for both eyes to focus simultaneously on the same point. Far from making either figure less photogenic or suitable for portraiture, the slight disunion draws us into the irresolvable riddle of their vision. Something happens when an image becomes so familiar that its aura expands beyond the borders of its material self. It begins to break down and become a thing on which our eyes can no longer focus or clearly see. In that sense, the confounding compound image is really a reflection of each and every one of us.

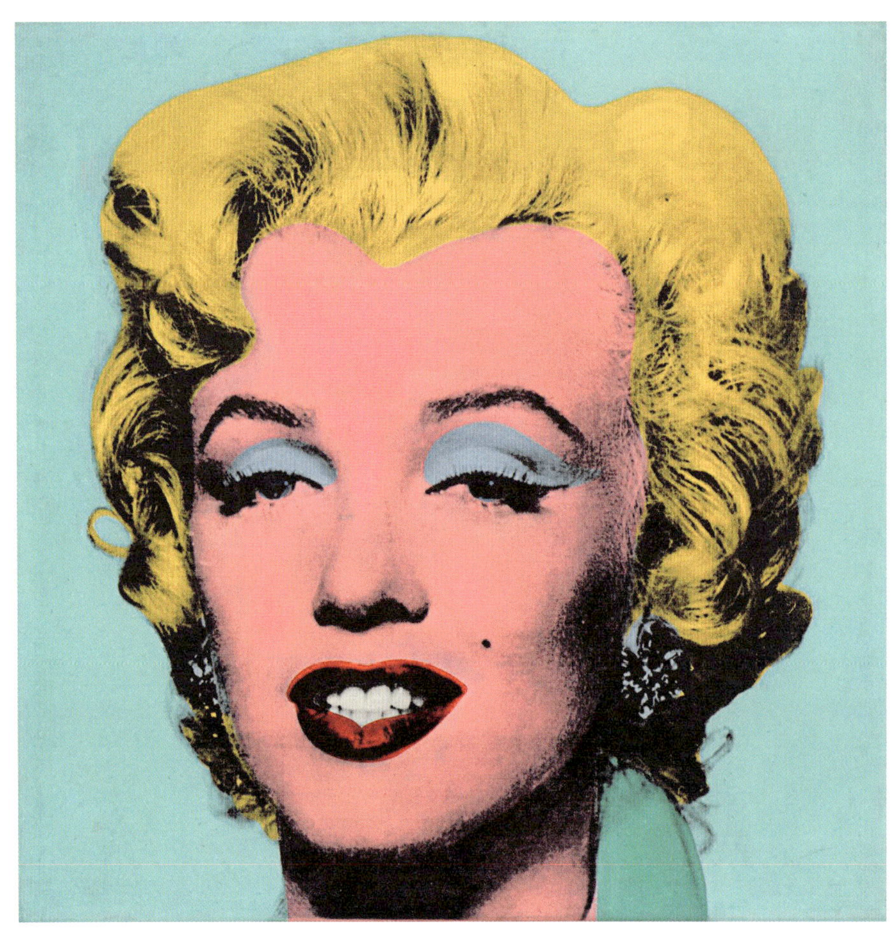

Andy Warhol, *Shot Sage Blue Marilyn*, 1964

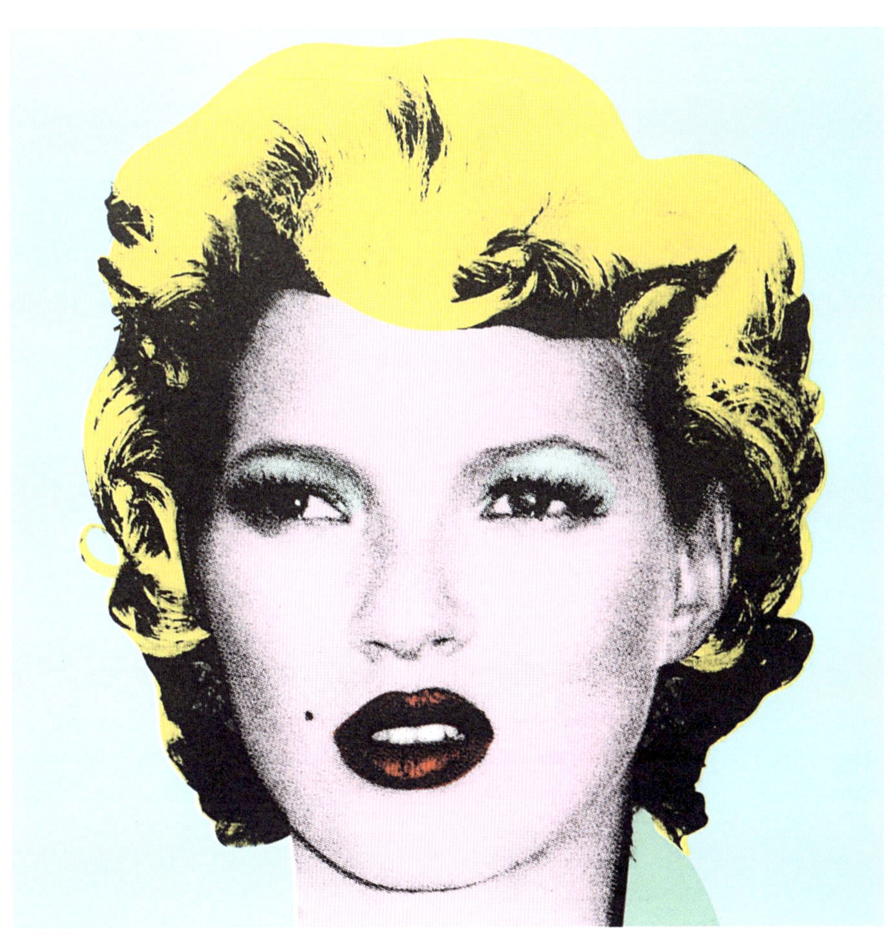

Kate Moss, 2005

WHERE I CAN SEE THEM

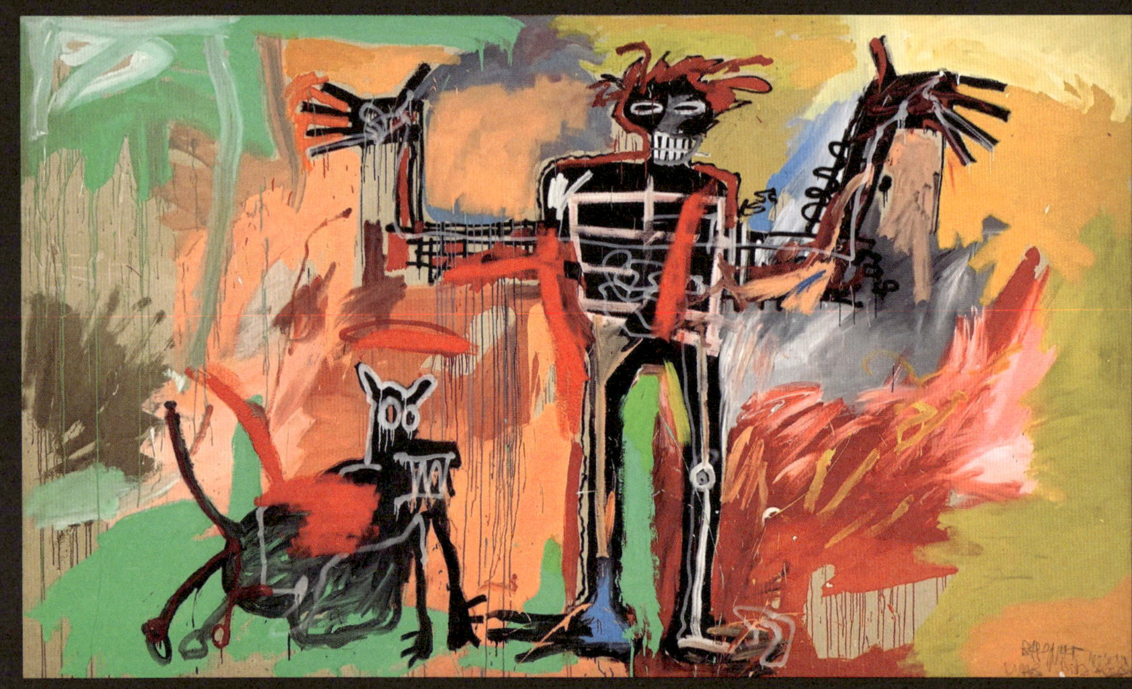

Jean-Michel Basquiat, *Boy and Dog in a Johnnypump*, 1982

In a healthy world, the phrase 'stop and search' might be read simply as a benign description of what we do whenever we look at art. But ours isn't healthy. In the United Kingdom, the power to stop and search any person deemed suspicious was first given to police officers in 1984, at roughly the same moment that American painter and former street artist Jean-Michel Basquiat created one of his most famous and enduring works, *Boy and Dog in a Johnnypump*. In a healthy world, that electric image of a child with arms flung aloft and akimbo against the an apricot haze of humid heat, as his body is quenched by a burst of water geysering from an open fire hydrant on the street, would be perceived as unambiguously joyful – an exuberant snapshot of lazy summer abandon. But a simple stop and search of Basquiat's complex canvas, examined through the lens of America's struggle with racism, finds plenty of evidence that the painting is anything but unequivocally jubilant: the invasive interrogation of the boy's X-rayed body, his skeletal grin, and the angular rigidity of his petrified limbs, frozen midway between a mugging at gunpoint and a crucifixion.

Although the work was not among those shipped to London in 2017 for a major exhibition at the Barbican, 'Basquiat: Boom for Real', Banksy determined it was not an image that should slip the attention of visitors. In the light of ongoing concerns in the UK over the abuse by police of stop-and-search powers, particularly against people of colour, which results in as many as a quarter of a million illegal detainments each year, Banksy went to work on a wall in central London beside the Barbican itself before dawn on 17 September. The resulting mural is an audaciously unsanctioned collaboration with Basquiat, who died of a heroin overdose in August 1988 at the age of twenty-seven. In a manner reminiscent of Banksy's earlier conspiratorial invocation of Keith Haring, *Choose Your Weapon*, the Barbican mural is a mash-up of Basquiat's aerosolized expressiveness, in which the boy and dog are convincingly expressed, and Banksy's own signature stencil style, in which a pair of monochromatic cops, surreally frisking the portrait, are rendered. In the years since Basquiat's untimely death, his paintings have attracted some of the highest prices ever paid for works of art – stratospheric sums that the artist himself, needless to say, did not live to enjoy. Four months before the Barbican show opened, a still-life skull by Basquiat, *Untitled* (1982), sold at auction for $110.5 million (£85.2 million) – the highest price ever paid for a work by an American artist in a public sale. Seen in that shadow, it is difficult not to read Banksy's mural not merely as a comment on the treatment of Black citizens (and how Basquiat might himself have been greeted by police on his way to the show's opening, had he lived to see it), but as a reflection too on the shameless shakedown of artists, who can do little more than throw up their hands in despair.

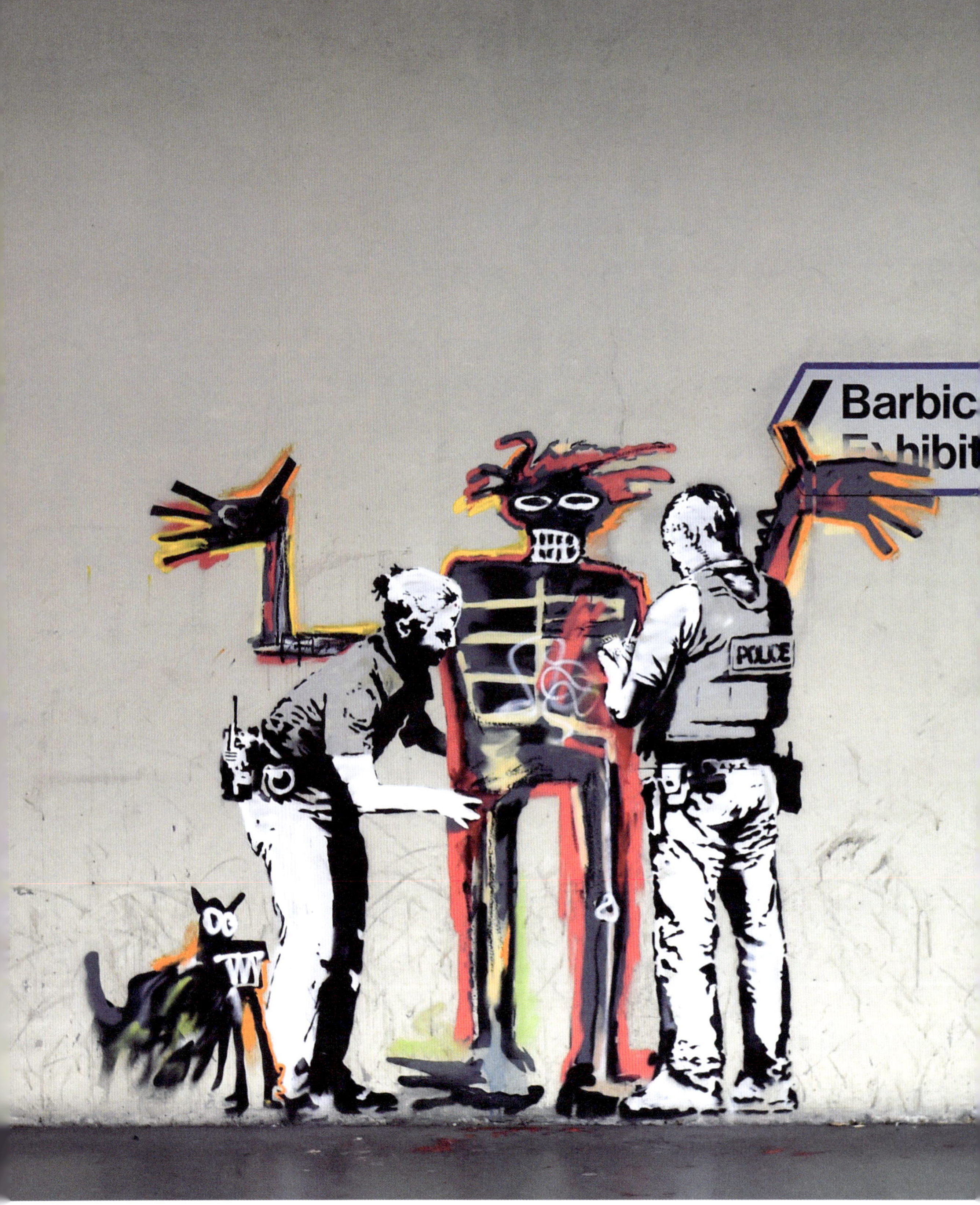

Barbic
Exhibit
POLICE

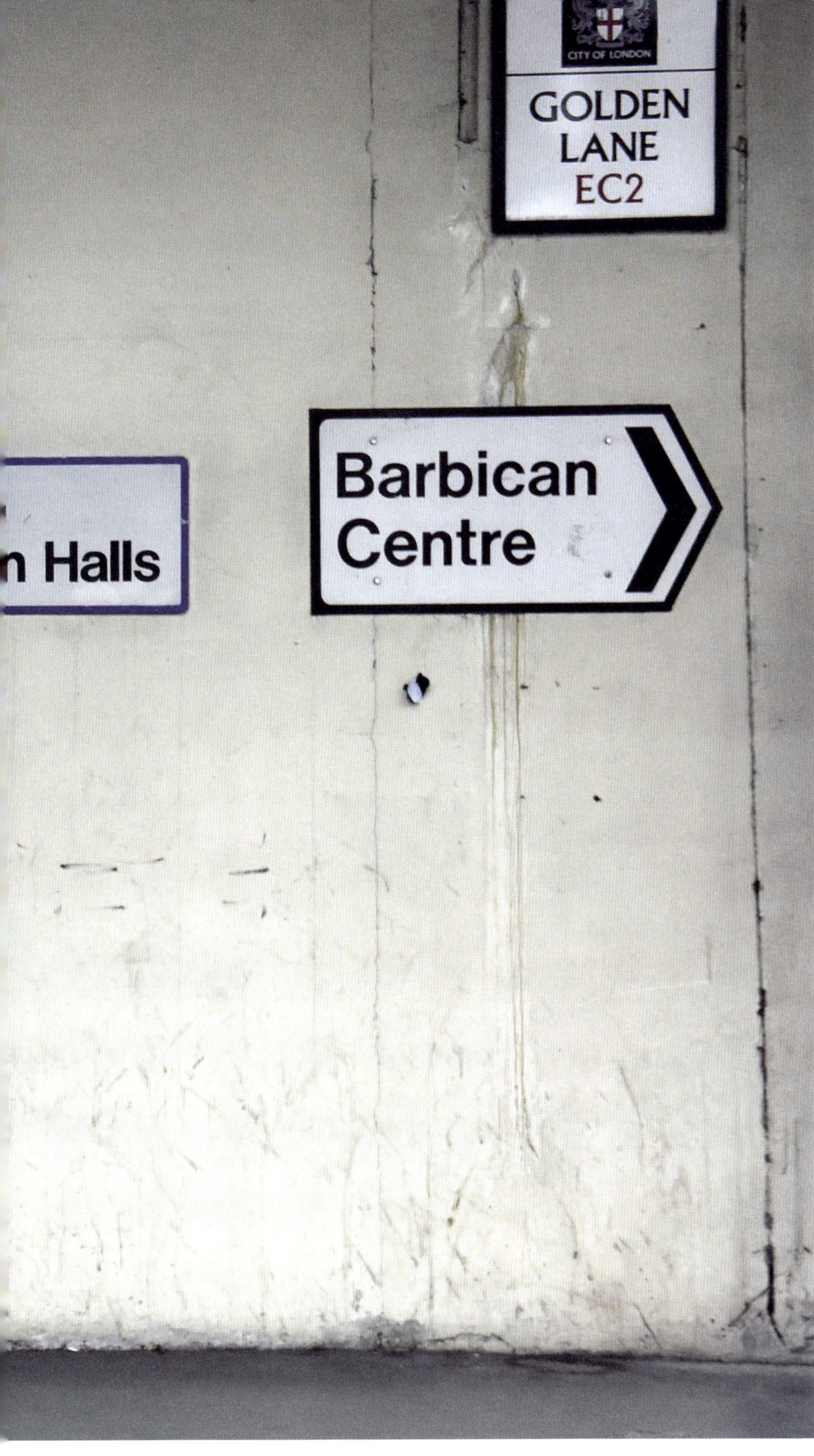

Barbican, London, 2017

WARP AND WOOF

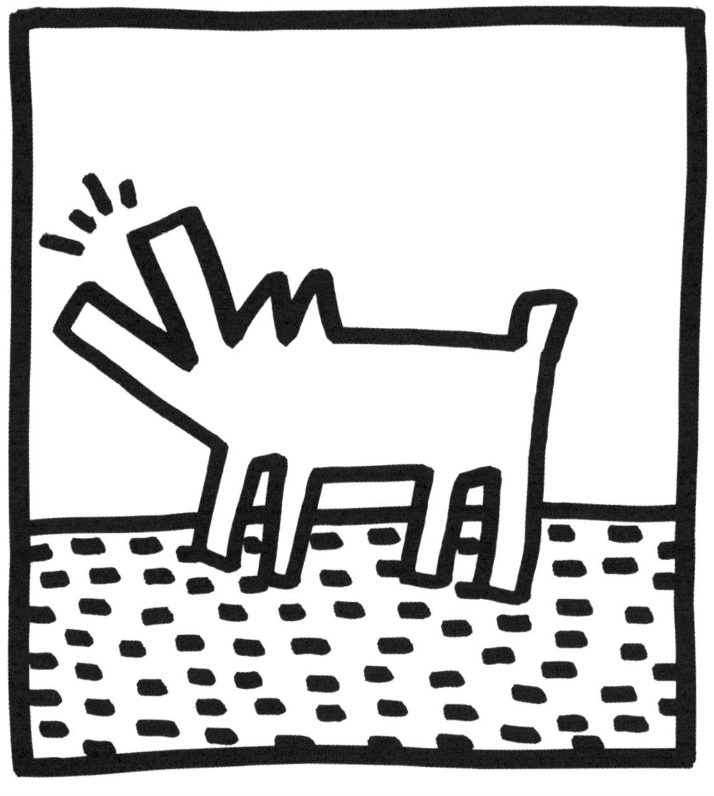

Keith Haring, *Untitled*, 1984

How you perceive a dog's bark depends a great deal on whether you are holding its leash or whether its chain is straining straight in your direction. The same snarl and vicious yap can evoke both fear and fortitude in equal measure. So too with any weapon – and with art. In the decade leading up to his death from AIDS-related complications in 1990, American artist Keith Haring succeeded in creating an ambiguous archetype in the shape of a barking dog whose blunt rhomboid physique and mute angular yowl – with hieroglyphic attributes that helped define the visual vocabulary of New York's art scene in the 1980s – were seen variously as censorious of authority or assertive of inner verve, depending on your perspective. Twenty years after Haring's death, Banksy borrowed his iconic dog and took it for a fresh stroll around cultural consciousness by tethering its cartoonish shape incongruously to a detailed stencil of a masked and hooded youth whose aura we recall from the famous flower thrower mural of a few years earlier. At first glance, the hybrid image may seem merely an obliquely amusing comment on a growing concern in some urban communities in the UK over the wielding of menacing Bully dogs as weapons by disaffected youths desperate to project a semblance of power. Look closer, however, and the work may be a more intriguing statement on the very nature of political speech.

When Haring first unleashed his dog on the walls of New York's subway in the early 1980s, the illegally scrawled motif, which appeared in many of Haring's works, was widely interpreted as mocking politicians and authorities who abuse their power. To many, the aggressive dog's bark symbolized the yammer of elected officials who preach sanctimoniously about their moral righteousness while displaying indifference to those who suffer, especially from AIDS. Over time, Haring complicated the resonance of his striking canine cipher, so that it became anything but two-dimensional. Recasting the barking beast in various guises – now riddled with infectious spots howling at UFOs, now spinning records at a DJ mixing deck as an ecstatic totem of creative expression – Haring refused to allow his work to remain static or to curdle into cliche. Constantly adjusting the significance of his complex symbol, Haring demanded of those who encountered his work that they read it with fresh eyes and not assume it expressed a predictably branded meaning. We hear in the dog's bark what we want to hear. By placing a shadowy surrogate of himself, masked and stencilled on a street wall, at the other end of the lead from Haring's indeterminate dog, Banksy draws a parallel with his own shifting and unfixed significance. Whether you see his work as a weapon pointed at you or a voice speaking for you depends on where you decide to stand. The choice is yours.

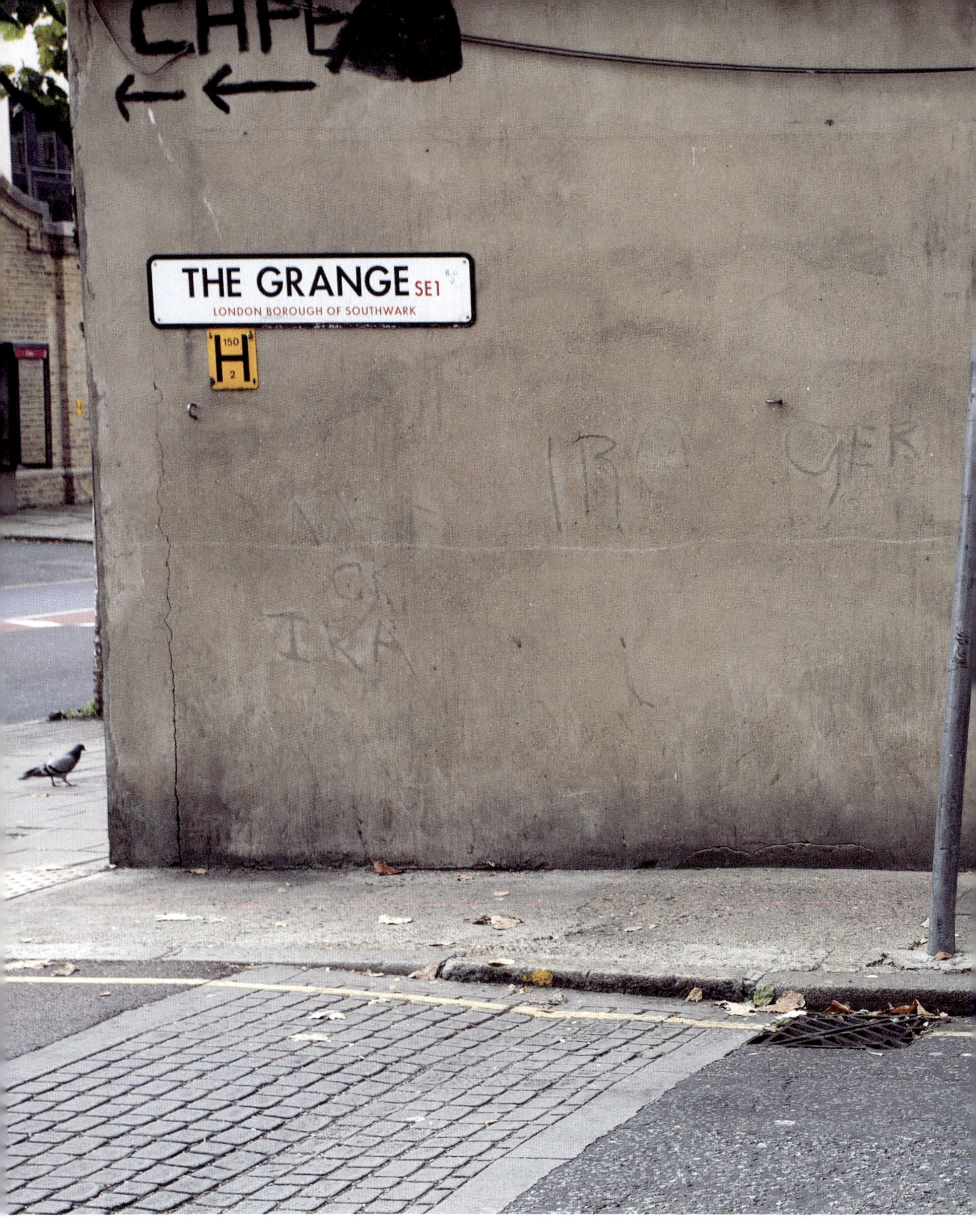

THE GRANGE SE1
LONDON BOROUGH OF SOUTHWARK
150
H
2

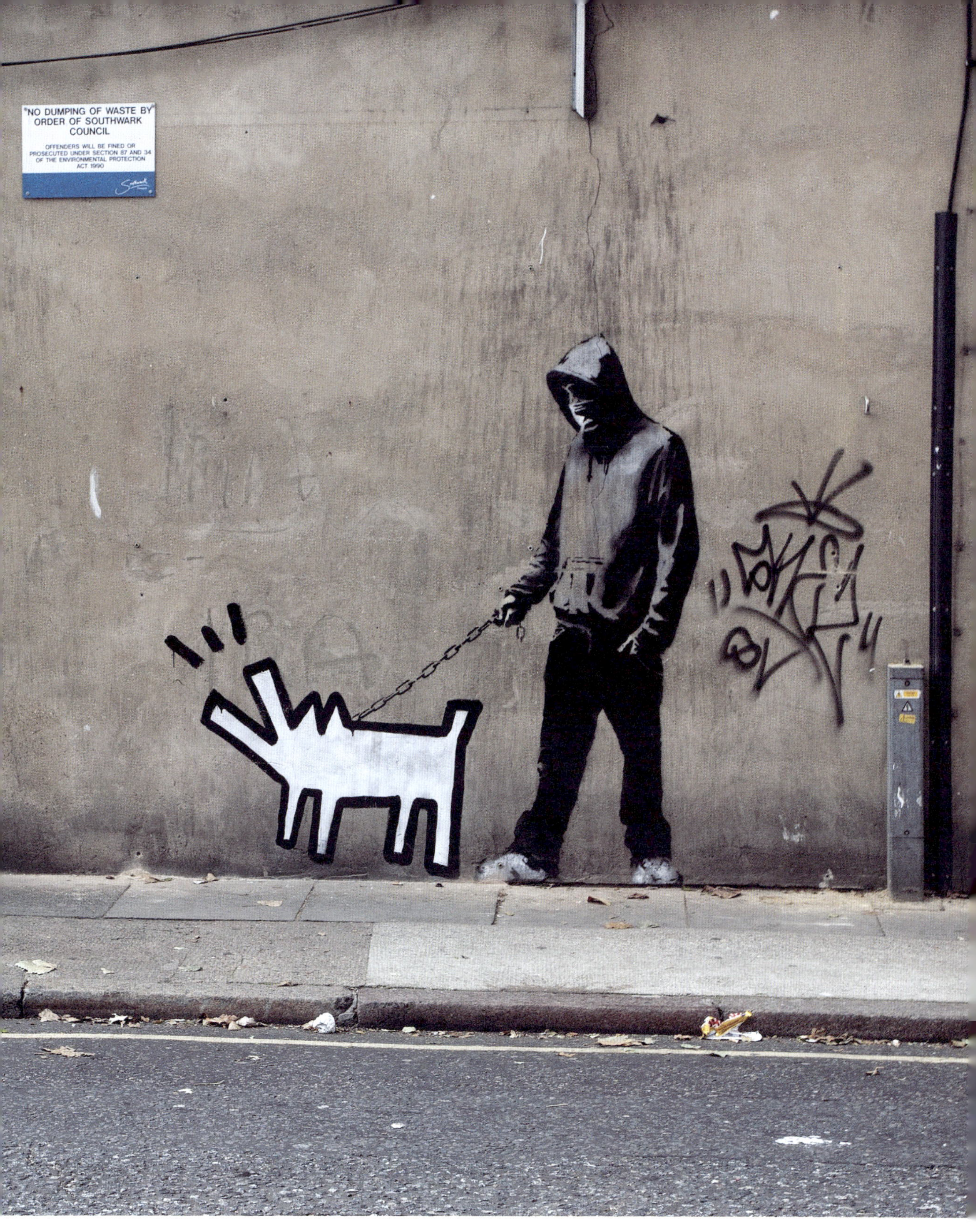

Bermondsey, London, 2010

SPOTS OF TIME

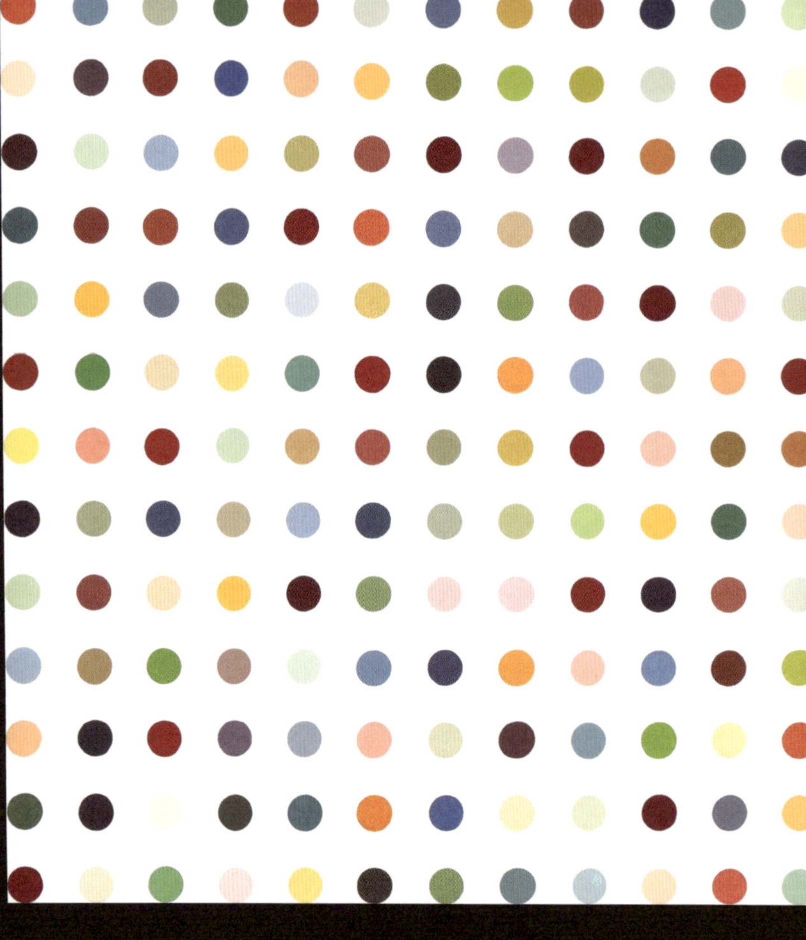

Damien Hirst, *Methoxyverapamil*, 1991

What greater sign of respect can you show another artist than popping open a can of the drabbest paint you can find, grabbing a DIY roller, and furiously obliterating their work? Oh, and not some flimsy facsimile or parody of their painting, either – the thing itself. For all his incorrigible irreverence, surely even Banksy would regard such a display of contempt for another creator beyond the *pail*, as it were? But in 2007 Banksy did just that when he got his hands on a work by fellow British artist Damien Hirst, who came to prominence in the early 1990s as a key figure in the Young British Artist (YBA) movement that dominated the UK art scene at the end of the millennium. Rather than demonstrating disdain for the efforts and imagination of his contemporary, however, Banksy's blotting out of one of Hirst's signature 'spot paintings' is tinged with unexpected poignancy.

Immediately recognizable, Hirst's spot paintings, of which he has created upwards of 2,000 since the series began in the late 1980s, are comprised of coloured dots, of uniform size within each work, evenly spaced and arranged in neat rows and columns. No two spots in any given painting are exactly the same colour. Highly sought-after by collectors today, Hirst's ever-growing blizzard of dots began humbly enough, painted directly onto the whitewashed concrete walls of an empty building owned by the Port of London Authority in the Docklands, where in 1988 Hirst had helped to organize the seminal exhibition of his peers from Goldsmiths College, 'Freeze' – a legendary display that would prove instrumental in launching the YBAs.

Though the very first incarnations of Hirst's series were executed by his own hand, he soon saw the infinitely reproducible potential of his works as an opportunity to invoke the spirit of Andy Warhol's factory-style production and began allowing assistants to generate the paintings' prised-open pixelations. In 2009, Hirst permitted Banksy to 'deface' one of his spot paintings for the major display of the street artist's work, 'Banksy versus Bristol Museum'. Two years earlier, the pair had collaborated, if collaboration it might be called, in a similar manner for a piece that was auctioned to support AIDS charities in Africa. That work, *Keep it Spotless*, a spot painting onto which Banksy had super-imposed the image of a maid lifting the canvas's edge to sweep dust under it, sold for a jaw-dropping $1.8 million at Sotheby's New York in February 2008.

For his exhibition at the Bristol Museum in June 2009, Banksy took things in a different direction. Here, the superimposition onto Hirst's spots takes the shape of an oversized rat, Banksy's steadfast proxy, who wields a paint roller on a long pole and appears to be exterminating Hirst's spots with a fumigation of grey paint. That's one way of perceiving it, anyway. Another is to see the rat as a restorer of raw innocence, a rewinder of clocks, who takes us back in time to that moment just before the crude walls of the Port Authority were about to be painted white, just about to hold those first feracious spots from which so much would soon burst forth – to that instant just before the British art world changed.

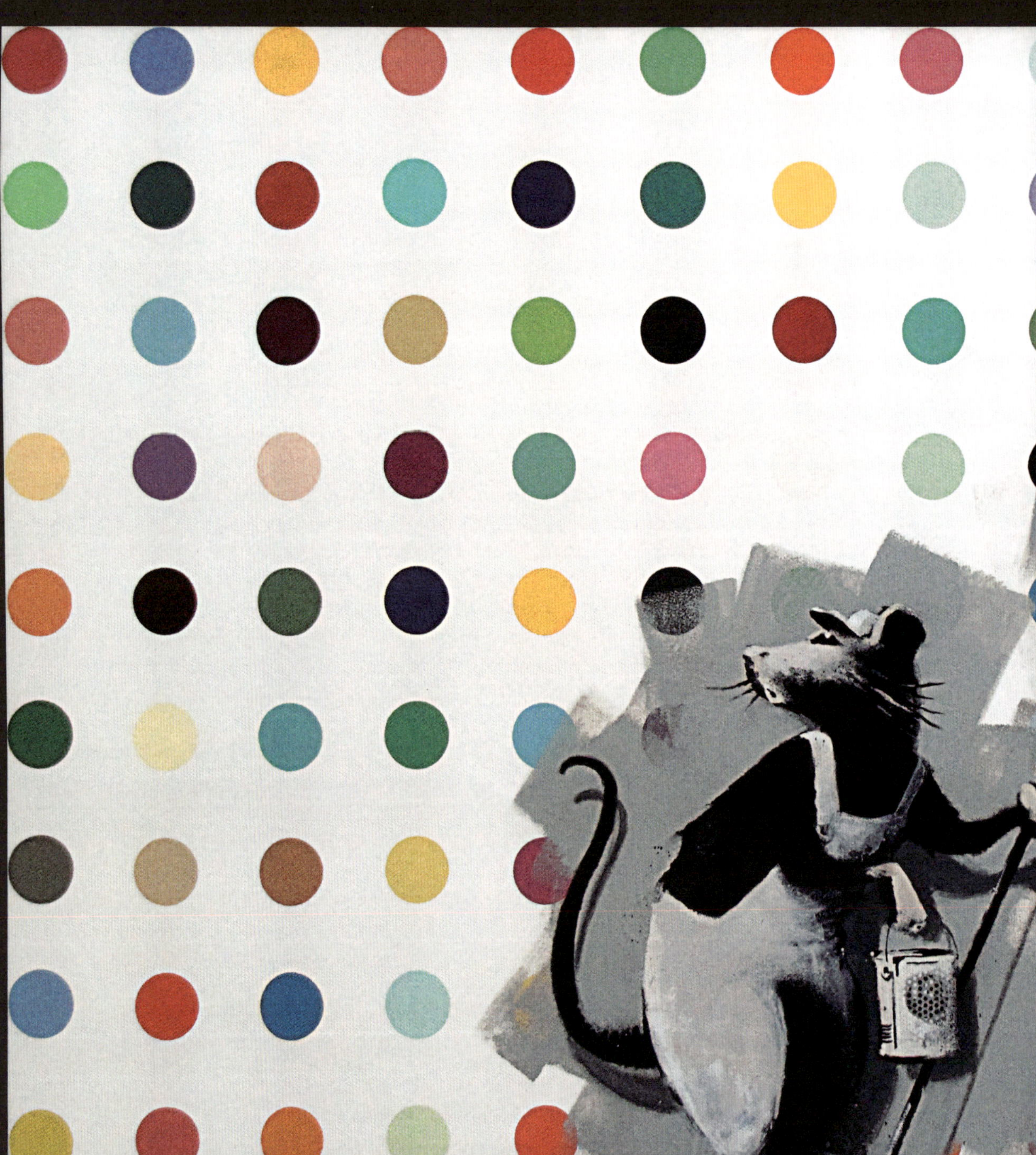

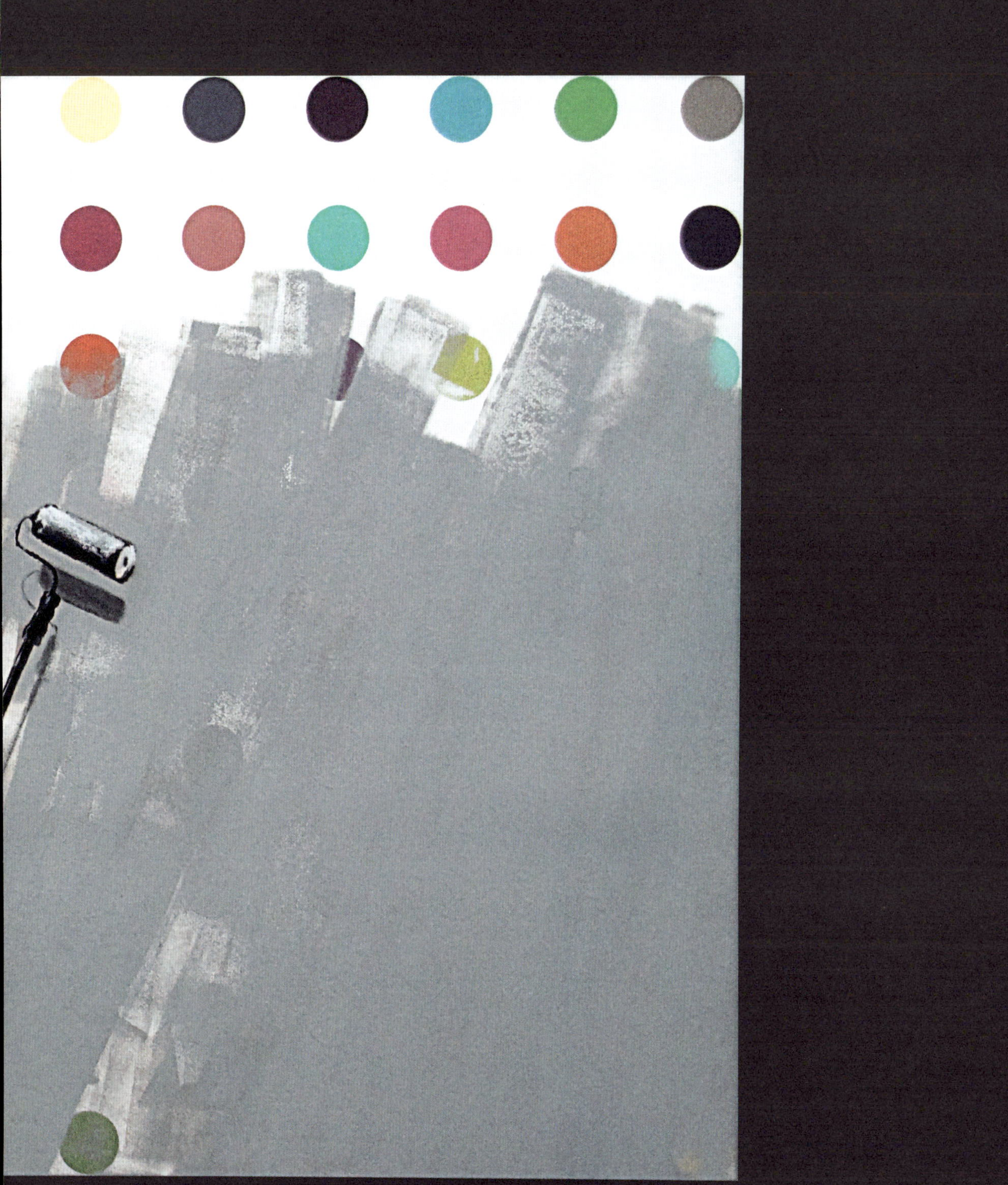

RAIN CHECK

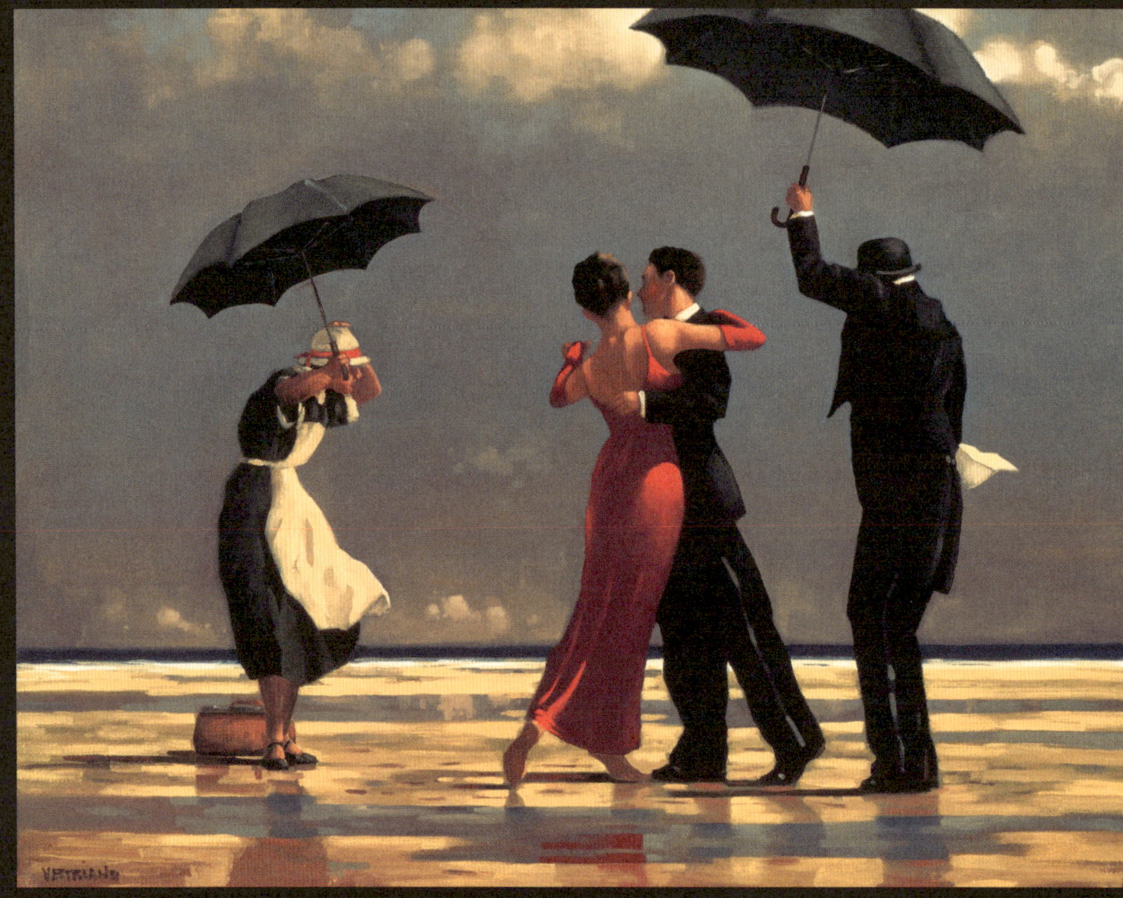

Jack Vettriano, *The Singing Butler*, 1991

W ho decides what is and isn't art? Who determines what we look at, treasure, and spend precious public resources preserving? Esteemed museum directors? Over-educated historians? Pretentious critics? You? Consider the case of Lot 169 of an auction devoted to the sale of Scottish paintings, which made international news when the hammer fell on 19 April 2004. The snippy headline that sat atop the article that ran in the British newspaper *The Guardian* the morning after the Sotheby's sale at the stately Hopetoun House, outside of Edinburgh, was indicative of the tone that the coverage took: 'Painting by ridiculed but popular artist sells for £744,800 [or $1.3 million]'. The striking sum fetched by Fife-born artist Jack Vettriano's cinematic canvas of a glamorous couple dancing on the glossy shore of a wind-swept beach, *The Singing Butler* (1991), following 'frenzied bidding'[40] by keen collectors, made it the most expensive painting ever sold in Scotland. Not a bad showing for a work by a self-taught artist whose entire oeuvre of sleek physiques posturing in sensual shadows has been brutally dismissed as 'toneless, textureless, brainless slick corpses of paintings'.[41]

Despite the remarkable popularity of Vettriano, who has been colloquially crowned 'the people's painter', and the ubiquity of cheap reproductions of his work on dorm-room posters and Christmas calendars, kitschy tea towels and mugs, his canvases are almost impossible to find on the walls of prestigious museums and galleries. While Vettriano, in style, subject and message, is by no means a street artist and the mentality of his works may seem at the furthest possible remove from that of Banksy's, the disconnection between his enthusiastic reception by ordinary people, on the one hand, and his derisive rejection by the art establishment, on the other, may have struck a nerve in Banksy, who has long assailed the hegemony of the pompous art world elite. Certainly Banksy's bold decision the year after *The Singing Butler* sold spectacularly at Hopetoun House to include an intriguing intervention into the headline-stealing painting in his exhibition 'Crude Oils' – thereby inserting Vettriano, when no one else would, into a conversation that included Monet and Van Gogh, Constable and Rembrandt – was itself a thumb in the eye of those who manipulate what we are allowed to see and admire. Nothing in Banksy's send-up of the popular painting, which removes the breeze-embattled maid on the left of the canvas to allow our gaze to reach a luxury liner that is slowly sinking in the distance and a pair of hazmat-suited figures in the middle distance, tangoing with a salvaged canister of toxic waste, suggests he has singled Vettriano out for extra scorn. While Banksy's oil-on-canvas work is often read as a comment on how the world waltzes on, oblivious to the damage it has inflicted on the earth, it is difficult not to see the image too as a statement on the toxicity of the art world generally and the landscape of looking it rigidly controls. The egregiously elegant pair at the centre of the work could easily be wealthy patrons at an expensive gala, helping grease the wheels of museums' out-of-step machine. Meanwhile, the rest of us, locked outside, blown about by life's winds, foist flimsy umbrellas against the gathering storm.

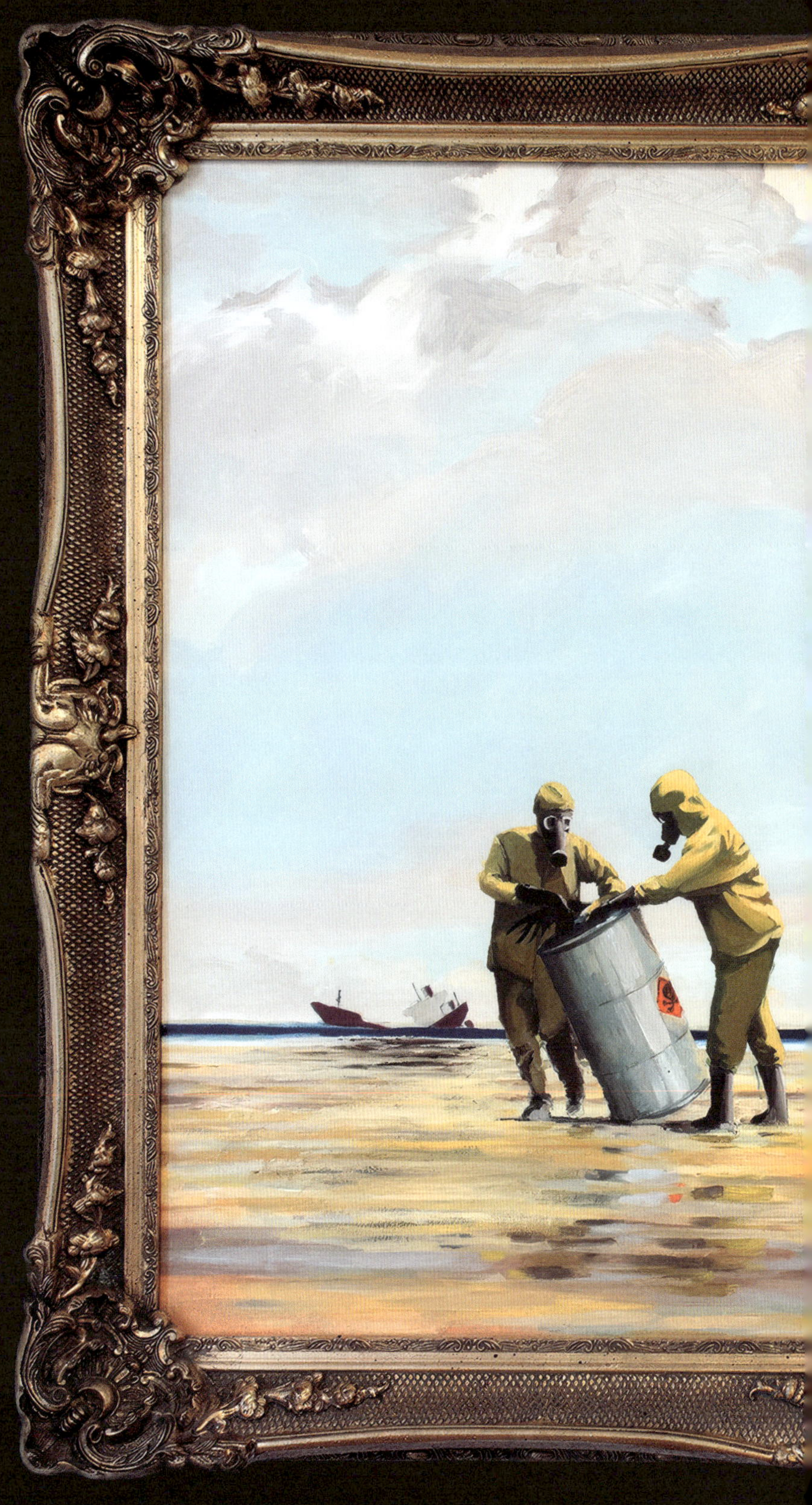

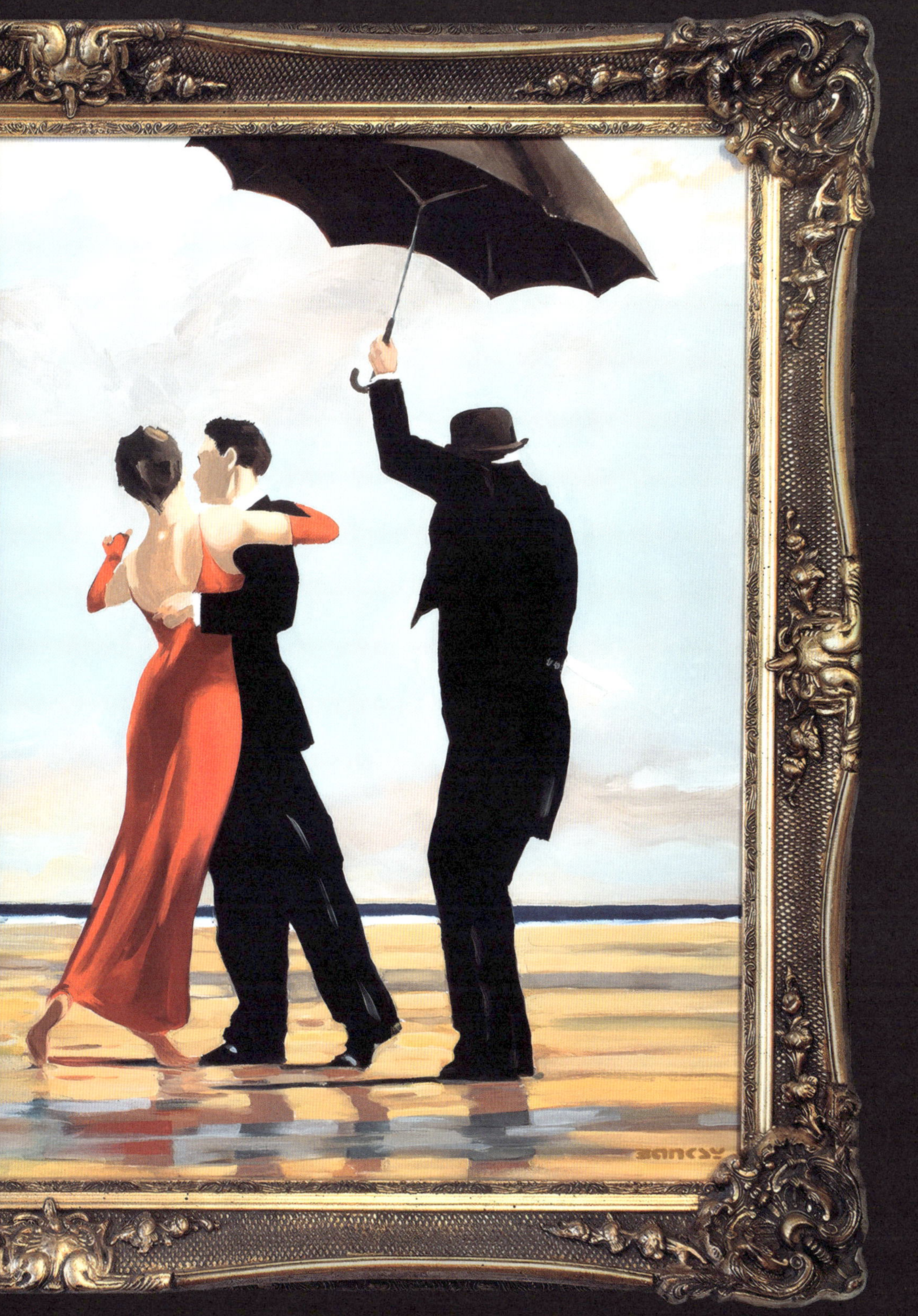

PAINT IT BLACK

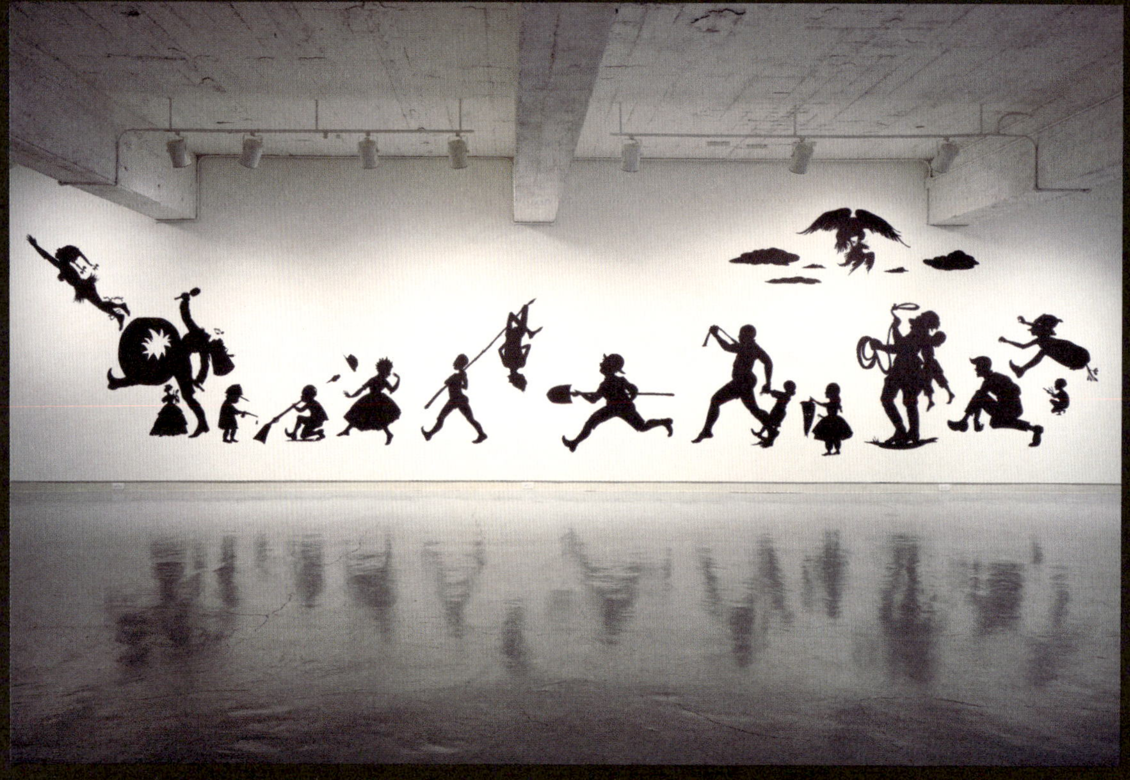

Kara Walker, *Virginia Lynch Mob*, 1998

Nothing is ever simple. Especially simple things. Take, for example, silhouettes. At first blush, the whispery word seems ideally suited to that sparest of art forms: pared-back profiles in purest black against pristine white backgrounds. Probe a little deeper, however, and the seemingly straightforward tradition of image-making vibrates with surprising complexity. The term itself is a one-word paradoxical poem. Basque in origin, it is thought to be related to the name 'Zuloeta', which is comprised of the prefix 'zulo', meaning 'hole' and the suffix '-eta', meaning 'abundance'. A silhouette is literally an abundance of nothing. But enticing etymology has little to do with how the technique actually got its name, or why it resonates so profoundly in the work of Banksy.

Though examples of silhouettes in art history stretch back at least to antiquity, it wasn't until the 18th and 19th centuries that the technique really took off. The frugality of the form – cut-outs of profiles cast by candlelight against a sheet of paper, an evocative craft that even people of modest means could undertake – found itself inextricably caught up in the politics of the moment. When the French Controller-General, Étienne de Silhouette, began implementing a programme of strict economic austerity after taking office in 1759, his name quickly became synonymous with all things cost-cutting. As it happens, it was to the making of cheap, shadowy portraits, snipped in dim light, that the sneer really stuck, henceforth and forever thereafter inflecting 'silhouettes' with political and economic protest.

In our own era, the complex simplicities of the silhouette have invigorated the imaginations of several artists, from Canadian Kristi Malakoff to South African William Kentridge, from Japanese-born Kumi Yamashita, to Banksy himself – creators whose works carry a rich cultural resonance that belies the monochromaticity of their making. In the hands of African–American artist Kara Walker, who has been fascinated with the form since the early 1990s, the silhouette has exploded beyond the conventional and circumscribed perimeters and parameters of humble busts staring askance into a white void. Her powerful panoramic friezes explore the corrosive legacy of slavery on contemporary consciousness, compressing centuries of complex abuse into deceptively spare, black-and-white narratives.

In March 2018, on a return visit to New York where, five years earlier, he had completed a month-long residency, Banksy unveiled a mural in Coney Island Avenue in Brooklyn, whose disquieting drama unfolded with a violent verve reminiscent of Walker's sprawling friezes. Scurrying forward in apparent fear, a group of random citizens, young and old – one carrying a child, another a walking stick – is whipped into action by a man in a suit – perhaps a property-site developer, judging from his hard hat. To intensify the scene and transform it into something truly archetypal, Banksy has replaced the shadowy whip wielded by the man with the soaring trend-line of a financial forecast, making it clear that greed motivates the panic. More than a mere wisecrack, Banksy's blood red whip echoes the dispiriting reality that for most people who propel economic booms, the profits seen from rising revenues are disproportionately paltry – an abundance of nothing.

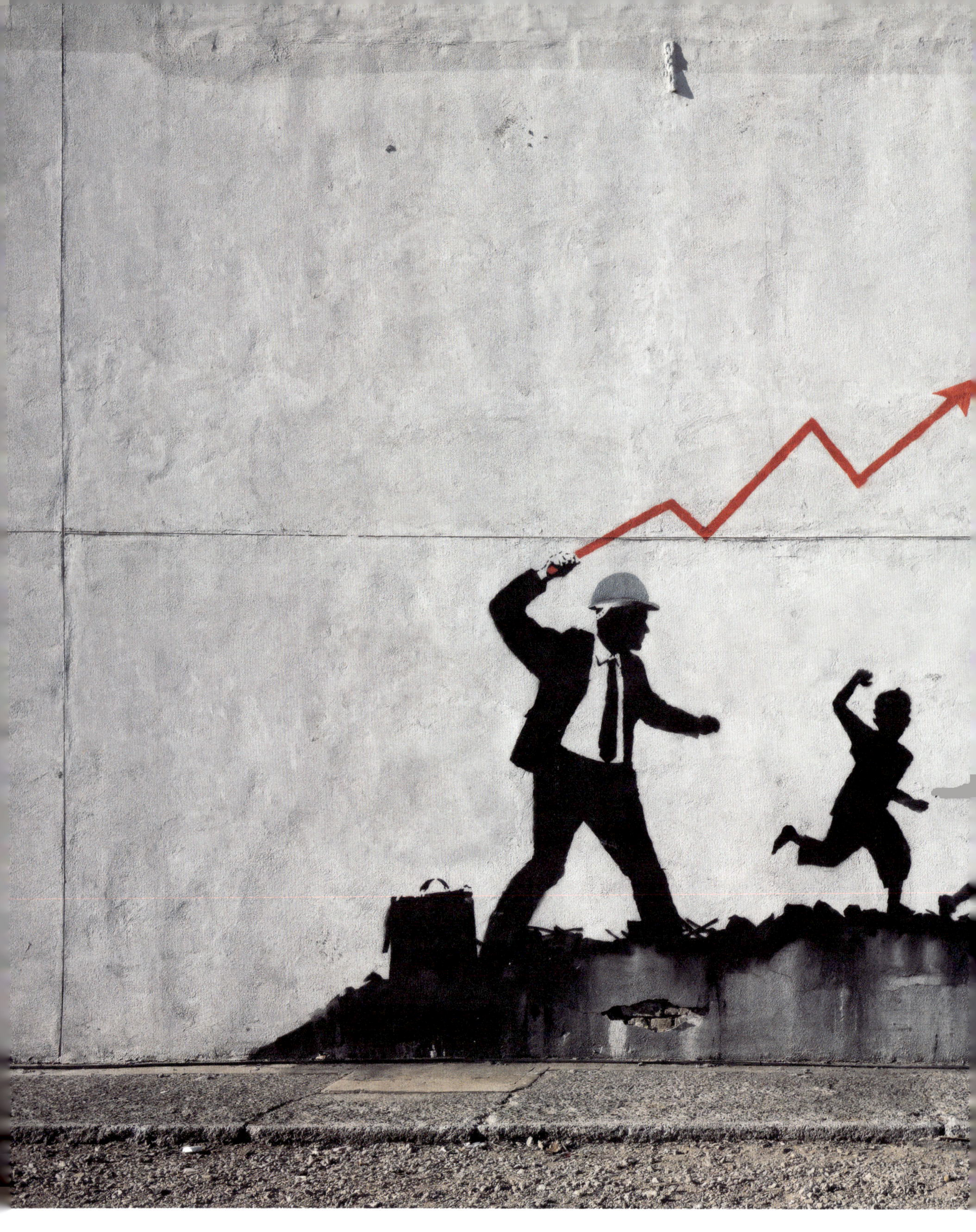

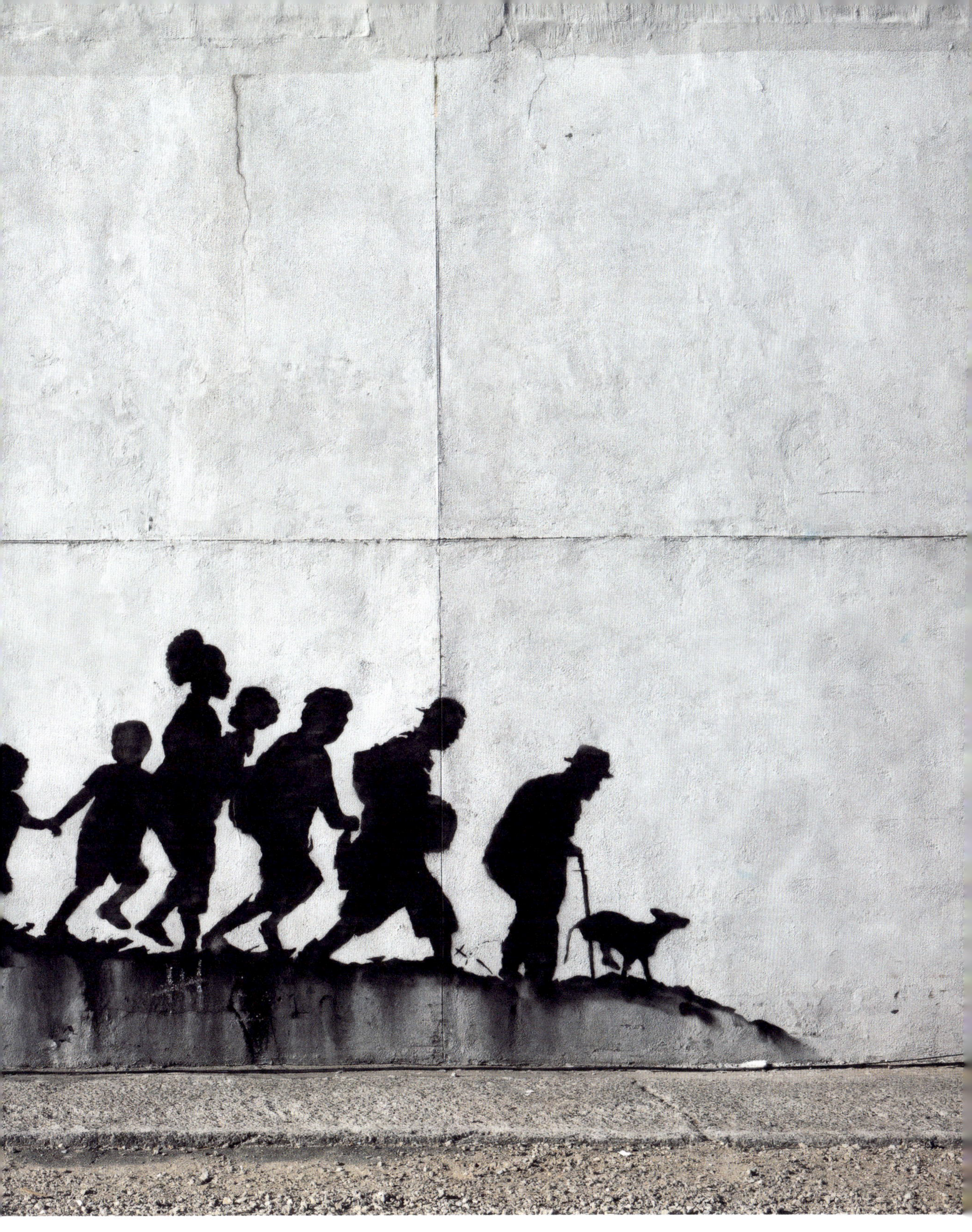

Brooklyn, New York, 2018

NOTHING TO SEE HERE

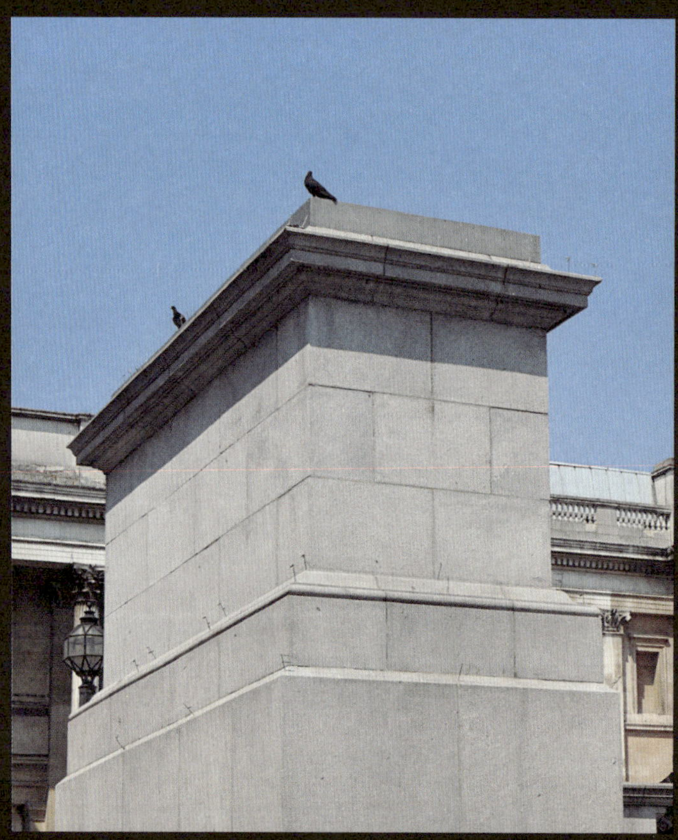

The empty Fourth Plinth in Trafalgar Square

Since 1999, one of the four plinths that rise in each of the corners of Trafalgar Square, overlooked by the National Gallery of London from the north, has played a unique role in showcasing the very essence of the art of our age by permanently elevating nothing at all. Where the three stone pedestals in the northeastern, southwestern and southeastern corners of the sprawling plaza have long been occupied by statues of military and regal figures of the sort that one expects to find overseeing a civic space, the northwestern plinth had stood conspicuously bare for a century and a half, ever since the square was opened to the public in 1844. It wasn't supposed to be that way. Plans for an imposing equestrian statue of King William IV were perennially postponed due to a chronic lack of funds to complete the project. After much deliberation in the 1990s, including the launch of an official commission seeking suggestions from prominent curators and critics, it was decided in 1998 that the plinth should, in fact, remain empty but for the occasional display of works by contemporary artists.

There is something sweetly philosophical, of course, about preserving at the heart of a thrumming metropolis a recurring emptiness as a subject on which to pause and meditate amid the cacophonies of city life – the jubilant celebrations and defiant protests, the riotous rustle of brollies and prams and pigeon wings. Something soulfully mindful, if a pinch postmodern. Something, shall we say, pompously pretentious. I mean, seriously. Surely there is some morally dubious historical figure with an appallingly exploitative past that we can all agree deserves to be eternally effigied in bronze and placed on a pedestal to sneer down at us snobbishly from on high?

The 'Fourth Plinth' does not represent the first occasion on which the art world has stood enraptured by the nothing that is not there and the nothing that is – an absurdity that Banksy seems to be mocking in his mural *Art Buff*, which appeared on a street wall in Folkestone, England, in 2014. In 1960, Italian conceptual artist Piero Manzoni dared his collectors to take an interest in a small rubber balloon (they could choose between red, white or blue) that he had blown up himself and tethered with a short string to a wooden base with two lead seals. Affixed to the pedestal is a small bronze plaque that reads 'PIERO MANZONI / Fiato d'artista [The Artist's Breath]'. It didn't take long, of course, before the balloon deflated, as balloons predictably do, and buyers were left, like the old lady in Banksy's mural, squinting to see something that has slipped away – dissipated into thin air if not actually painted over. It is thought that Manzoni succeeded in selling over a dozen copies of the work that, he claimed, would preserve his very essence. 'When I blow up a balloon', he insisted, 'I am breathing my soul into an object that becomes eternal.'[42] And how much, exactly, was his soul worth? 200 lire per litre, apparently. That is what he had previously charged collectors who hired him to blow up a flaccid balloon that he had placed in a box for an earlier work he called *Bodies of Air*. (If you think Manzoni was taking the piss, you might be right. In 1961, he released a line of shop-ready tins filled with his own excrement that he nattily labelled in four languages 'Artist's Shit'.) Banksy's mural, like Manzoni's piece before it, challenges us to consider whether, when we place a work on a pedestal, there is really anything there at all.

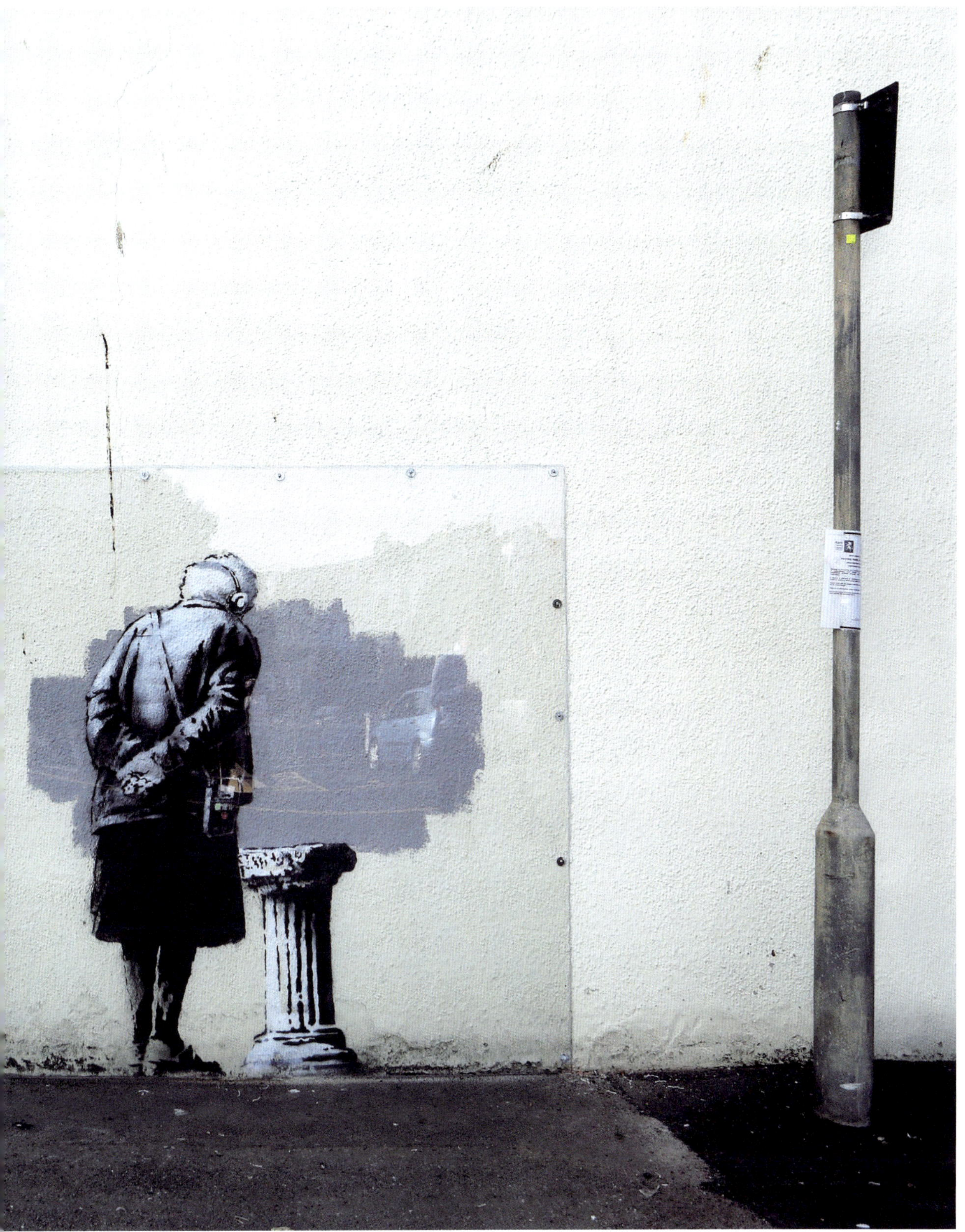

Folkestone, 2014

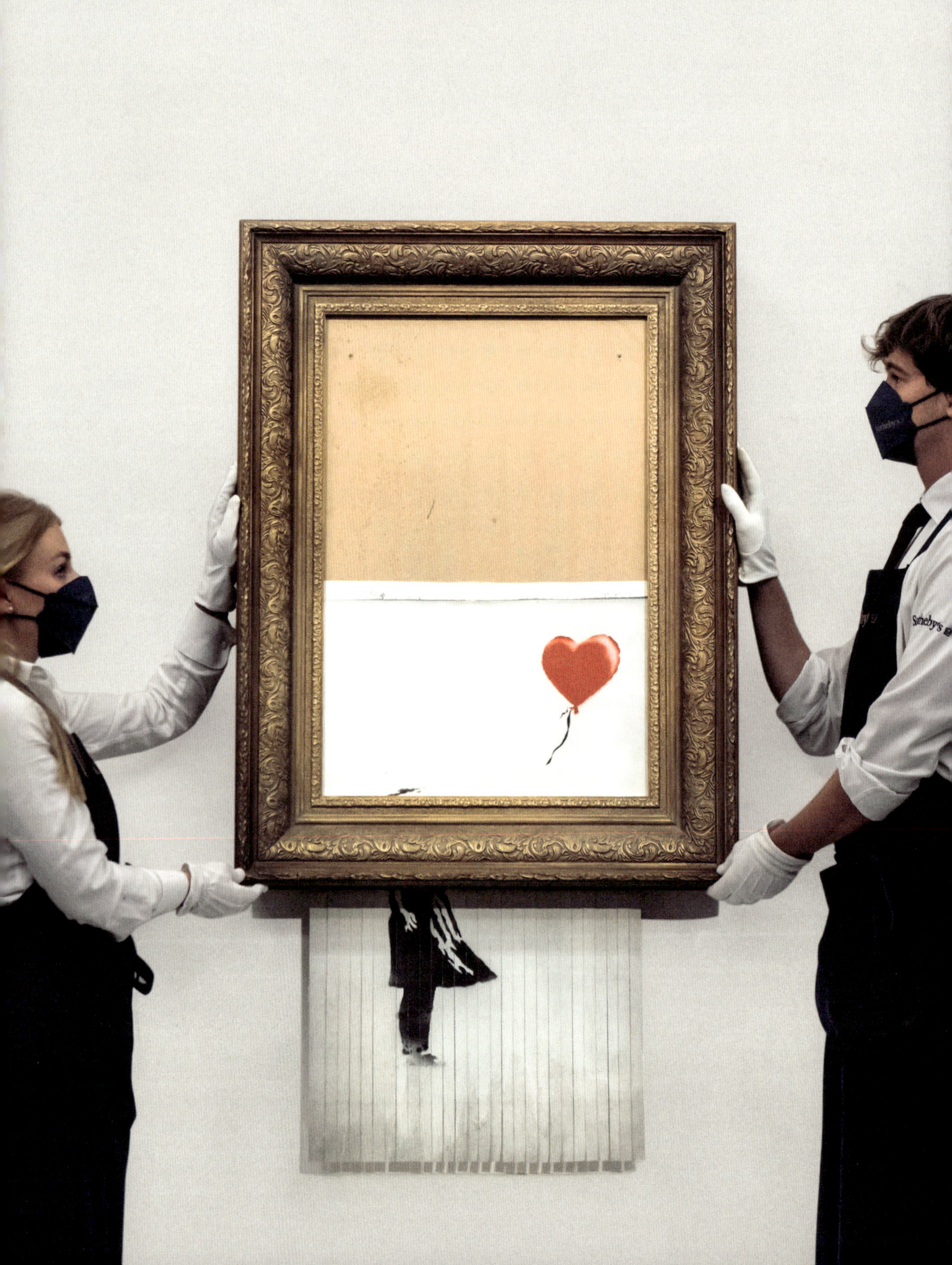

CHRONOLOGY OF BANKSY WORKS

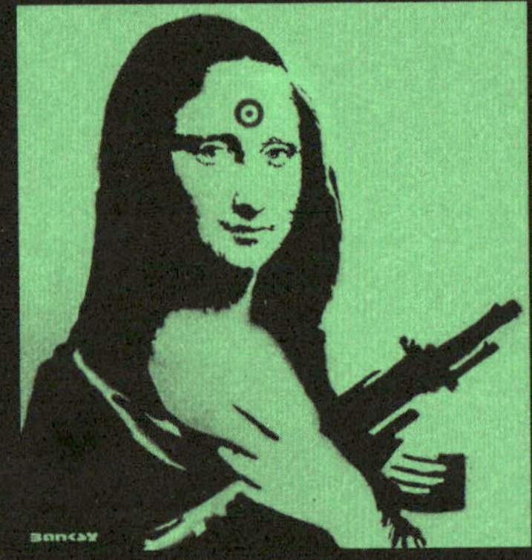

Mona Lisa with AK47, 2000

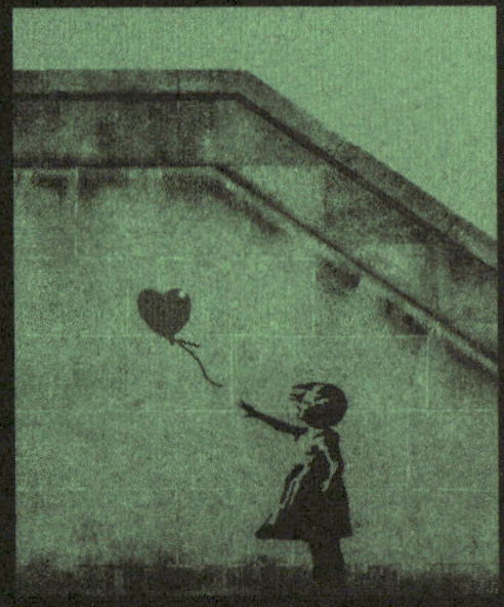

Waterloo Bridge, South Bank,
London, 2002

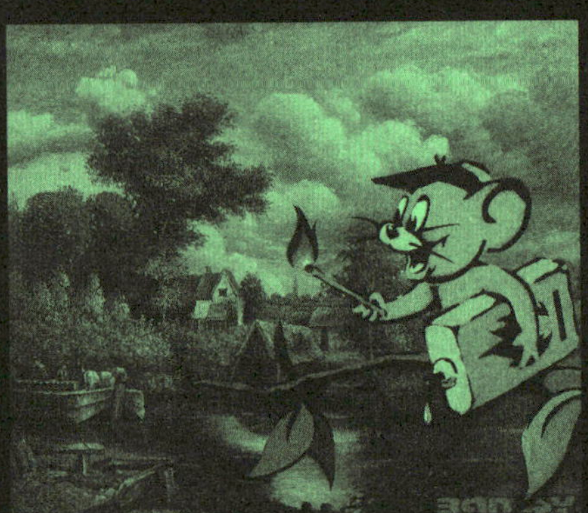

Crude Oil Jerry, 2003

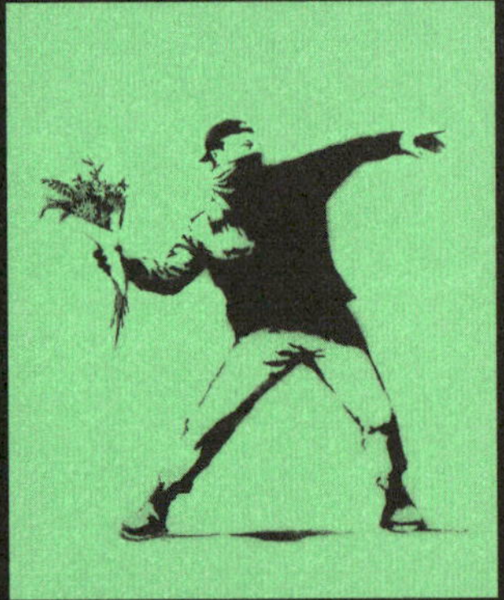

Love is in the Air, 2003

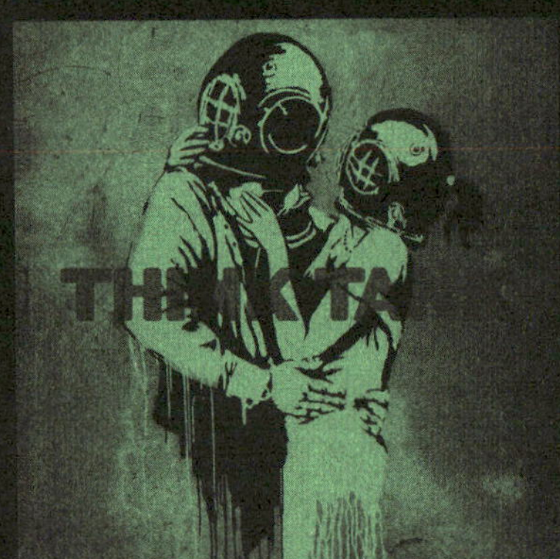

Think Tank, 2003

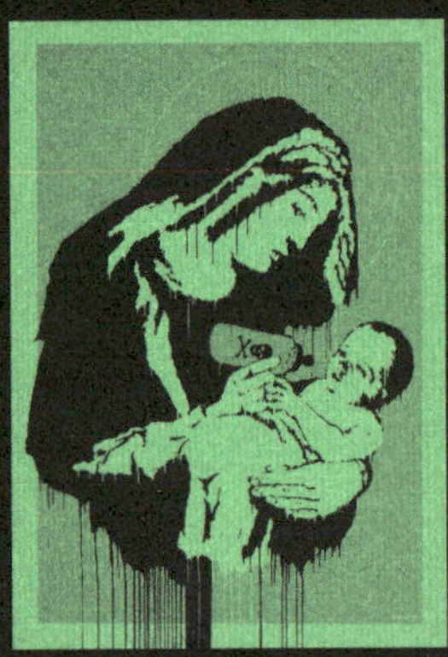

Toxic Mary, 2003

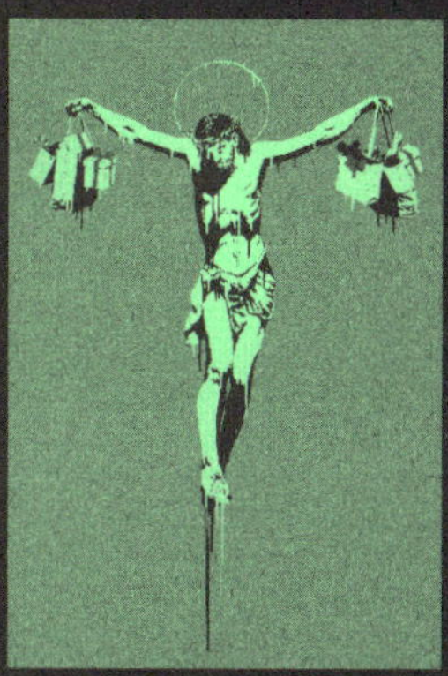

Christ with Shopping Bags, 2004

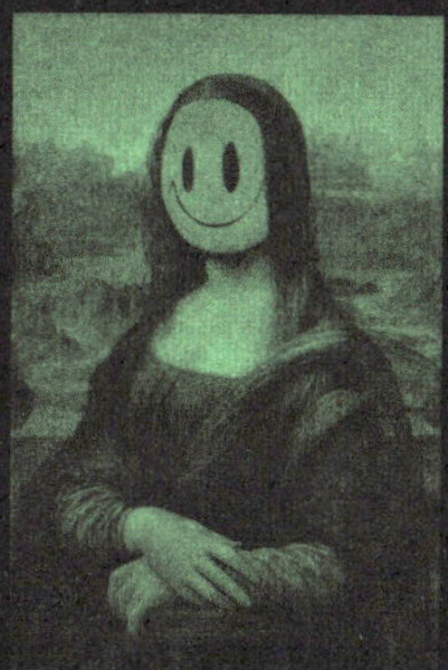

Mona Lisa Smile, 2004

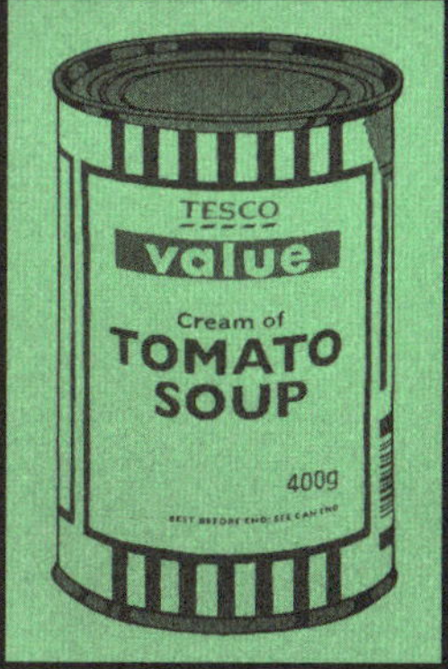

Tesco Value Soup Can, 2004

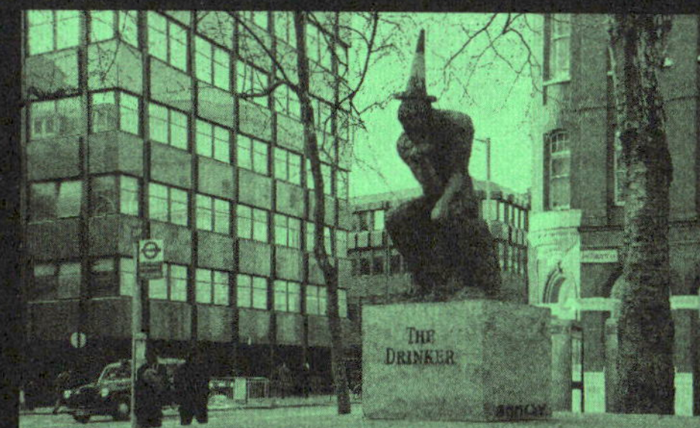

The Drinker, 2004

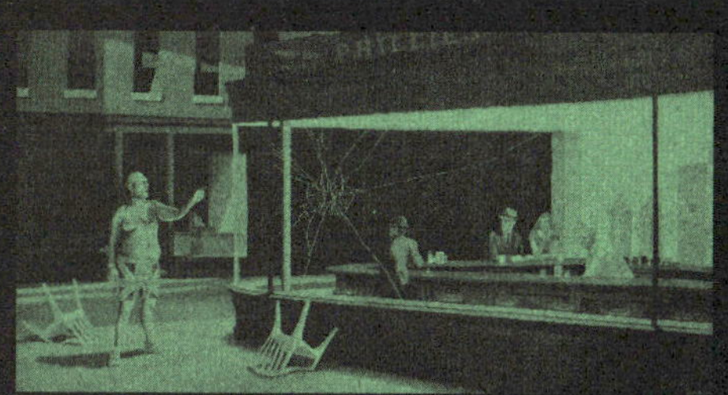

Are You Still Using That Chair?, 2005

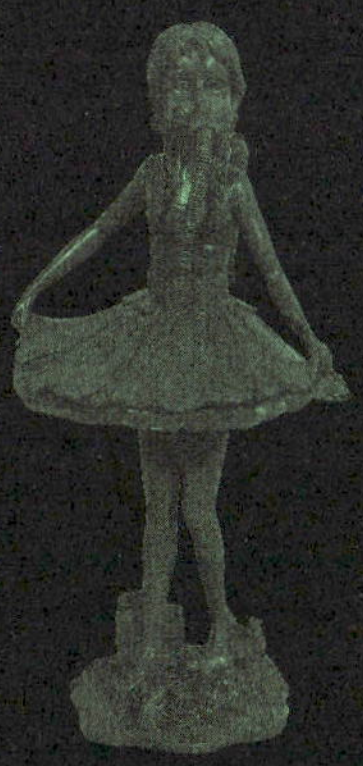

Ballerina with Action Man Parts, 2005

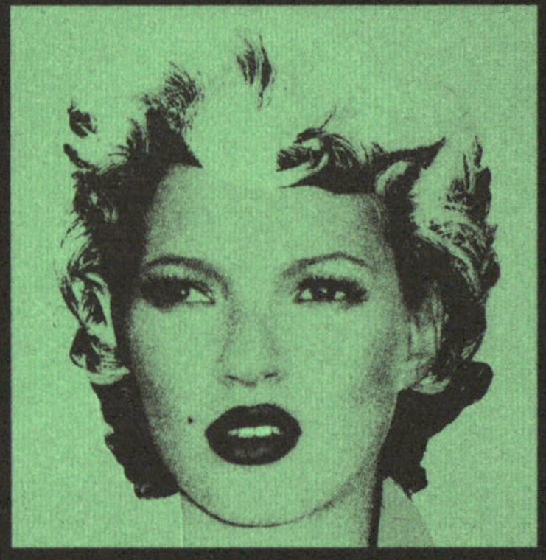

Kate Moss, 2005

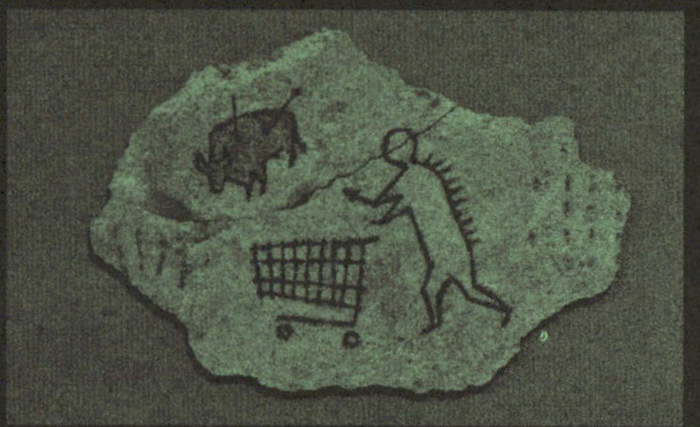

Peckham Rock, retitled *Wall Art*, 2005

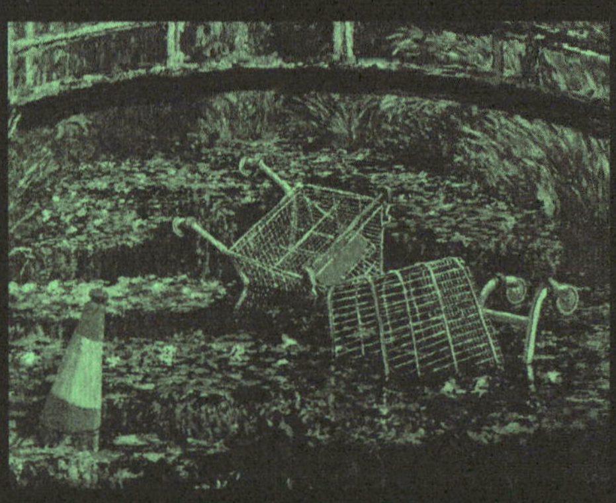

Show Me the Monet, 2005

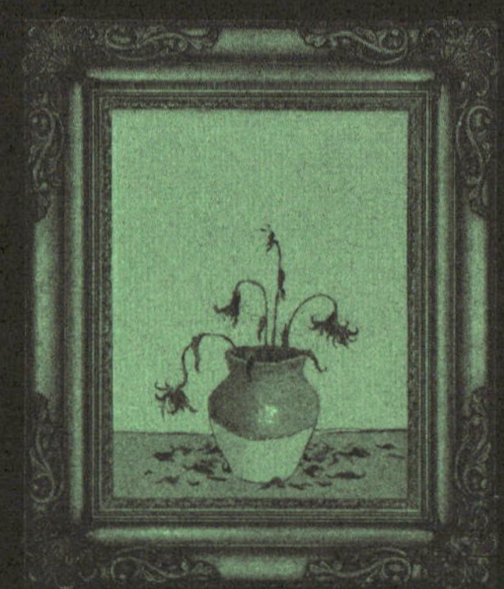

Sunflowers from Petrol Station, 2005

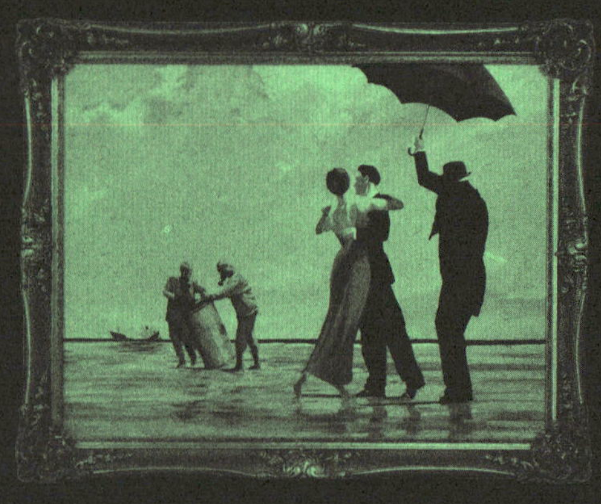

Toxic Beach, 2005

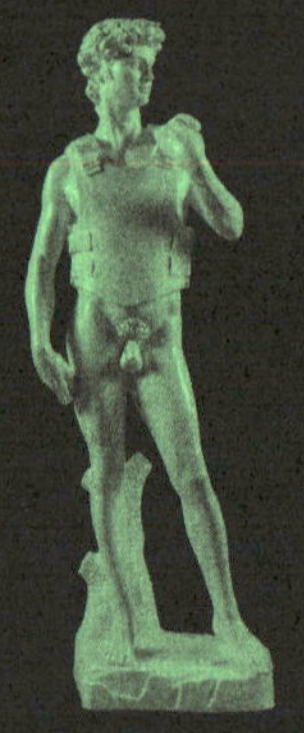

Bullet-Proof David, 2006

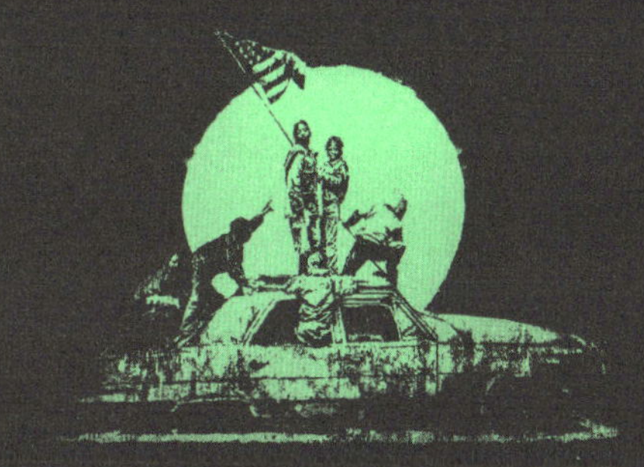

Flag, 2006

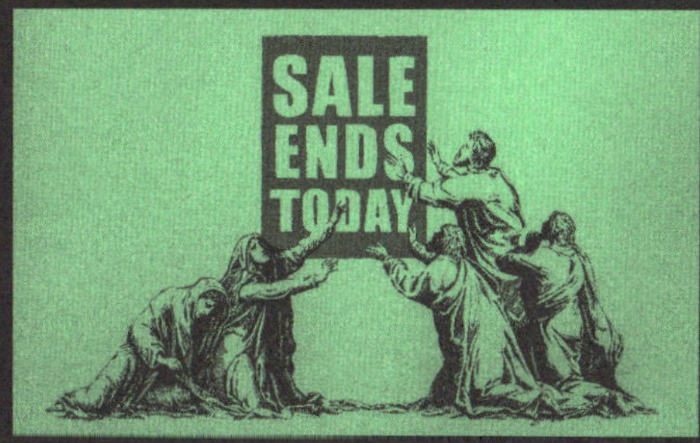

Sale Ends Today, 2006

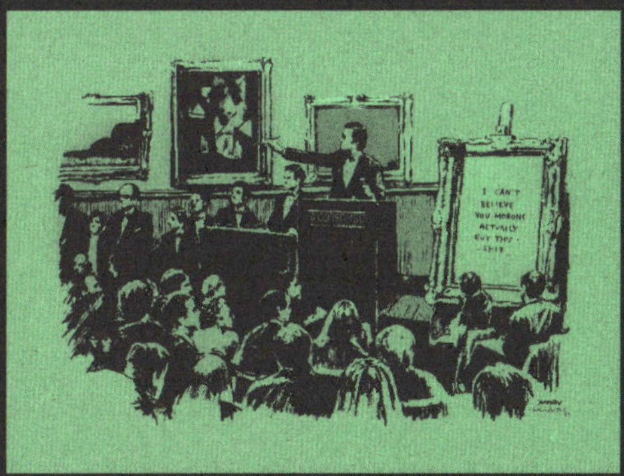

Morons, 2007

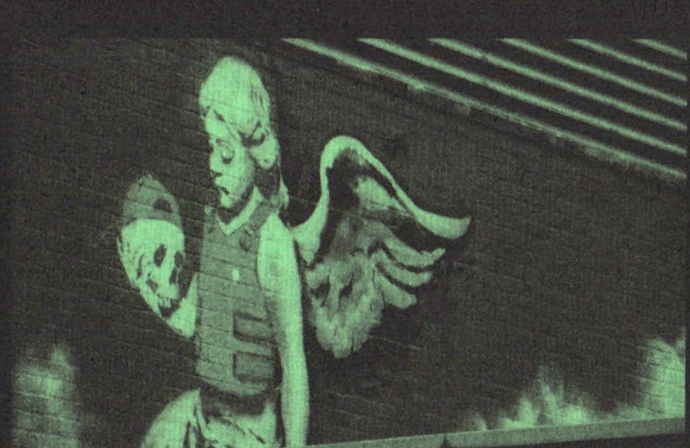

Shoreditch, London, 2007

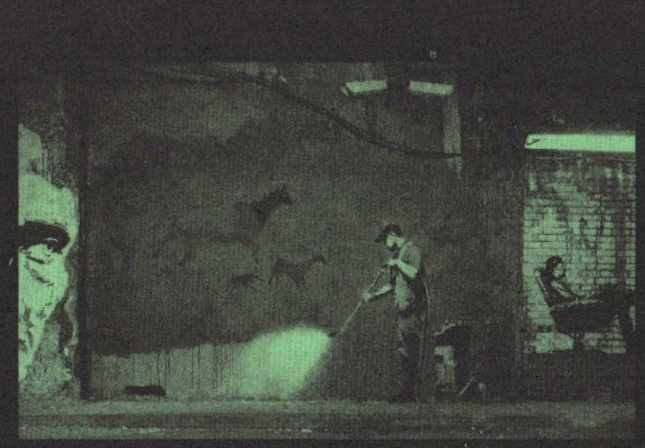

South Bank, London, 2008

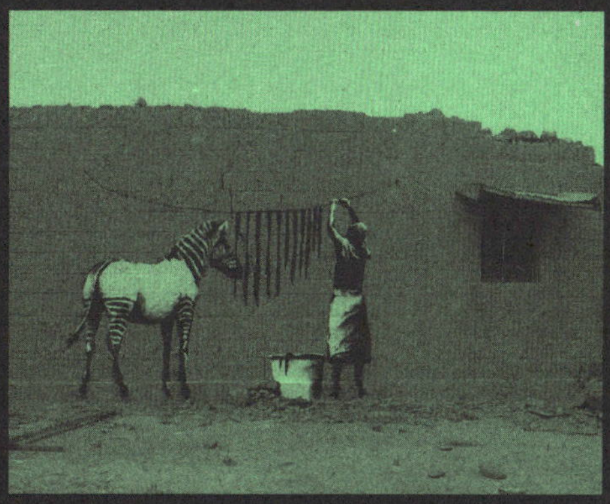

Timbuktu, 2008

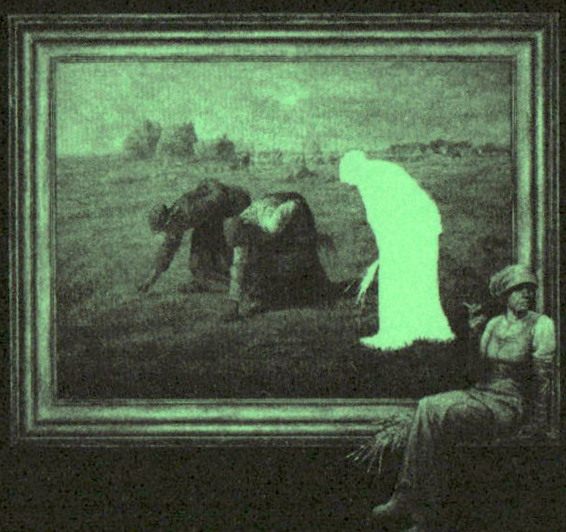

Agency Job, 2009

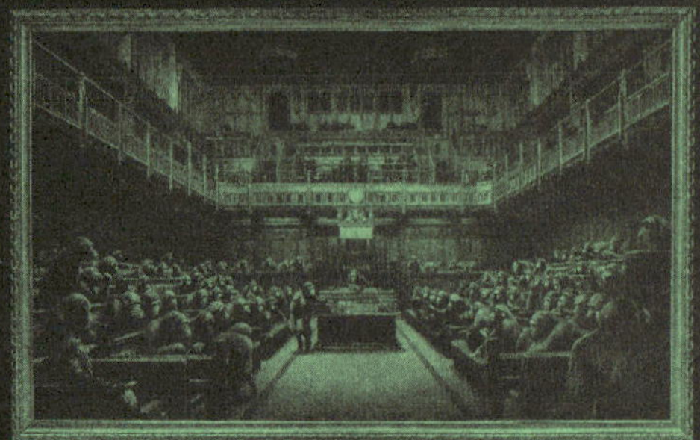

Devolved Parliament, 2009

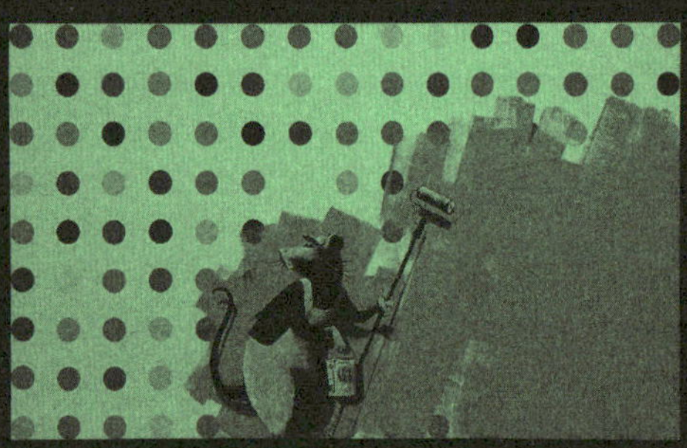

Rat with Roller on Spot Painting, 2009

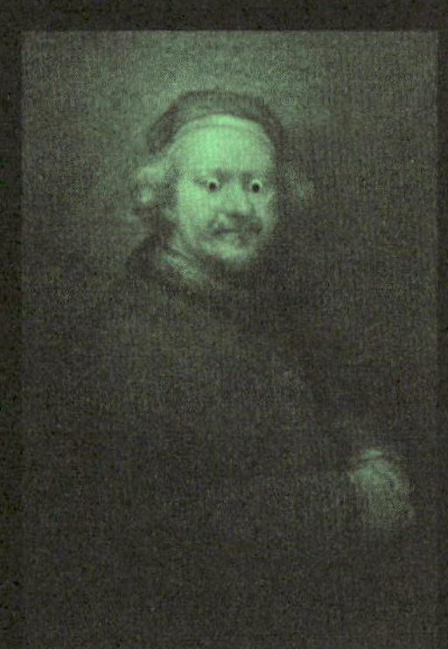

Rembrandt, 2009

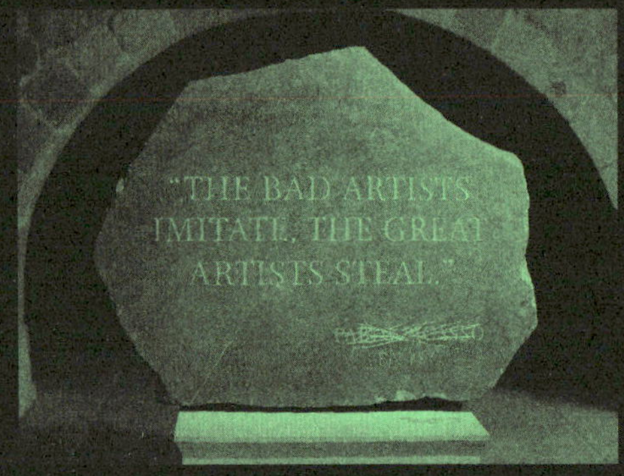

The Bad Artists Imitate, 2009

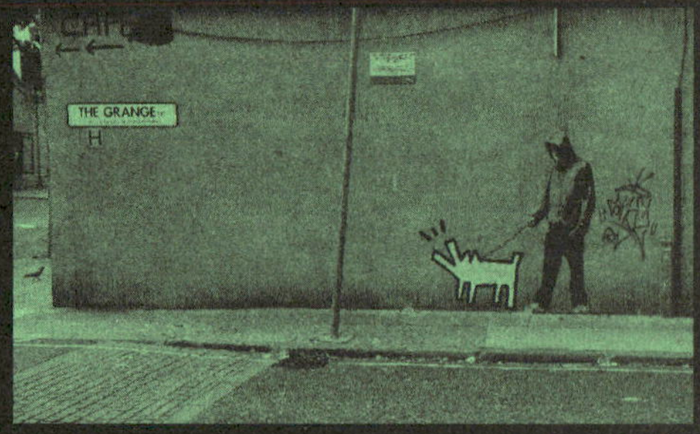

Bermondsey, London, 2010

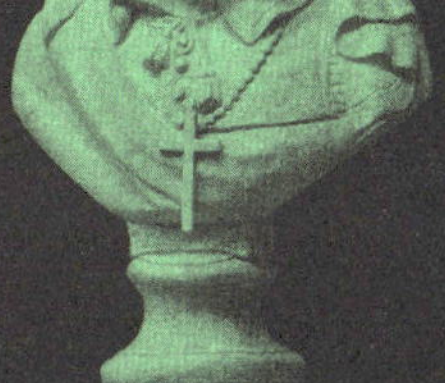

Cardinal Sin, 2011

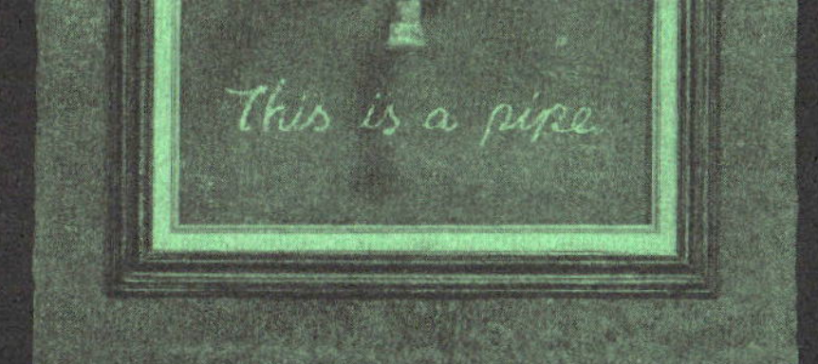

This is A Pipe, 2011

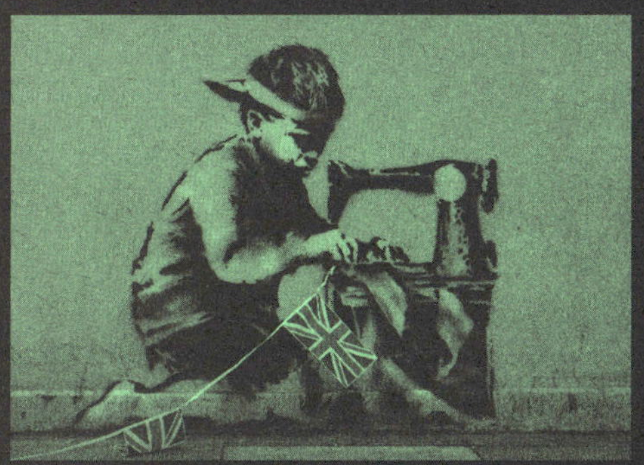

Wood Green, London, 2012

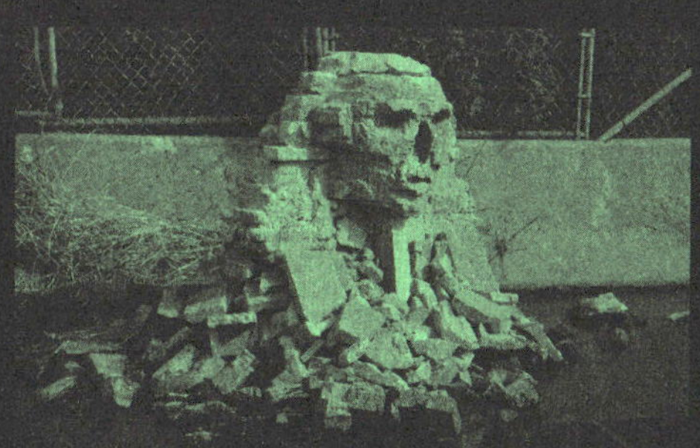

Everything but the Kitchen Sphinx, 2013

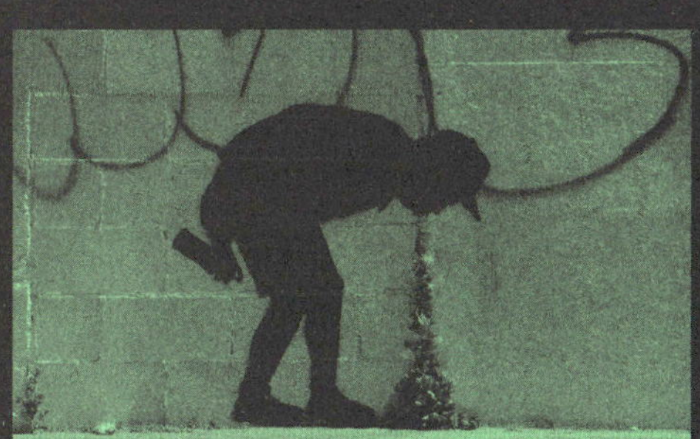

New York, 2013

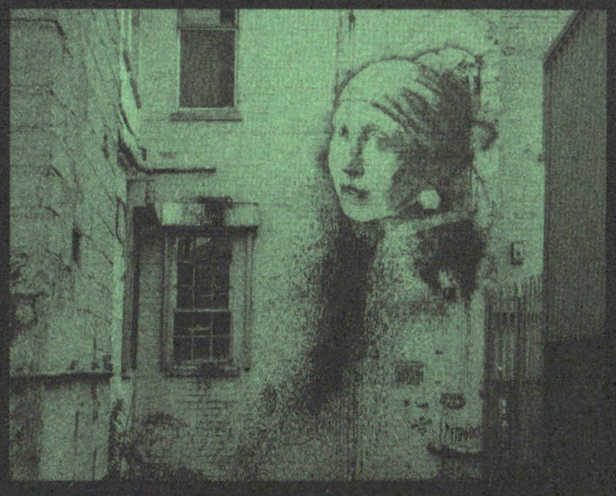

Bristol, 2014

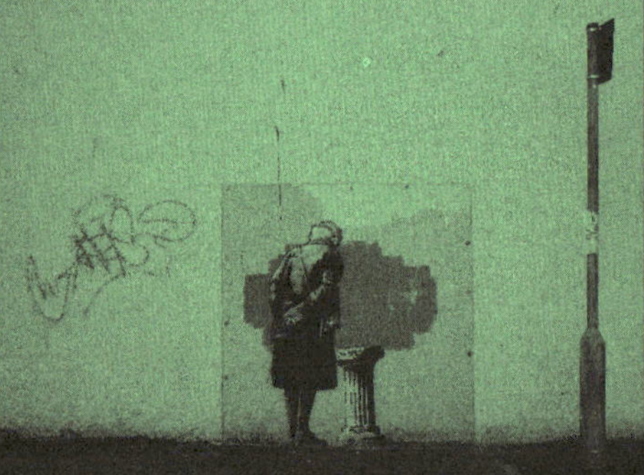

Folkestone, 2014

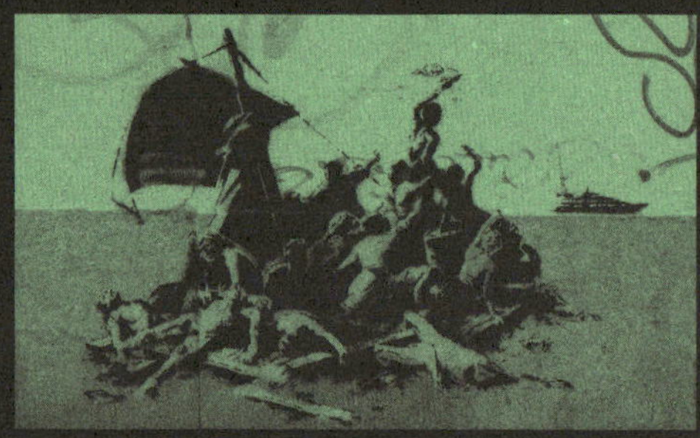

Calais, 2015

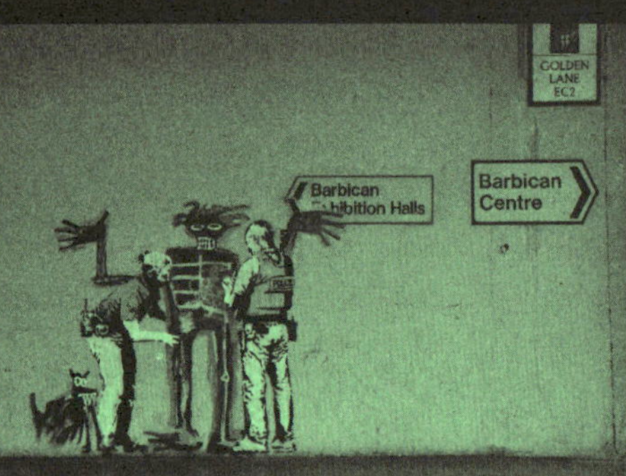

Barbican, London, 2017

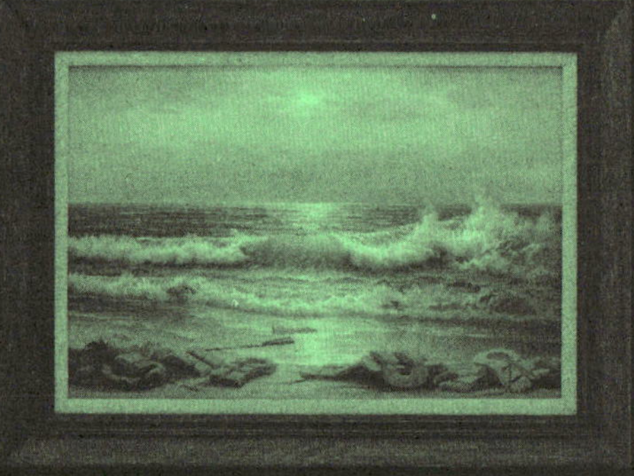

Mediterranean Sea View, 2017

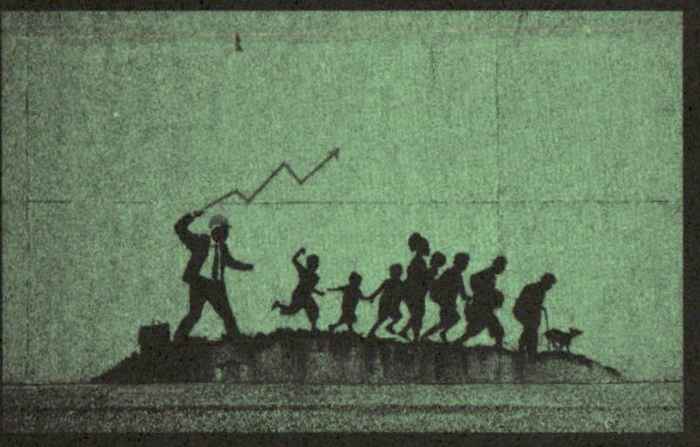

Brooklyn, New York, 2018

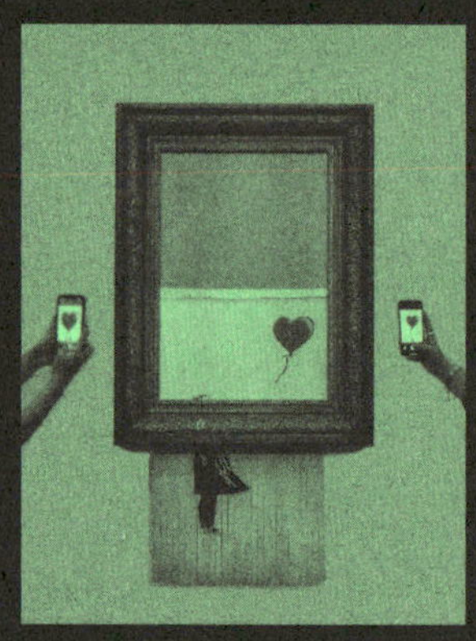

Love is in The Bin, 2018

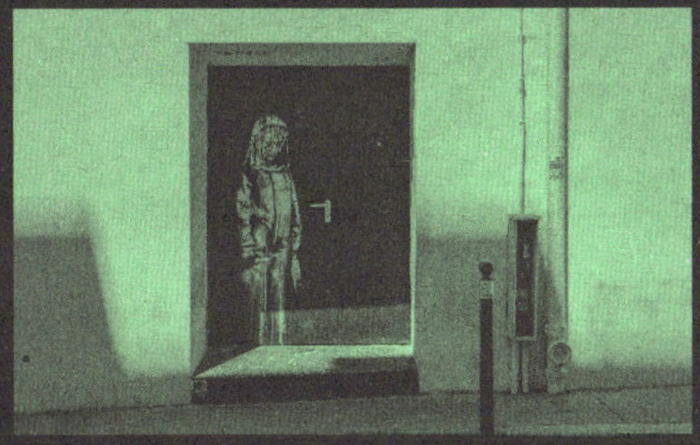

Bataclan theatre, Paris, 2018

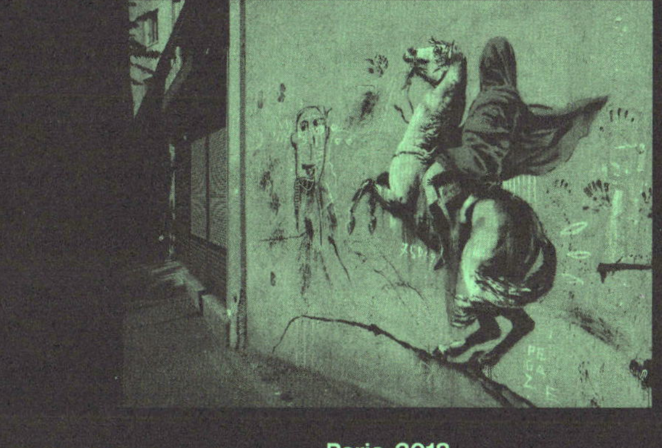

Paris, 2018

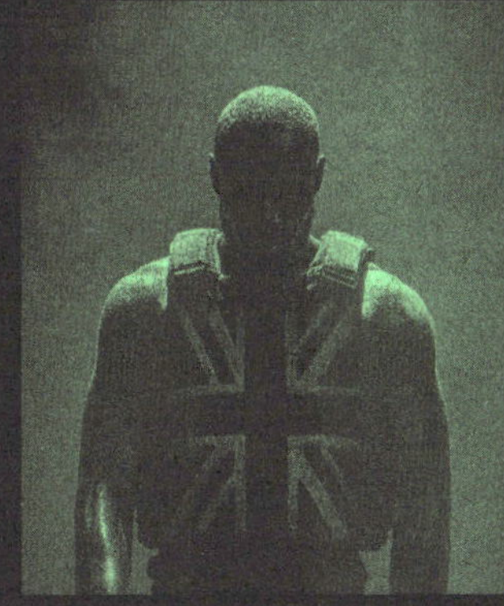

Stab-proof vest designed by Banksy
for Stormzy's headline performance at
Glastonbury, 2019

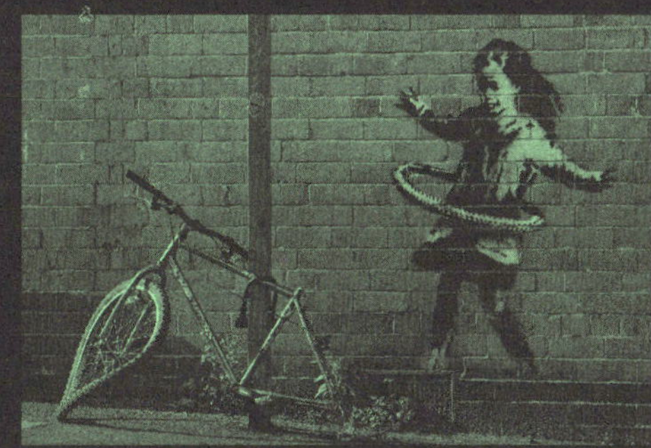

Nottingham, 2020

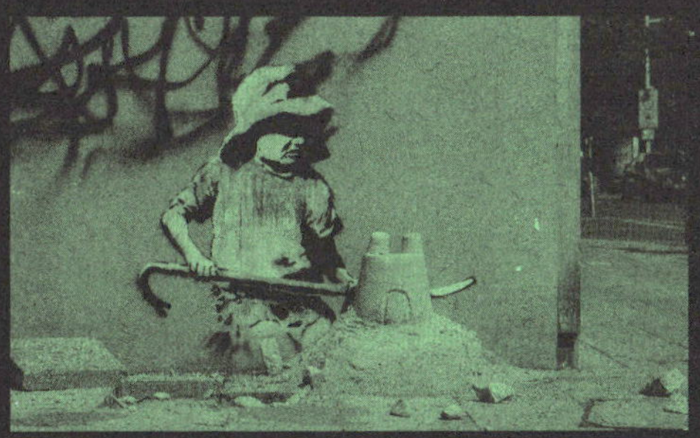

Lowestoft, 2021

ENDNOTES

1 Originally featured on Banksy's official website. Quoted in Cameron McAuliffe & Kurt Iveson, 'Art and Crime (and Other Things Besides …): Conceptualising Graffiti in the City'. *Geography Compass* 2011 (5), p. 130.

2 Rudolf Arnheim, *To the Rescue of Art*. United Kingdom, University of California Press, 1991, p. 10.

3 Arthur Danto, 'The End of Art', in *The Philosophical Disenfranchisement of Art*. United States, Columbia University Press, 1986.

4 Miroslava Hajek et al., *Bruno Munari: My Futurist Past*. Italy, Silvana, 2012, p. 21.

5 Francis Fukuyama, *The End of History and the Last Man*. Spain, Free Press, 1992.

6 For a fuller analysis of how works leave traces on works that came before them in a literary context, see my article 'Keats and the Holocaust: Notes Towards a Post-Temporalism'. *Literature and Theology*, 2003, 17(4), pp. 361–73.

7 Denise Murrell, *Posing Modernity: The Black Model from Manet and Matisse to Today*. United States, Yale University Press, 2018.

8 Quoted in Peter Brooks, *Body Work: Objects of Desire in Modern Narrative*. United States, Harvard University Press, 1993, p. 132.

9 Banksy, *Wall and Piece*. Germany, Random House UK, 2006, p. 13.

10 Waldemar Januszczak, 'Blek le Rat, the man who gave birth to Banksy'. *The Sunday Times*, 8 June 2008.

11 Quoted in Matilda Battersby, 'Blek le Rat: Streetwriting Man'. *The Independent*, 25 April 2012.

12 Interview with AJ Schnack, 'Banksy (Yes, Banksy) on Thierry, *EXIT* Skepticism & Documentary Filmmaking as Punk.' edendale.typepad.com/weblog 21 December, 2010.

13 Banksy, *Wall and Piece*. Germany, Random House UK, 2006, p. 170.

14 Albert Bigelow Paine, *Mark Twain, A Biography: The Personal and Literary Life of Samuel Langhorne Clemens*. United States, Harper, 1912, p. 112.

15 Thomas Stearns Eliot, *The Sacred Wood: Essays on Poetry and Criticism*. United Kingdom, Methuen & Company Limited, 1920, p. 114.

16 Tom Hockenhull, quoted in Mark Brown, 'Ian Hislop picks Banksy hoax for British Museum dissent show'. *The Guardian*, 16 May 2018.

17 L. Dickens, 'Placing post-graffiti: the journey of the Peckham Rock'. *Cultural Geographies*, 2008, 15(4), p. 472.

18 Giorgio Vasari, *The Lives of the Artists*, translated by Julia Conway Bondanella and Peter Bondanella. United Kingdom, Oxford University Press, 1998, p. 428.

19 Ibid., p. 427.

20 Darren R. Flower, *Bioinformatics for Immunomics*. The Netherlands, Springer New York, 2010, p. 15.

21 Banksy, *Wall and Piece*. Germany, Random House UK, 2006, p. 204.

22 Richard Dawkins, *A Devil's Chaplain: Reflections on Hope, Lies, Science, and Love*. United States, Houghton Mifflin Harcourt, 2004, p. 158.

23 Steve DiPaola, Caitlin Riebe and James T. Enns, 'Rembrandt's Textural Agency: A Shared Perspective in Visual Art and Science'. *Leonardo*, 2010, 43 (2), pp. 145–51.

24 Stacy Schiff, 'Know It All'. *The New Yorker*, 23 July 2006, p. 43.

25 Antoine-Clair Thibaudeau, *Histoire générale de Napoléon Bonaparte*. France, Ponthieu & Comp., 1828, p. 330.

26 Oscar Wilde, *The Happy Prince and Other Stories*. United Kingdom, Pan Macmillan, 2008, p. 75.

27 Penelope Jackson, *The Art of Copying Art*. Switzerland, Springer International Publishing, 2022, pp. 124–25.

28 J. K. Smith and L. F. Smith, 'Spending Time on Art' *Empirical Studies of the Arts*, 2001, 19(2), pp. 229–36.

29 Quoted in Millet Bacou, *One Hundred Drawings*, translated by James Emmons. United States, Harper & Row, 1975, p. 12.

30 For Degas's severe treatment of his models see Jill Devonyar et al., *Degas and the Dance*. United Kingdom, Harry N. Abrams, 2006.

31 Sue Roe, *The Private Lives of the Impressionists*. United Kingdom, Vintage, 2007, p. 183.

32 Letter to Vincent's sister, 19 February 1890, in Vincent van Gogh, *Ever Yours: the Essential Letters*. United Kingdom, Yale University Press, 2014, p. 726.

33 Thomas Jefferson, *The Writings of Thomas Jefferson: Being His Autobiography, Correspondence, Reports, Messages, Addresses, and Other Writings, Official and Private*. United States, Taylor & Maury, 1854, p. 361.

34 P. G. Wodehouse, *Cocktail Time*. United Kingdom, Random House, 2009, p. 41.

35 'Everybody's a critic'. *New York Magazine*, 16 December 1996, p. 17.

36 Paul Smith, *Interpreting Cezanne*. United States, Stewart, Tabori & Chang, 1996, p. 21.

37 'Jerry Saltz Ranks Banksy's New York City (So-Called) Artistic Works'. *Vulture*, 31 October 2013.

38 Quoted in Xavier Pavie, *L'innovation à l'épreuve de la philosophie: le choix d'un avenir humainement durable?* France, PUF, 2018, p. 71.

39 Comte de Lautréamont, *Les Chants de Maldoror*, translated by Guy Wernham. United States, New Directions Publishing, 1965, p. 263.

40 Gerard Seenan, 'Painting by ridiculed but popular artist sells for £744,800'. *The Guardian*, 20 April 2004.

41 Jonathan Jones, 'A picture of poor taste'. *The Guardian*, 5 October 2005.

42 *Piero Manzoni: Serpentine Gallery, London, 28.02 - 26.04.98*. Kiribati, galleriet, 1998, p. 144.

LIST OF ILLUSTRATIONS

Little Dancer Aged Fourteen, 1880–81. Partially tinted bronze, cotton tarlatan, silk satin, and wood, 97.8 × 43.8 × 36.5 (38½ × 17¼ × 14⅜). The Metropolitan Museum of Art, New York. H. O. Havemeyer Collection, Bequest of Mrs. H. O. Havemeyer, 1929 **103, 195** Banksy, *Ballerina with Action Man Parts*, 2005. Painted resin, 31 × 20 × 18 (12¼ × 8 × 7). Edition of 6. Private Collection **104** Mary Cassatt, *Children Playing on the Beach*, 1884. Oil on canvas, 97.4 × 74.2 (38⅜ × 29¼). National Gallery of Art, London **106–7, 201** Banksy mural, Lowestoft, 2021. Painted as part of The Great British Spraycation, 2021 **110** Vincent Van Gogh, *Sunflowers*, 1888–89. Oil on canvas, 95 × 73 (37½ × 28¾). Van Gogh Museum, Amsterdam (Vincent van Gogh Foundation) **111, 196** Banksy, *Sunflowers from Petrol Station*, 2005. Oil on canvas in artist's frame, 102.6 × 87.5 (40⅝ × 34⅜). Private Collection **112** Claude Monet, *Japanese Footbridge*, 1899. Oil on canvas, 81.3 × 101.6 (32 × 40). National Gallery of Art, Washington DC **114–15, 196** Banksy, *Show Me the Monet*, 2005. Oil on canvas, 143.1 × 143.4 (56⅜ × 56½). Private Collection **116** Auguste Rodin, *The Thinker*, 1904. Bronze sculpture, 200.7 × 130.2 × 140.3 (79⅛ × 51⅜ × 55¼). Musée Rodin, Paris. Bequest of Jules E. Mastbaum, 1929. Photo Penta Springs Limited/Alamy Stock Photo **118–19, 195** Bansky, *The Drinker*, London, 2004. Metal. **120** Marcel Duchamp, *Bicycle Wheel*, 1913. 1964 (replica of 1913 original). Wheel, painted wood, 128.3 × 63.5 × 31.8 (50½ × 25 × 12½). Philadelphia Museum of Art. Gift of Galleria Schwarz, 1964. © Association Marcel Duchamp/ADAGP, Paris and DACS, London **122–23, 201** Banksy mural, Nottingham, England, 2020. Photo PA Images/Alamy Stock Photo **124** John Lavery, *The Right Honourable J. Ramsay Macdonald Addressing the House of Commons*, 1923. Oil on canvas, 127 × 101.6 (50 × 40). Glasgow Museums Resource Centre (GMRC), gift from the artist, 1930. Photo Painters/Alamy Stock Photo **126–27, 198** Banksy, *Devolved Parliament*, 2009. Oil on canvas, 250 × 420 (98⅜ × 165⅜). Private Collection. Photo Guy Bell/Alamy Stock Photo **128** Joan Miró, *Dancer II*, 1925. Oil on canvas, 116 × 89 (45¾ × 35⅛). Private Collection. © Successió Miró/ADAGP, Paris and DACS London **130, 200** Banksy, *Love is in the Bin*, 2018. Spray paint

and acrylic on canvas mounted on board, framed by the artist, 142 × 78 × 18 (56 × 30¾ × 7⅛). Private Collection. Photo Stephen Chung/Alamy Stock Photo **131, 194** Banksy mural, Waterloo Bridge, South Bank, London, 2002. Photo Dmytro Surkov/Alamy Stock Photo **132** René Magritte, *The Lovers*, 1928. Oil on canvas, 54 × 73.4 (21⅜ × 28⅞). The Museum of Modern Art, New York. Gift of Richard S. Zeisler. Rene Magritte © ADAGP, Paris and DACS, London **134–35, 194** Banksy, *Think Tank*, 2003. Acrylic and spraypaint on steel, 155 × 134 (61 × 52¾). Private Collection **136** René Magritte, *The Treachery of Images*, 1929. Oil on canvas, 60 × 81 (23¾ × 32). Broad Contemporary Art Museum, Los Angeles. Purchased with funds provided by the Mr. and Mrs. William Preston Harrison Collection. René Magritte © ADAGP, Paris and DACS, London **138–39, 199** Banksy, *This is a Pipe*, 2011. Paint, vintage frame and reclaimed metal, 87.6 × 99 (34½ × 39). Private Collection **140** Piet Mondrian, *Composition with Red and Blue*, 1933. Oil on canvas, 41.2 × 33.3 (16¼ × 13⅛). The Museum of Modern Art, New York. The Sidney and Harriet Janis Collection **142–43, 199** Banksy mural, New York City, 2013. **144** Victor Vasarely, *Zèbres-A*, 1938. Screenprint in black on wove paper, 26.9 × 34 (10⅝ × 13½). Private Collection. Photo Album/Alamy Stock Photo. Victor Vasarely © ADAGP, Paris and DACS, London 2024 **146–47, 197** Banksy mural, Timbuktu, 2008. **148** Salvador Dalí, *Sewing Machine with Umbrellas in a Surrealist Landscape*, 1941. Oil and gouache on panel, 22.5 × 30.5 (8⅞ × 12⅛). Private Collection. © Salvador Dali, Fundació Gala-Salvador Dalí, DACS **150–51, 199** Banksy mural, Wood Green, London, 2012. Photo Brendan Bell/Alamy Stock Photo **152** Edward Hopper, *Nighthawks*, 1941. Oil on canvas, 84.1 × 152.4 (33⅛ × 60). Art Institute of Chicago. Friends of American Art Collection **154–55, 195** Banksy, *Are You Still Using That Chair?*, 2005. Oil on canvas, 200 × 400 (78¾ × 157½). Photo WENN Rights Ltd/Alamy Stock Photo **156** thal, *Raising of the Flag at Iwo Jima*, 1945. National Archives and Records Administration, Maryland, USA **158–59, 197** Banksy, *Flag*, 2006. Screenprint, 49.9 × 70 (19⅝ × 27½). Photo imageBROKER.com GmbH & Co. KG/Alamy Stock Photo **162** *Campbell's Soup Can (Pepper Pot)*,

1962. Casein and graphite on linen, 50.8 × 40.6 (20 × 16). Private Collection. © The Andy Warhol Foundation for the Visual Arts, Inc. /DACS, London, 2017. Trademarks Licensed by Campbell Soup Company. All Rights Reserved **163, 195** Banksy, *Tesco Value Soup Can*, 2004. Oil on canvas, 121.9 × 91.5 (48 × 36). Private Collection. Photo MK Vienna/Alamy Stock Photo **166** Andy Warhol, *Shot Sage Blue Marilyn*, 1964. Acrylic and silkscreen ink on linen, 102 × 102 (40 × 40). Private Collection. © 2024 The Andy Warhol Foundation for the Visual Arts, Inc./Licensed by DACS, London **167, 196** Banksy, *Kate Moss*, 2005. Screen-print in colors on wove paper, 70 × 70 (27½ × 27½). Photo Jan Fritz/Alamy Stock Photo **168** Jean-Michel Basquiat, *Boy and Dog in a Johnnypump*, 1982. Oil on canvas, 240 × 420 (94½ × 165⅜). Private Collection. © Estate of Jean-Michel Basquiat. Licensed by Artestar, New York **170–71, 200** Banksy mural, Barbican, London, 2017. Photo Stephen Chung/Alamy Stock Photo **172** Keith Haring, *Untitled*, 1984. Silkscreen, Various Dimensions. © Keith Haring Foundation **174–75, 198** Banksy mural, Bermondsey, London, 2010. Photo Shutterstock **176** Damien Hirst, *Methoxyverapamil*, 1991. Household gloss on canvas, 190.5 × 175.3 (75 × 69). Photo Prudence Cuming Associates Ltd. © Damien Hirst and Science Ltd. All rights reserved, DACS 2024 **178–79, 198** Banksy, *Rat with Roller on Spot Painting*, 2009. Banksy vs. Bristol Museum, Bristol Museum, Bristol, 2009 **180** Jack Vettriano, *The Singing Butler*, 1992. Oil on canvas, 71 × 81 (28 × 32). Private Collection. © Jack Vettriano **182–83, 196** Banksy, *Toxic Beach*, 2005. Oil on canvas. Private Collection **184** Kara Walker, *Virginia Lynch Mob*, 1998. Cut paper on wall, approximately 304.8 × 1127.8 (120 × 444). Installation view. Kara Walker, Forum for Contemporary Art, St. Louis, MO, 1998. Photo David Kingsbury. © Kara Walker. Courtesy Sikkema Jenkins & Co. and Sprüth Magers **186–87, 200** Banksy mural, Brooklyn, New York, 2018. Photo Steven Ferdman/Shutterstock **188** The empty Fourth Plinth in Trafalgar Square, 1999–present. Photo Matthew Chattle/Alamy Stock Photo **190–91, 200** Banksy mural, Folkestone, 2014. Photo PA Images/Alamy Stock Photo **192** Banksy, *Love is in the Bin*, 2018. Photo Stephen Chung/Alamy Stock Photo

<h1 style="text-align:center">INDEX</h1>

ACKNOWLEDGMENTS

I am very grateful to my perennially brilliant editor Roger Thorp,
who backed this project from the start, and to his incredible colleagues at
Thames & Hudson, who made these pages come alive. My sincerest thanks
is owed too to my wonderful editors at BBC Culture, Fiona Macdonald
and Rebecca Laurence, for generously allowing me to hone my ideas about
Banksy in many articles over the past decade. This book is dedicated to
my wife, Sinéad, and to our little boy, Caspar, for their limitless love and
encouragement along the way. Anything wrong here is entirely their fault.

Kelly Grovier is a columnist and feature writer for BBC Culture and his
writings on art have appeared in the *Times Literary Supplement*, *Independent*, *Sunday
Times*, *Observer*, *RA Magazine* and *Wired*. He is the author of several books,
including *A New Way of Seeing: The History of Art in 57 Works* (2018),
On the Line: Conversations with Sean Scully (2021) and *The Art of Colour* (2023),
all published by Thames & Hudson. He is co-founder of the scholarly
journal *European Romantic Review*.

For Sinéad & Caspar

First published in the United Kingdom in 2024 by
Thames & Hudson Ltd, 181A High Holborn, London WC1V 7QX

First published in the United States of America in 2024 by
Thames & Hudson Inc., 500 Fifth Avenue, New York,
New York 10110

How Banksy Saved Art History © 2024 Thames & Hudson Ltd, London

Text © 2024 Kelly Grovier

British Library Cataloguing-in-Publication Data
A catalogue record for this book is available from the British Library

Library of Congress Control Number 2024934342

ISBN 978-0-500-02705-9

Printed in China by Shenzhen Reliance Printing Co. Ltd

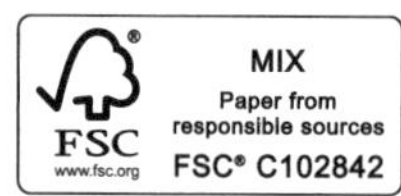

Be the first to know about our new releases,
exclusive content and author events by visiting
thamesandhudson.com
thamesandhudsonusa.com
thamesandhudson.com.au